THE GERMAN LANGUAGE

CONSONANTS (PULMONIC)

	Bilabial	Labiodental	Dental	Alveolar	Postalveolar	Retroflex	Palatal	Velar	Uvular	Pharyngeal	Glottal
Plosive	p b			t d		ʈ ɖ	c ɟ	k ɡ	q ɢ		ʔ
Nasal	m	ɱ		n		ɳ	ɲ	ŋ	N		
Trill	ʙ			r					ʀ		
Tap or Flap				ɾ		ɽ					
Fricative	ɸ β	f v	θ ð	s z	ʃ ʒ	ʂ ʐ	ç ʝ	x ɣ	χ ʁ	ħ ʕ	h ɦ
Lateral fricative				ɬ ɮ							
Approximant		ʋ		ɹ		ɻ	j	ɰ			
Lateral approximant				l		ɭ	ʎ	ʟ			

Where symbols appear in pairs, the one to the right represents a voiced consonant. Shaded areas denote articulations judged impossible.

CONSONANTS (NON-PULMONIC)

Clicks	Voiced implosives	Ejectives
ʘ Bilabial	ɓ Bilabial	ʼ Examples:
ǀ Dental	ɗ Dental/alveolar	pʼ Bilabial
ǃ (Post)alveolar	ʄ Palatal	tʼ Dental/alveolar
ǂ Palatoalveolar	ɠ Velar	kʼ Velar
ǁ Alveolar lateral	ʛ Uvular	sʼ Alveolar fricative

OTHER SYMBOLS

ʍ Voiceless labial-velar fricative

w Voiced labial-velar approximant

ɥ Voiced labial-palatal approximant

ʜ Voiceless epiglottal fricative

ʢ Voiced epiglottal fricative

ʡ Epiglottal plosive

ɕ ʑ Alveolo-palatal fricatives

ɺ Alveolar lateral flap

ɧ Simultaneous ʃ and X

Affricates and double articulations can be represented by two symbols joined by a tie bar if necessary.

k͡p t͡s

VOWELS

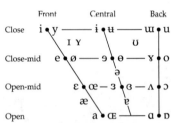

Where symbols appear in pairs, the one to the right represents a rounded vowel.

SUPRASEGMENTALS

ˈ Primary stress

ˌ Secondary stress

ˌfoʊnəˈtɪʃən

ː Long eː

ˑ Half-long eˑ

˘ Extra-short ĕ

| Minor (foot) group

‖ Major (intonation) group

. Syllable break ɹi.ækt

‿ Linking (absence of a break)

DIACRITICS   Diacritics may be placed above a symbol with a descender, e.g. ŋ̊

̥ Voiceless	n̥ d̥	̤ Breathy voiced	b̤ a̤	̪ Dental	t̪ d̪
̬ Voiced	s̬ t̬	̰ Creaky voiced	b̰ a̰	̺ Apical	t̺ d̺
ʰ Aspirated	tʰ dʰ	̼ Linguolabial	t̼ d̼	̻ Laminal	t̻ d̻
̹ More rounded	ɔ̹	ʷ Labialized	tʷ dʷ	̃ Nasalized	ẽ
̜ Less rounded	ɔ̜	ʲ Palatalized	tʲ dʲ	ⁿ Nasal release	dⁿ
̟ Advanced	u̟	ˠ Velarized	tˠ dˠ	ˡ Lateral release	dˡ
̠ Retracted	e̠	ˤ Pharyngealized	tˤ dˤ	̚ No audible release	d̚
̈ Centralized	ë	̴ Velarized or pharyngealized ɫ			
̽ Mid-centralized	e̽	̝ Raised	e̝	(ɹ̝ = voiced alveolar fricative)	
̩ Syllabic	n̩	̞ Lowered	e̞	(β̞ = voiced bilabial approximant)	
̯ Non-syllabic	e̯	̘ Advanced Tongue Root	e̘		
˞ Rhoticity	ɚ a˞	̙ Retracted Tongue Root	e̙		

TONES AND WORD ACCENTS

LEVEL			CONTOUR		
e̋ or ˥	Extra high		ě	˩˥	Rising
é	˦ High		ê	˥˩	Falling
ē	˧ Mid		e᷄	˧˥	High rising
è	˨ Low		e᷅	˩˧	Low rising
ȅ	˩ Extra low		e᷈	˧˩˧	Rising-falling
ꜜ	Downstep		↗		Global rise
ꜛ	Upstep		↘		Global fall

THE INTERNATIONAL PHONETIC ALPHABET (revised to 1993, corrected 1996)

Source: Reprinted by permission of the International Phonetic Association (http://www2.arts.gla.ac.uk/IPA/ipa.html).
The IPA can be contacted through the Secretary, John Esling (esling@uvic.ca).

THE
GERMAN
LANGUAGE

A Linguistic Introduction

Jean Boase-Beier and Ken Lodge

Blackwell
Publishing

© 2003 by Jean Boase-Beier and Ken Lodge

350 Main Street, Malden, MA 02148-5018, USA
108 Cowley Road, Oxford OX4 1JF, UK
550 Swanston Street, Carlton South, Melbourne, Victoria 3053, Australia
Kurfürstendamm 57, 10707 Berlin, Germany

First published 2003 by Blackwell Publishing Ltd

Library of Congress Cataloging-in-Publication Data

Boase-Beier, Jean.
    The German language : a linguistic introduction / Jean Boase-Beier and Ken Lodge.
        p. cm.
    Includes bibliographical references and index.
        ISBN 0-631-23138-2 (alk. paper) — ISBN 0-631-23139-0 (pbk. : alk. paper)
        1. German language—Study and teaching.   2. Linguistics.   I. Lodge, K. R. (Ken R.)   II. Title.
    PF3066 .B63 2003
    438'.0071—dc21

                                                                        2002007794

A catalogue record for this title is available from the British Library.

Set in 10/12½pt Sabon
by Graphicraft Limited, Hong Kong

For further information on
Blackwell Publishing, visit our website:
http://www.blackwellpublishing.com

CONTENTS

PREFACE

We have always found that university students are interested in the research their teachers do, and also that the answers to the kinds of specific practical questions students ask ('When do I put the verb at the beginning of a German sentence?', 'How do I understand a word I have never seen before?') make much more sense when they are given in the context of current thinking on the issue. This book arose out of the need to combine some of our own research interests in German and linguistics with a thorough description of German which will not only provide that context to its readers but will also give them practice in possible ways of thinking about language. While we do not give details of different theories and approaches, we do try to justify and illustrate our own view, and thus to give a clear background to the general framework – that of generative grammar – which we use. We have also tried, in the exercises which follow each chapter (except the first), to encourage readers to expand on what they have read in the chapter by finding further examples for themselves. We suggest that to do this they question native speakers of German (such as fellow-students, friends or teachers), use novels, dictionaries and the internet and thus gain a greater sense of how a linguistic description helps understand language as it is actually used. It is our experience that students of a language benefit greatly from seeing and making these links between description and use and that students of linguistics need to see linguistics applied to a particular case to make sense of it. This book is aimed mainly at second- and final-year undergraduates of German, and also at postgraduates in the broad area of German studies. There is no need for any prior knowledge of linguistics as all linguistic terms are clearly defined on their first usage, given in the text in bold. Glosses and translations are provided for all German examples (except in chapters 4 and 5) so that it is also possible to use this book with little or no prior knowledge of German, or, for students with more advanced German, without worrying about the meanings of words or the need to look them up. This means that students of linguistics with only very minimal knowledge of German, wishing to see what a linguistic description can tell us about a language, will also be able to profit from this book.

Over the past ten years we have, jointly and singly, taught several units on German which explore and make use of this link between linguistic description and practical application, examining contemporary and older texts, discussing examples, uses, research questions and practical applications, and have thus been able to incorporate feedback from our students into the book. We would like to thank all students who have thus, in their various ways, contributed to our teaching and research and to the class notes which eventually formed part of the book. We would also like to thank many colleagues both in the School of Language, Linguistics and Translation Studies at UEA and elsewhere for their help and suggestions, especially Stephen Barbour, Dieter Beier, Martin Durrell, Michael Harms, and the late Colin Good. Thanks are also due to several anonymous readers for Blackwell, whose comments we have discussed at great length and have integrated into our final version to the great improvement, we are convinced, of the resulting book. We would also like to thank Blackwell Publishing (especially Tami Kaplan and Beth Remmes) for their help and advice. And we would most particularly like to thank Mary Fox, who has spent many hours, especially in the final stages of preparing the manuscript, wrestling with all manner of semi-legible inserts, re-arrangements and changes of mind with efficiency and good humour. It goes without saying that shortcomings are our responsibility, and we welcome any comments from readers who would like to offer suggestions for improvement.

J. B.-B. and K. L.

ABBREVIATIONS

A	adjective	NHG	New High German
acc	accusative	nom	nominative
Adv	adverb	NP	noun phrase
AP	adjective phrase	O	object
Aux	auxiliary	OHG	Old High German
C	consonant	P	preposition
COMP	complementizer	PGmc	Proto-Germanic
conj	conjunction	pl	plural
D	determiner	PP	prepositional phrase
dat	dative	pron	pronoun
det	determinative	S	subject
f	feminine	SOV	subject–object–verb
gen	genitive	SVO	subject–verb–object
m	masculine	V	verb
MHG	Middle High German	VP	verb phrase
n	neuter		

CHAPTER ONE

Introduction

1.1 What is the German Language?

What is the German language? This is the way most textbooks on German start. The answer we want to give is perhaps rather surprising, namely that 'German' is not a useful linguistic concept when the question is looked at from the perspective of modern linguistics. First of all, however, we should consider some of the answers other writers have provided (for instance, Barbour and Stevenson 1990; Russ 1994; Stevenson 1997; Barbour 2000) and the different perspectives they involve.

The starting point for most people is that the answer is obvious: German is the language spoken by Germans. In other words language is tied to nationality. But this is not the full picture. Obviously, German is spoken in Austria and Switzerland, too. In addition, there are a small number of citizens of the Czech Republic who speak German as their first language and bilingual French citizens live in Alsace. So, nationality is not really the answer.

There is also the historical dimension: German is the modern development of the language spoken by various Germanic tribes, for instance, the Saxons, the Franks, the Langobards, in the first millennium AD. Certain changes occurred which differentiated German from the parent language. The Germanic languages include English, Dutch, German, Danish, Norwegian and Swedish, and if we compare them we can see consistent relationships of sound in the vocabulary, for instance English [p] as in *pound, hop* corresponds to German [pf] as in *Pfund; hüpfen*, English [t] as in *ten, net* corresponds to German [ts] as in *zehn, Netz*. In chapter 8 we shall look at the historical aspect of the language with more examples, but for the moment we have to be aware that languages do not change uniformly and variation of form is the norm. Furthermore, the different tribes referred to above did not speak a common language and settled in different parts of Europe, too: a group of the Saxons invaded England, the Franks settled in northern France and central Germany and the Langobards ended up in northern Italy, giving their name to Lombardy. So we would not expect uniformity of development in languages as widespread as these. (Consider, for instance, the lack of uniform development evidenced by the differences between British and American English which were separated over 300 years ago.) Another aspect of linguistic history that we should note is that native speakers have little awareness of the history of their language and we shall see instances of this later, but a simple example will suffice here. The German word *fertig* was originally derived from *Fahrt* and meant 'ready to travel'; if this connection was still made by native speakers we would expect the adjective to be spelled *fährtig*. So, historical development will not provide the answer, either, to the question of what constitutes the German language.

In an attempt to overcome some of these problems, writers have tried to define a language using a combination of social and political factors and in some cases have added linguistic considerations such as mutual comprehensibility in order to deal with the problem of variation. But if we consider what are usually regarded as varieties of German, we find that many of them are mutually unintelligible, as much as English and Dutch are. The fact that they are closely related languages does not mean that speakers of each can understand one another. Let us take a speaker from the German side of the Dutch–German border and one from Bavaria. If they are speakers of the local dialects, they will understand one another only with the greatest difficulty. In some respects the Plattdeutsch speaker from the North has more in common linguistically speaking with an English speaker than with a Bavarian. For example, the former may well have initial [p] and [t] as in English, where the latter has [pf] and [ts]. Despite the fact that they live in the same political entity, Germany, pay the same central taxes, owe allegiance to the same flag, serve in the Bundeswehr, if they do military service, they do not seem to speak the same language. So mutual comprehensibility, it seems, is of little help in defining a language. Indeed, northern speakers will be able to understand their Dutch neighbours far better than they can understand their Bavarian compatriots, and in this important sense the North German and the Dutch speaker speak the same language. This means that from a linguistic point of view their national allegiance is irrelevant. Of course, they are each taught a different standard language in school, but this, too, is a political and social matter, not a linguistic one. The picture we end up with, if we look at geographical variation in language, is of a dialect continuum, a slowly changing set of partially overlapping linguistic systems which at the extremities may be very different indeed.

We shall return to the notion of nation and language in chapters 8 and 9 but for the moment we note that social, political and geographical factors will not help us to demarcate what it is we want to describe as the German language.

1.2 A Linguistic Description

The perspective of modern linguistics referred to in the first paragraph, sometimes called the generative enterprise, which we are using as the basis for much of what is said in this book, makes a clear distinction between political and social concerns and those that are purely linguistic. This is the view put forward in Chomsky (1980), who explains that for him the expression 'language X' (for example, 'German') is of no help and of no interest because a linguist's main concern is with the nature of language itself. This is also our view; and so to take up again the question we asked at the beginning of this chapter, we would reiterate that the notion of the 'German language' defined historically, geographically, or socially is simply not helpful in deciding what constitutes a particular language. What we are concerned with are the structural properties and relationships internal to the system. To return to our simple example of initial consonants, what is important is that in one linguistic system [p] contrasts meaningfully with [t] and in another [pf] contrasts with [ts]. It does not matter that we call the first one English and the second one German, as far as linguistics is concerned.

So what sort of a view of language is the one we are putting forward here? Developed from the views of Chomsky and other generative grammarians, it sees language as one of the human cognitive systems, the one that we alone as a species have developed. Human beings develop language because they are genetically preprogrammed to do so; language is a biological function of humans just like bipedal gait. A young child will naturally get up onto her legs and walk. Of course, she has help from her carers but nevertheless at the right time under the right circumstances the child will be ready to walk. So, according to this theory, children will acquire language when they are ready to do so. Help is provided by the surrounding adult language, but we must note that this is not a teaching situation, merely a provision of material (linguistic data) for the children to work on, and they will acquire whichever language they are presented with. There is no gene to learn German; people learn German, rather than Swahili or Malay, as their native language because of an accident of birth.

Since the surrounding adult language determines which specific linguistic system a child learns in the first months of acquisition, we can see quite easily how variation is perpetuated. Many North German children

acquire initial [p] and [t] where Bavarian children acquire initial [pf] and
[ts]; similarly, a child from Hamburg will grow up saying *Brötchen* and
Guten Tag, whereas a child from Munich will say *Semmel* and *Grüß
Gott*. It is only at a much later stage, that of schooling, that the influence
of the standard language will be brought to bear on the child's linguistic
development. Contact with other varieties relates to mobility, too; changing social groups brings speakers from different backgrounds together,
whether children or adults. So as a person develops, linguistic development occurs at the same time. In most cases speakers do not have one
homogeneous linguistic system, but end up using a number of variants,
usually overlapping ones in linguistic terms. These overlapping systems
are what are usually referred to as dialects. It is the grammatical systems
of these dialects that are the main concern of theoretical and descriptive
linguistics.

Linguistic description of the kind we want to introduce in this book is
focused on the language itself and its structural characteristics. Out of all
the possible features found in human language we want to present those
features that are specific to German. This will enable us to offer at least
a partial linguistic definition of German. The social and political aspects
of German that we considered briefly in the previous section must not be
forgotten, though. These are aspects of language use, how the linguistic
system we shall be describing is used by native speakers in their everyday
lives. We make a clear distinction between the language itself and the use
that is made of it. This distinction has a long history, going back to
Saussure's (1916) distinction of **langue** (the linguistic system) and **parole**
(actual speech). A somewhat similar distinction is made by Chomsky
(1965) with respect to an individual speaker: here the terms are **competence** and **performance**. Competence is the term used for a native
speaker's knowledge of language, as represented in the mental grammar.
Performance is the way this knowledge is put to use. Performance is
what we see (or hear); competence is the underlying linguistic system we
make inferences about. We shall be looking at the former in particular in
chapters 2–3 and 5–7, and in this sense most of what we have to say
about the competence of a native speaker of German is contained in
these chapters. Chapter 4 is an introduction to basic articulatory phonetics; this enables the linguist to talk about speech in an objective way and
carry out phonological analyses. Chapter 8, which discusses the historical dimension, covers both language-internal and external aspects of the
linguistic development, that is to say, both general principles of language
change and the social and political circumstances that brought about
change. In chapter 9 we will be concerned with performance, not just
with linguistic performance, but also with communicative performance.
The process of socialization gives the native speaker a set of rules to
govern his or her behaviour, including linguistic output, according to the

particular situation, and in this sense it is possible to take over the notion of competence to this area by describing such sets of rules as communicative competence. This is not, however, a notion we shall be particularly concerned with in this book.

A further distinction drawn in the theory proposed here was made by Chomsky (1986): that between **E-language** and **I-language**. This has to do with the relevance ascribed to data within linguistics, and its relation with the theoretical orientation of the discipline. E-language is the language outside the speaker, collected as data for analysis. This was virtually the only approach to language before what is generally referred to as the Chomskyan revolution, the radical change in the way language was viewed which was initiated with Chomsky's (1957) work *Syntactic Structures* and led to the development of generative grammar. This is the notion that a set of rules and principles exists which allows all utterances (and only those) of a particular language to be formed, or generated, and that, furthermore, there is an even more general set of universal principles underlying the grammars of all languages. This is why describing natural languages in these terms is often referred to as the generative enterprise. I-language, on the other hand, relates to the knowledge of those specific and general rules and principles of language a native speaker has; it is internal to the speaker and can only be studied indirectly. Characterization of I-language is, for all those concerned with the generative enterprise, the research programme of linguistics. Before linguists can look at how language is used in context or acquired by children, they have to know the nature of the faculty being used or acquired.

1.3   The Grammar and Grammatical Knowledge

We referred in the previous section to grammar and to grammatical systems. We must say something more here about what we mean by the term **grammar**. In non-technical and language-teaching contexts this word usually refers to the way in which sentences are put together and the use of the right form of words in the sentence, for example, the appropriate ending on the verb. In modern linguistics, especially that inspired by Chomsky's work, the term has a broader application: it means the whole of the linguistic system stored in the brain of a native speaker. It therefore covers the way in which sentences are constructed, the way words are constructed, the systematic relationships of meaning in words and sentences, and the sound system of a language. As mentioned above, we shall be taking these separately and devoting a chapter to each, in their particular relations to the German language. The technical terms for each are the chapter titles: chapter 2 deals with **syntax**, the way sentences are put together; chapter 3 deals with **morphology**, the internal structure of words; chapter 4 deals with **phonetics**, or German pronunciation, and chapter 5 with **phonology**, the system of meaningful distinctions of sounds; chapter 6 deals with **lexis**, the structure of the system of words and their semantic relationships; chapter 7 deals with **stylistics**, that is, the additional ways in which the language encodes meaning and creates particular effects.

To return to our notion of grammar as the total native-speaker knowledge of the language, we are assuming that this knowledge is of two types: universal and language-specific. Universal characteristics may themselves be of two types: substantive, which apply identically to all languages and are called **principles**, and variable, which apply in different ways across languages and are called **parameters**. It is the existence of these two types of principle which explains the term 'principles and parameters theory', frequently used to define this type of theory. An example of the former type is **structure-dependency**. All human languages have this characteristic; any operation in syntax depends on knowledge of the structure of the sentence. Take, for instance, the relationship between statements and questions in German. (1) and (2) are related in just this way.

(1)   Hans geht morgen in die Stadt
      Hans will go to town tomorrow

(2)   Geht Hans morgen in die Stadt?
      Will Hans go to town tomorrow?

All native speakers of German know that, in the formation of a question, it is the verb that moves to the front of the sentence. 'Verb' is an element of syntactic structure; it does not mean 'the second word', for instance, even though in (1) it is the second word. It does not matter how many words occur before the verb, it is still the verb that is moved. Consider examples (3)–(8):

(3)   Die Frau geht morgen in die Stadt
      The woman will go to town tomorrow

(4)   Geht die Frau morgen in die Stadt?
      Will the woman go to town tomorrow?

(5)   Die alte Frau geht morgen in die Stadt
      The old woman will go to town tomorrow

(6)   Geht die alte Frau morgen in die Stadt?
      Will the old woman go to town tomorrow?

(7) Die alte Frau, die eine Freundin meiner Mutter ist, geht morgen in die Stadt
The old woman, who is a friend of my mother's, will go to town tomorrow

(8) Geht die alte Frau, die eine Freundin meiner Mutter ist, morgen in die Stadt?
Will the old woman, who is a friend of my mother's, go to town tomorrow?

The questions in (4), (6) and (8) all begin with the verb *geht*, even though the corresponding statements in (3), (5) and (7) have different numbers of words before the verb, showing that the verb must be something we define in a way dependent on sentence structure, and not merely in relation to the linear structure – the actual number and position of words – in a sentence. Chapter 2 deals with such matters in detail. All that has to be noted here is that this kind of relationship, structure-dependency, is a characteristic of all languages. It contrasts with simple mathematical operations such as order reversal, as in (9) and (10), which never occur in human languages.

(9) 1 2 3 4 5 6
(10) 6 5 4 3 2 1

The other kind of universal, a parameter, is a characteristic of all languages which is variable in its manifestation in any particular language. A very good example of this is the **Pro-drop** parameter, which encapsulates the information that all languages can have subjects in sentences, but some do not require the position of subject to be filled. Compare the German example in (11) with the Italian one in (12).

(11) Ich spreche mit Ihrer Frau
      I   speak   with your wife

(12) Parlo   con la   Sua signora
      I-speak with (the) your wife
      I'm talking to your wife

The German sentence requires the subject pronoun *ich*; Italian does not require *io*; use of the pronoun in Italian indicates an emphatic contrast. Languages can be divided into two sorts: the Pro-drop languages like Italian, Spanish and Arabic, where the subject position need not be filled, and the non-Pro-drop languages like English, French and German. It is assumed that during acquisition of their native language children know that languages can be of either sort and that the input data of the language used around them gives them the evidence as to which type their particular language belongs to. In such cases the parameter is said to become fixed one way or the other. We shall briefly mention the Pro-drop parameter again in chapter 2 but it will not be a subject of much concern to us; here it is used merely for illustration of what is meant by a parameter.

There are universals at all linguistic levels. There are phonological ones relating to syllable structure, for instance, which we shall consider in chapter 5, and others requiring certain feature co-occurrences; for instance, if a language has nasals, they will be voiced. Semantics in particular is an area of universal features of language structure: meanings and their relationships are for the most part common to all languages, though they are encoded lexically in entirely language-specific ways, as the examples in chapter 6 will show.

Although we have separated out the various levels of linguistic structure, we have not asked the question as to how these levels are incorporated into the grammatical knowledge of the speaker. The traditional divisions are to some extent arbitrary: as we shall show in the chapters that follow, morphology and syntax are not neatly separated, nor are phonology and morphology. Syntactic structure encodes some of the meaning of the sentence. What has to be recognized is that all the different levels interact with one another in a number of ways and this has to be reflected in any model of grammatical knowledge. We shall take up this point again when we discuss modularity below.

It is necessary at this point to say something about linguistic models, which are a type of scientific model. A scientific model is like a metaphor (describing one thing in terms of another) in that it describes an object of study in a way which can be understood. But, unlike a metaphor, it does not merely involve description. It also potentially enables the investigator to make appropriate generalizations about the nature of the object. Some scientific models deal with the physical world, such as molecular structure. In the case of linguistics, however, our theories are about the structure and nature of knowledge, a representation of a mental capacity. There is not necessarily a direct relationship between the model and the object of study, though it could be argued that the more sophisticated a model becomes through constant refinement, the closer it might come to providing an actual picture of the object it represents. But on the whole the way linguistic knowledge is represented is to some extent independent of the knowledge itself, and over the past forty years many competing models have been proposed. In some cases the model may be a convenient way of stating what can be said in normal language; for instance, the observations relating to syntactic structure in (13) and (14) are equivalents.

(13)   S → NP VP
(14)   A sentence is made up of a noun phrase followed by a verb phrase

On the other hand, though representations in particular models cannot claim to mirror directly the structure of the stored knowledge, they do often make theoretical claims about it, and in such cases are not merely equivalent versions of the same claim. An example of this kind is provided by the difference between models that trade on notions of process and those that do not. This can be seen clearly in current theoretical work in phonology (see Lodge 1997). In German, native speakers know that there is a subset of the lexicon in which the stem-final consonant varies between voiceless and voiced, for example, *Rad* 'bicycle', 'wheel', pronounced [ʀaːt], of which the genitive is [ʀaːdəs]. (We consider the details of this phenomenon in chapter 5.) How are we to represent this knowledge? One way is to say that certain voiced consonants are devoiced at the end of a syllable, and that consonants that occur in such words, /b d g v z/, are stored in the **lexicon** (the list of words of the language) as voiced and that there must be a rule changing voiced to voiceless as appropriate. Such a theory claims that native speakers have phonological elements stored complete with their features (such as 'voiced') and rules of feature-changing.

This is quite different from the alternative view, which excludes such feature-changing rules from the outset as a matter of principle. (This kind of a priori or 'from the outset' requirement is usually referred to as constraining a theory.) In such an approach the stored forms have no specification of features such as 'voiced', which is added in the appropriate circumstances. Note that the data are the same and they instantiate the knowledge that German speakers have. It is the theoretical models that are different. A similar distinction between approaches to syntax can be found in the transformational approach (Chomsky 1965) and that of Generalized Phrase Structure Grammar (Gazdar et al. 1985).

This book is not the place to pursue these matters any further. It is our intention merely to draw the reader's attention to the theoretical issues involved. As a general rule, we will not present alternative analyses of the data we discuss.

At this point we should point out that the term **rule** refers to a statement of observable regularities in linguistic structure; it is not used in a prescriptive sense. Thus (13) and (14) are rules to the extent that they specify what we find in all sentences of German. They are not on a par with commands such as 'Thou shalt not kill' or 'Give way'.

We must now turn to a consideration of the status of the different areas (levels) of linguistic structure that are reflected in the separate chapters of our book. One of the assumptions of modern generative grammar is that certain areas of syntax, morphology and phonology are best seen as sub-areas or modules of linguistic knowledge. We are assuming that the brain organizes its knowledge into separate modules. One of these is responsible for sight, one for motor ability, one for language, and so on. This would explain how a particular area may be damaged while leaving the others intact. A person may have a stroke and be unable to move his or her right arm but be perfectly able to speak. People may even be born with certain abilities impaired while others develop normally or even exceptionally well. See Smith and Tsimpli (1995) for a discussion of a young man with astonishing linguistic abilities but who was unable to carry out simple tasks such as dressing himself.

It seems that not only is the language module separate from other modules in the brain but that it is also specific to humans. As Felix and Fanselow (1987: 105) point out, a dog growing up in the same German family as a child, listening to roughly the same linguistic input, will not begin to speak German, nor will it respond only to German. And despite many attempts to teach animals such as chimpanzees to speak, or, more precisely, use language, the results, though fascinating, indicate that though the animals clearly possess semantic abilities, they cannot manipulate syntax. Syntactic knowledge, at least, is clearly only available to humans.

What we are assuming is thus that there are different levels of modularity. Language, like sight and hearing, is a module (see Smith and Tsimpli 1995: 30ff), but within the language module there are modules of a different type, sub-areas of interacting knowledge, each governed by its own specific universal principles and parametric variation of the kind we exemplified above. Modules at this level can be equated with sub-theories of language, such as the theory governing argument structures of lexical items, known as **theta theory** and discussed in chapter 6, or the theory governing the hierarchical ordering of syntactic phrases, known as **X-bar theory**, which is discussed in chapter 2. Not all linguists working within the principles and parameters theory share the same view about what constitutes a module, but we shall make the assumption here that in fact such sub-theories are autonomous modules of the language, representing separate, though interacting, areas of linguistic knowledge. Which parts of the language are taken to be separate modules has few consequences for the details of the linguistic principles themselves, as many linguists such as, for example, Stechow and Sternefeld (1988: 14ff.) point out.

Because the areas traditionally distinguished in linguistics such as syntax and morphology do not have the status of modules in terms of the overall theory of grammatical knowledge, we would expect to find that some modules of grammar relate to several such areas. Phonology furnishes good examples of the interrelationship of different modules and indeed the separateness or otherwise of a phonological component has been a focus of debate for a long time. For instance, the phonetic realizations of morphemes have to be accounted for. We have to decide what the status of a phenomenon like Umlaut is. How does it fit into the grammatical structure as a whole? We shall see in chapters 3 and 5 that it is morphologically unpredictable but phonetically regular. Furthermore, it is not merely a question of morphological additions to a basic lexical form, as in *Schuh – Schuh+e*, but a phonetic feature, frontness, that carries a grammatical function. Intonation has both a semantic and a pragmatic function. In some instances it is the only means of knowing the meaning of a sentence. If we take the sentence in (15), when spoken it may have a falling intonation and main stress on *morgen* or a rising intonation and main stress in the same place:

(15)   Hans kommt morgen
       Hans will come tomorrow

With a falling intonation it is a statement, with a rising one a question. (For a treatment of German intonation, see Fox 1984.) Intonation interacts with syntax and with meaning. In chapter 3 we shall show that syntactic principles might be said to apply to what is traditionally called morphology. And in chapter 6 we shall see that syntactic principles such as those governing the representation of argument structures are at work in areas of what is traditionally assumed to be the lexicon. Terms like 'morphology', 'syntax' or 'lexicon' are therefore convenient terms for talking about language but they are not meant to represent the structure of linguistic knowledge. In this sense, they do not necessarily have what is sometimes referred to as psychological reality in terms of the way linguistic knowledge is organized.

1.4   Other Linguistic Knowledge

There is another area generally included in the discipline of linguistics, namely **pragmatics**. Pragmatics is the study of language use and as such is not part of the purely grammatical knowledge of native speakers. It is assumed that there are general principles governing language use, but they are not of the same kind as those we referred to above and will be discussing in chapters 2–3 and 5–7; language use is not subject to purely linguistic principles. Linguistic knowledge interacts with a speaker's mental encyclopaedia (Sperber and Wilson 1995), whenever we use language in a context. This division between language in isolation and language in use underlies important divisions within linguistics in terms of sub-areas of the discipline such as syntactic theory on the one hand, which is concerned with how humans put sentences together, and sociolinguistics on the other, which investigates the variable linguistic usage in various

contexts, something we discuss in chapter 9. This division is also an area
of theoretical debate. For instance, those who have a functional view of
language, that is that the forms are determined by the use we put them
to (for example, Halliday 1973, 1994), question whether it even makes
sense to consider linguistic knowledge as an object of study out of context. Our view is that a cognitive theory of language and a functional
one are quite compatible, provided the function is not seen as *determining* the forms of language. The theories in this case relate to different
aspects of language, its nature and its use, respectively.

To return to pragmatics, we can see that it has to do with certain types
of meaning. We have already noted that semantics deals with meaning,
so let us consider the difference between semantics and pragmatics. In
(16) we give a simple German sentence:

(16)   Das Wasser ist heiß
       The water is hot

As it stands on the page, this sentence has a meaning which is recognizable to all native speakers despite the fact that it is not being used by
anyone (except by us as a linguistic example). *Wasser* refers to a particular liquid with the chemical formula H_2O; *das* means that it is a specific
volume of water that is being referred to; *ist* has a relational meaning
indicating that the subject noun phrase has the characteristics specified
by the following adjective; *heiß* means that some object has a relatively
high temperature. These meanings hold good irrespective of context;
they may be said to be the linguistic meanings of these words. But now
let us consider a context in which this sentence could be used.

One of two people who live together is sitting reading. The other
person enters the room and utters (16). We can legitimately ask the
question: what does this person mean by that? Note that we are in this
case asking about the speaker not the words; a speaker's intentions may
be various and they do not equate directly with any one particular sentence or sentence-type. In other words, the speaker of (16) may have any
number of intentions, and indeed more than one at a time. The following are at least possible in our context:

(17)   a.   It's time for your bath
       b.   Why not make a cup of tea?
       c.   Why not get up off your backside and do something useful like the
            washing-up?

For the most part people who live together will know what intentions
each of them is likely to have when they speak to one another. Notice
that linguistic meaning can be found in a dictionary, but speaker meaning

cannot. None of the meanings in (17) would be found in the dictionary entry for any of the constituent words of (16). The former type of meaning is the realm of semantics and the latter of pragmatics. Some of the variation discussed in chapter 9 is pragmatic variation.

We have so far referred to sentences in all circumstances, that is, (16) is in syntactic terms a sentence and it is used by speakers with this form in a context. In this particular instance there is no problem, but in reality a German might equally well produce something like (18):

(18)   Ich . . . du . . . was hat er gesa . . . ?
       I . . . you . . . what did he sa . . . ?

It is interrupted, unfinished and clearly indicates two changes of mind. But there is nothing unusual about this; such utterances are commonplace. How does this fit in with our views on grammar presented so far? This question relates directly to the notion of competence that we introduced above. Sentences in the strict sense are abstract entities representing the grammatical knowledge of a native speaker. This is not what speakers actually utter. Real speech may be like (3)–(8), (15) or (16) but it is just as likely to be full of hesitations, false starts, omissions and interruptions. In chapter 2 we give further examples of actual speech and consider how the incompleteness and defectiveness (in grammatical terms) of such utterances affects language acquisition in children. Such characteristics are so common that we as hearers filter them out and ignore them (unless they are used excessively by a particular speaker and then they become a hindrance to communication). Linguists do not generally write grammars which try to see regularities in utterances such as (18); we assume that they are unpredictable and not subject to rule in the same way as sentences, which are abstract entities, are.

However, some characteristics of real speech relate to the construction of texts and there are regularities to be observed here. Consider the exchange between two speakers in (19):

(19)   *A:* Wer kommt morgen?
             Who is coming tomorrow?

       B: Hans.
             Hans.

If the rule given in (13) applies to German, then B's reply to A is not a sentence. Yet, again, there is nothing unusual about such an exchange. What native speakers of German know is that B's reply 'stands for' example (15). This is what is understood. So B's reply is actually part of (15) and not, for instance, part of (20).

(20)   Hans hat einen neuen Mantel
       Hans has a new coat

Note that this specific meaning attaching to *Hans* only occurs in the
context of (19); it is context-determined. The rules of text construction tell us not to repeat given information; *kommt morgen* is therefore suppressed in B's reply. (This is usually referred to as **ellipsis**; it is
discussed further in connection with **gapping** (deleting only what is
recoverable in context) in chapter 7.) The meaning, however, is quite
clear. To distinguish between the grammatical system of knowledge and
its use in texts we refer to structures in the former as **sentences**, as
discussed in chapter 2, and instances of the latter as **utterances**. Strictly
speaking, written texts are also utterances, that is, instantiations of the
linguistic system, but, as we shall see in chapters 8 and 9, the written
form is standardized in a way that makes it seem closer to the structures
specified by the system. For instance, most written sentences have complete syntax, so they look like (15), (16) and (20) above. Certainly, they
do not look like (18). Similarly, in chapters 4 and 5 we shall show that
detailed phonetic descriptions of speech relate to actual utterances,
whereas the phonological system deals with the storage of abstract
information.

   We have given a brief exposition of the approach we are taking in this
book. In what follows we can only deal with a fraction of each topic
covered in the individual chapters. It is hoped that the reader will follow
up the references, both those in the text and those in the 'Further Reading' sections, for herself.

1.5   Further Reading

For a discussion of language change, see Aitchison (1981), McMahon
(1994) and Trask (1996). On the problems of defining a speech community, see Romaine (1982), and Dorian (1982); see also Fasold (1984), on
nations and languages.

   Pinker (1994) is an accessible introduction to the broadly Chomskyan
view of language we put forward in this book. Cook and Newson
(1996) is an introduction to Universal Grammar. Smith and Wilson (1979)
discuss what we refer to in section 1.2 as the Chomskyan revolution.
Another useful overview of the development of generative grammar is
van Riemsdijk and Williams (1986). Studies of generative grammar
using German data can be found in Toman (1984) and a specific application of Generalized Phrase Structure Grammar to German is Nerbonne,
Netter and Pollard (1994). Recent theoretical work in phonology can
be found in Coleman (1995), Kaye (1995), Bird (1995). Discussions of

the differences between derivational and non-derivational (declarative) phonology can be found in Coleman (1995), Kaye (1995) and Bird (1995).

On language change, see Aitchison (1981) or Kiparsky (1982a), Downes (1988) discusses social determinants of language change.

For an interesting study of language and the mind, read Jackendoff (1993). Pinker (1997) is a discussion of the mind which goes beyond linguistics and linguistic knowledge. The relevance of brain damage to linguistic theory is discussed by Pinker (1994), Jackendoff (1993) and Caplan (1987).

Aitchison (1992) gives a survey of attempts to teach language to animals, an issue also discussed by Pinker (1997). Another book which deals with talking animals, though not from a linguistic point of view, is Bright (1990).

For discussion of the general principles governing the use of language, see Blakemore (1992) and Sperber and Wilson (1995). Hymes (1972) has developed notions of communicative competence and communicative performance.

Books (besides this one!) which deal with the linguistic description of the German language are Fox (1990) and Beedham (1995). A good German grammar is Durrell (1996).

CHAPTER TWO

Syntax

2.1 The Concept of Syntax

Syntax is, broadly speaking, the name given to the area of grammar concerned with the way in which words are put together to form sentences. While general syntactic theory explains how differences in structure between languages relate to one another, the syntactic theory of German could be seen as a theory of the knowledge a native speaker of German has about forming sentences, about understanding sentences and about judging whether or not sentences are well-formed. It is important to realize that making such judgements does not relate to judgements about whether a sentence is true or not, nor indeed about whether there is any basis for such judgements. A sentence

(1) Die Frau schrieb einen Brief
     The woman wrote a letter

would be judged both syntactically well-formed and comprehensible, though it may not be true, or speaker and hearer may have no evidence for whether it is true or not. The following sentence may be judged false, or unlikely, or impossible to pronounce upon:

(2) Die Blume hat einen Hallimasch gegessen
     The flower has eaten a honey agaric

but a speaker of German would normally judge it to be a syntactically well-formed sentence of German even if he or she does not know the meaning of *Hallimasch* and suspects that it cannot be eaten by flowers, or perhaps even that flowers cannot eat anything. The three sentences which follow are all, however, ill-formed:

(3) a. *Frau die Brief schrieb einen
     b. *Hallimasch gegessen Blume die einen hat
     c. *Die Blumen hat einen Hallimasch gegessen

and are marked with an asterisk (*) to indicate this. Such judgements can be made independently of the fact that, as mentioned in chapter 1, an adult native speaker of German (or of any other language, for that matter) may often produce ill-formed utterances. The following is an authentic example:

(4) *Das kommt mir so lange her, dass wir in Schottland waren
     (roughly: *It seems such a long time we were in Scotland*)

When the speaker was made aware that the verb is *vorkommen* and that therefore (4) should have had the form:

(5) Das kommt mir so lange her **vor**, dass wir in Schottland waren
     It seems such a long time since we were in Scotland

he accepted that his statement had contained a grammatical slip, so clearly the fact that such slips occur does not affect the speaker's ability to give judgements on the well-formedness of sentences such as this and of those in (3) above. (See chapter 1 on the difference between a sentence and an utterance.)

What the examples given above suggest is that judgements about the syntactic well-formedness of sentences of German differ from semantic judgements about German. From a semantic point of view, (2) may be judged unacceptable because *Blume* cannot be the subject of the verb *essen*. In contrast to this, (3a), (3b) and (3c) would be judged unacceptable for syntactic reasons. (3a) and (3b) both violate the requirements of German word-order although

(6) Einen Brief schrieb die Frau
     The woman wrote a letter

does not and is a perfectly acceptable alternative to (1). Example (3c), on the other hand, violates agreement rules for subject and verb, which we judge to apply independently of whether we know what a *Hallimasch* is, or even whether such a word exists at all.

Looking more carefully at (6), it appears that, although the order of (1) has been changed, certain elements have been kept together: *einen* and *Brief* have been kept in the same order with respect to one another as in (1), and so have *die* and *Frau*. Indeed, it appears that the change in the respective order of these elements, as in (3a), repeated here:

(7)   *Frau die Brief schrieb einen

has rendered it syntactically ill-formed, even though some kind of meaning might be attached to it more easily than to (2), which is syntactically
well-formed.

These judgements suggest that not only is there a limited number of
options for the word order of a sentence in German (and, we might
assume, in any other language), but that there is also a structure within
the sentence which is more complex than mere linear ordering. This is
the notion of structure dependency, mentioned in chapter 1.

Clearly there are principles governing the way in which words are
put together to form sentences. A moment's comparison between the
examples in (3) and the following two examples in English show that
similar considerations apply here too:

(8)   a.   The woman wrote a letter
      b.   *Woman the letter a wrote

Sentence (8a) is syntactically well-formed, whereas (8b) is not. However,
we cannot simply change the order of (8a) above to correspond to the
order of the German words in (6), which was also acceptable, and meant
the same thing, or the result is

(9)   A letter wrote the woman

Although this sentence is in fact grammatically well-formed, it does not
mean the same as (8a), and would generally be considered unacceptable
on semantic grounds. This suggests that though there is a principle,
perhaps universal in nature, of structural organization within sentences,
the ways in which this principle is implemented may well vary from
language to language. The question of particular variation among languages is mentioned in chapter 1; it is referred to as parametric variation. Universal principles, or principles of **Universal Grammar**, apply in
all languages, but there is parametric variation in their application in any
individual language.

We also noted in chapter 1 that the syntax of a language is just one
area of a native speaker's knowledge of language, along with others such
as the phonology and the lexicon. When a child first begins to speak
German as her native language, it will soon become clear that she is
using knowledge of the syntax, the phonology and the lexicon of German, and we will just digress briefly at this point to consider the situation of such a child because this has consequences for our understanding of syntax. By the age of about four years, the child will be able to
speak German fluently, though she may make errors with words, have

difficulty with certain sounds, or even occasionally produce utterances which contravene the syntax of German. However, the child has in a very short time reached a point which could not, presumably, have been reached purely by observation nor even by conscious teaching on the part of others. This fact has formed the basis for many studies of child language acquisition, especially those, such as Clahsen (1988) or the papers in Baker and McCarthy (1981), which are mainly concerned with the acquisition of syntax as opposed to studies such as Halliday (1975) or Bruner (1975) which are largely concerned with communicative aspects of language acquisition. There are a number of reasons for the assumption that neither observation by the child nor teaching by others, alone or in combination, could account for this quite extraordinary achievement.

Firstly, a child of four years, or even two and a half years, will produce sentences of German she has never heard before. The following is an authentic example produced by a three-year-old boy:

(10) Die Mami hat die Schmetterlinge in meinem Zimmer gemacht
Mummy made the butterflies in my room

It is extremely unlikely that this sentence has been spoken by anyone else, let alone heard and memorized by this little boy. The vast majority of his sentences, in fact, will be ones he has not heard before, and so he cannot have learned and be copying them.

Secondly, a child cannot have been taught all the syntactic constructions she uses. Many of them are structures of whose existence adults are not aware although they may use them intuitively. A child will understand that in a question such as:

(11) Was musst du fragen, bevor du zu essen anfängst?
What must you ask before you begin to eat?

the expected answer is something like

(12) Ob genug da ist
Whether there is enough

which could be expressed at length as

(13) Ich muss fragen, ob genug da ist
I must ask whether there is enough

and would not answer (11) by saying

(14) Süßigkeiten

meaning

(15) Ich muss fragen, bevor ich Süßigkeiten esse
      I must ask before I eat sweets

(15) is of course a perfectly acceptable sentence of German, and (14) a perfectly acceptable abbreviated form of it. But (14) is *not* an acceptable answer to (11), as a moment's consideration will show. The reason the child responds correctly to the question in (11) with (12) or something similar is not because someone has taught her the underlying principles of what *was?* in a sentence like (11) can be a question about. Most adults would not be in a position to explain this, nor even to see what it is that needs explaining. Indeed, the information that would need to be provided to a child if we were attempting to teach her such principles would include not only that (12) is a possible answer to (11) but that (14) is not. Now (11) and (12) can clearly constitute part of a conversation and the child may register (12) as a possible answer to (11), but (14) will never occur as an answer to (11), so she will never be provided with the evidence that this is not a possible sequence. Negative evidence, it seems, will be even thinner than positive evidence for both the universal principles of language and the parameters specific to German.

   There is also a third reason for assuming the child does not acquire syntax by observation. This is that the evidence would not be sufficient in view of the fact that, as we have already mentioned, people do not speak in complete sentences. The following are all authentic examples of conversation:

(16) a. Er sagt, er wollte . . . nein, er war es nicht
          He said he wanted to . . . no, it wasn't him

      b. Fährst du in die in die St . . . warum nicht?
          Are you going to to t . . . why not?

      c. Die hat einen . . . was sie nicht . . . sollte sie aber nicht, aber sie hat
          She has a . . . which she didn't . . . she shouldn't though, but she did

These, together with examples such as (4), provide evidence that the language spoken by German speakers, and thus heard by a child, does not consist only (or even mainly) of grammatically acceptable, complete sentences. And while the hesitations, indicated by dots in (16), may signal indecisiveness and therefore possible errors or gaps, there is nothing in the way (4) was said to tell a child that an utterance like this is not grammatical. This brief discussion suggests that neither observation nor explicit teaching could have enabled a child to speak German fluently by the age of four. There are other reasons for this assumption which are not directly relevant to our discussion here, including the fact that all German-speaking children's language will develop through very similar stages which have much in common with the stages a child goes through in the acquisition of English, Chinese or Russian. Whatever errors remain in a four-year-old German's language, it will not contain utterances like (3a). Certain types of errors, it appears, are never made.

In order to explain how a child acquires his or her native language in so short a time, bearing in mind the incompleteness, incorrectness or inaudibility of much of the data and the fact that it is not labelled with asterisks in the case of errors as in (4) (a situation often referred to as the **poverty of the stimulus**; see, for example, Hornstein and Lightfoot 1981), and bearing in mind also the fact that a child never makes certain types of error, it appears that we must assume that the universal principles mentioned in chapter 1 are **innate**, or present even before birth. If a child is born with knowledge of syntactic principles, then all she needs to learn in order for her syntax to function are the particular parameters of German. In addition, a complete knowledge of German will of course require the learning of particular elements of the lexicon, morphology and phonology which are peculiar to German. It is interesting to note that adults in fact seem to have little effect on their children's acquisition of syntax, though this is not a view shared by all researchers. Where there is little dispute, on the other hand, about the role played by other speakers is in certain areas of lexical knowledge; here tests have suggested that the first words children use are words used frequently by the parents (see Harris 1992). It is not surprising that in an area where the amount of knowledge to be learned can be assumed to be greater than that which could be subject to universal principles, as must be the case for the lexicon, then other speakers have quite a large influence on the child acquiring the language. In an area such as syntax, where much of the knowledge needed is assumed to be already present as universal principles, the effect of interaction with other speakers would be expected to be minimal, as indeed it appears to be. Nevertheless, without any language input from outside, a child will not acquire language, as studies of exceptional cases where children have grown up isolated from language input have shown. Implicit in what we have just been saying about the acquisition of German by a German child is the view that different areas of the language are acquired differently. This suggests that these different areas are governed by different principles, a view consistent with the assumption that certain areas of syntax, morphology and phonology are best seen as sub-areas or modules of linguistic knowledge, as discussed in chapter 1.

These various modules work together in a particular way in deriving the sentences of a language. Phrases and sentences are built up according to the principles of phrase structure, and movement of elements takes place during the derivation of sentences. At some point the structure is assigned a semantic interpretation on the one hand and a phonological interpretation on the other, so that a complete sentence, with meaning and sound, is the result. The latest generative theories, sometimes called minimalist theories, try to avoid having to assume a number of levels in the syntax as the output of the various modules and their interaction. Earlier theories posited a D-Structure or, even earlier, a Deep Structure level which was the result of phrase structure rules, as well as an S-Structure (earlier Surface Structure) which was the result of movements performed upon D-Structures. But the developments in syntactic theory and the differences between different stages of the theory will not be of direct concern to us in this book. The interested reader will find references in 2.6.

2.2   Phrase Structures of German

We have indicated several times in the preceding pages that all languages, including German, exhibit structure dependency. This is another way of saying that the elements of any sentence are ordered in a particular structure which is hierarchical in nature rather than linear. At this point we must make clear the distinction between the terms sentence, clause and phrase. A **sentence** is a connected group of clauses, often joined by a conjunction such as *und* or *weil*. A **clause** is a collection of phrases, consisting at least of a subject (a noun or noun phrase) and a verb (or verb phrase). A sentence may have only one clause. In this case the clause will be independent, that is, able to stand alone (*er lachte*, 'he laughed') as a main clause and the distinction between clause and sentence (not in any case present in German which uses *Satz* for both, though occasionally *Teilsatz* for clause) disappears. A subordinate clause (*weil es lustig war*, 'because it was funny') will be dependent on a main clause; it is introduced by a word such as a conjunction, and in German is typically characterized by having its verb at the end. To see what exactly a phrase is, let us look again at sentence (1) above, repeated here as (17). We note that certain elements go together:

(17)   Die Frau schrieb einen Brief
       The woman wrote a letter

Those elements which go together form the **phrases** or **phrasal categories** of the grammar. In sentence (17) *die* and *Frau* go together to make a phrase, traditionally called a **noun phrase** (or NP for short) because it consists of a noun (N) and, sometimes, a determiner (D) such as the definite article *die*. Much recent work in syntax considers the NP to be in fact a DP, or determiner phrase, but this is a technicality we shall not consider here; there are some references for this at the end of this chapter. We shall preserve the traditional terminology in calling it an NP in this book.

The NP *die Frau* could be replaced by a variety of other phrases, given in square brackets below, and the sentence would still make sense:

(18) a. [Die alte Frau] schrieb einen Brief
    The old woman wrote a letter

  b. [Die Frau, die ich gestern sah], schrieb einen Brief
    The woman I saw yesterday wrote a letter

  c. [Susanne] schrieb einen Brief
    Susanne wrote a letter

  d. [Die Frau in der Ecke] schrieb einen Brief
    The woman in the corner wrote a letter

These examples already give some indication of why it is that we speak of phrases as being the elements of a sentence. A word like *Susanne* and a phrase like *Die Frau, die ich gestern sah* clearly behave in the same way with respect to the structure of the sentence, because they are exactly interchangeable. Phrases or phrasal categories are the elements which combine to make sentences and the phrases themselves consist of words, or elements belonging to **lexical categories** such as *sah* (verb or V), *Frau* (N), *alt* (adjective or A), and so on. The other phrasal category in (17) is a **verb phrase** (VP) *schrieb einen Brief* which contains a further NP *einen Brief*. Again, we can tell that *schrieb einen Brief* belongs together as a VP because it could be replaced with other types of VP, in square brackets here:

(19) a. Die Frau [schrieb]
    The woman wrote

  b. Die Frau [schrieb furchtbar langsam]
    The woman wrote terribly slowly

  c. Die Frau [schrieb an einem Schreibtisch]
    The woman wrote at a desk

The VP *schrieb an einem Schreibtisch* in (19c) contains a further phrasal category PP or **prepositional phrase**, *an einem Schreibtisch*, which itself contains a preposition (P) *an* and an NP *einem Schreibtisch*.

It is possible to represent the structure of a sentence like (19c) by means of a **tree-diagram** or **phrase marker** as follows:

(20)

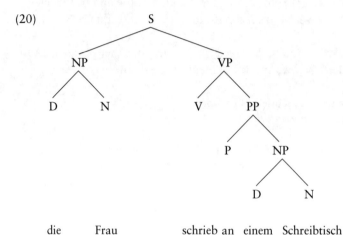

die   Frau   schrieb an einem Schreibtisch

A diagram like this enables us to see how the lexical categories – represented by the words at the bottom of the tree – are joined together to make phrasal categories such as NP, PP and VP and how these are joined together to make larger categories and finally the sentence.

Another way of representing the sentence in (19c) is to write rules which specify the structure of, or generate, sentences (see chapter 1). A generative grammar is a system of such rules. They may for example be written as:

(21)   a.   S   →   NP VP
       b.   VP →   V (NP) (PP)
       c.   PP →   P NP
       d.   NP →   (D) N (PP)

These rules, called **phrase structure rules** or **PS rules,** indicate that a sentence (S) can be rewritten as an NP and a VP and also show how each of these phrasal categories can itself be rewritten. The brackets in (21b) indicate that both the NP and the PP are optional, as can be seen by comparing (17), (19a) and (19b). The brackets in (21d) indicate that a determiner is optional as in (18c) above and that a PP may be present within an NP, as in *die Frau in der Ecke* in (18d), but need not be, as in the other examples in (18). The rules in (21a) to (21d) represent only a partial generative grammar; they will not generate sentences with auxiliaries (Aux) such as:

(22)   Die Frau hat einen Brief geschrieben
       The woman wrote/has written a letter

This sentence requires a PS rule including the element Aux. They will also not generate sentences with **adjective phrases** (AP) such as (18a) or

(23) Die sehr alte Frau schrieb einen Brief
The very old woman wrote a letter

and they will not generate sentences with a further embedded clause and a word such as *dass* (belonging to the category COMP, or **complementizer**), as in:

(24) Die Frau schrieb, dass Peter wieder gesund sei
The woman wrote that Peter was better

In principle, it would be possible to add to the list of PS rules in (22) so that all possible sentences of German can be generated by the set of rules. The history of the development of phrase structure rules, from single, language-specific rules such as those given in (21) for German, to the theory of unified phrase structure rules presented by Jackendoff in 1977 as X-bar rules and later integrated into the theory of universal grammar, cannot be gone into here, but the interested reader will find references in the final section of this chapter. In this chapter we shall not be concerned with this historical development nor with some of the interesting arguments about the nature of PS-rules, but we shall concentrate simply on the main features of German phrases.

The central concept of **X-bar Theory**, originally developed by Jackendoff (1977), based on an earlier idea suggested by Chomsky (1970), is that every phrase has a **head**, a lexical category which determines the nature of the phrasal category containing it. Let us look again at the sentence in (19c) and (20), repeated here:

(25) Die Frau schrieb an einem Schreibtisch
The woman wrote at a desk

We see that the phrases it contains are as follows:

(26) NP   die Frau
     VP   schrieb an einem Schreibtisch
     PP   an einem Schreibtisch
     NP   einem Schreibtisch

Both NPs both contain an N: *Frau* and *Schreibtisch* respectively. The VP contains the V *schrieb* followed by a **complement**, a PP, which may be optional, as here, or obligatory, as would be an NP following a transitive verb like *finden*, which must take an object NP such as *einen Schatz*

(treasure) or *das verlorene Buch* (the lost book). The PP contains a P
followed by an NP as complement.

Jackendoff (1977), observing that NPs contain Ns, VPs contain Vs,
and so on, proposed that there was a general principle of phrase structures, which could be represented as:

(27) a. XP   →   …X…

b.
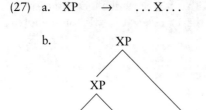

whereby XP is any phrase and X is its head, a word of the same category
but at a lexical level; the head of a noun phrase is a noun, of a verb
phrase a verb, and so on. The dots either side of X in (27a) indicate that
the other elements of the phrase may come before or after X. In (27b) we
see this represented at a tree diagram. In a PP like the following:

(28)   drüben an einem Schreibtisch
       over there at a desk

the head is the P *an*, which takes a complement *einem Schreibtisch* but it
also has what is known as a **specifier**, *drüben*, something which qualifies
the element *an einem Schreibtisch* but is part of the PP. Thus in a tree-
diagram, the PP in (28) would look like this:

(29)
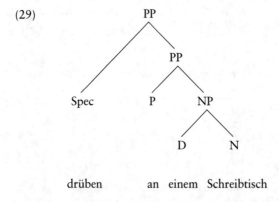

There are restrictions as to which categories can go into the dotted
areas in (27), but these are not in fact determined by the PS principle

itself, so they must be left open. However, they are not determined either by the parametric variation of the PS rules in German (or any other language), but rather by the interaction of other areas of the German (or other) grammar, such as **case-marking**, which will be mentioned later.

Because the formulation in (27) does not cope with levels of syntax between a PP such as *drüben an einem Schreibtisch* and its constituents NP (*einem Schreibtisch*) and (P) *an* – that is, it offers no way of labelling the intermediate phrase *an einem Schreibtisch* (as the fact that this is also PP in (29) and XP in (27b) indicates) – there are further refinements of the schema in (27) to be found in works such as Toman (1983) or Roberts (1997). But these need not concern us here; all we need to be concerned with is that there appears to be a universal principle of phrase structures at work here which we can call the **X-bar principle**. In universal terms it needs no further specification because the elements represented by the dots in (27) will be determined partly by the lexical properties of X and partly by other grammatical principles. The actual order of elements within phrases, in other words, whether *an einem Schreibtisch* follows *schrieb* as in (25) or precedes it, as in

(30)   Es passierte selten, dass die alte Frau an einem Schreibtisch schrieb
       It did not happen often that the old woman wrote at a desk

will be an issue specific to German. That is, it will be the result of German parametric variation of the universal principal (27a). In section 2.4 below, we shall argue that the subordinate clause introduced by *dass* in (30) represents the underlying order of the VP in German, that is, German syntax places the verb at the end of the VP. Another way of saying this is that German is a **head-final** language. Though this is the position taken by various writers such as Felix and Fanselow (1987), it is clear that German is not consistent in this. Within the PP *an einem Schreibtisch*, the head *an* is at the beginning, not at the end, though in NPs the N (such as *Frau* in *die alte Frau* in 30) is at the end.

What the discussion in this section indicates is that, in the view of German presented in this book, there is no really specific knowledge of German phrase structures which a native speaker of German will possess except, perhaps, that the head in a German phrase is (generally) at the end. Thus he or she will know that

(31)   a.   (dass) Peter ein Buch schrieb (VP)
       b.   eine sehr alte Frau (NP)
       c.   extrem alt (AP)

are possible German phrases but

(32) a. *(dass) Peter schrieb ein Buch (VP)
      b. *eine Frau sehr alte (NP)
      c. *alt extrem (AP)

are not. This clearly marks out German from other languages such as English, which would allow a corresponding structure to (32a):

(33) (that) Peter wrote a book

or French, which would allow those which correspond to (32b), for example:

(34) une dame très vieille

and whose speakers must thus have other versions of the parametric head position in phrases as part of their specific language knowledge. But apart from this knowledge about the position of the head, what to put in the gaps in the general schema (27) will be determined by the way it interacts with other types of knowledge, such as lexical knowledge, which we shall examine in chapter 6, and knowledge of case, which is considered in the following section.

2.3   Case in German

It is fairly common to hear people say that German has cases, whereas English does not. What they mean by this is that in a sentence such as

(35) Die Frau gab dem Mann den Brief
      The woman gave the man the letter

you can see by the forms of the determiners that *dem Mann* is in the dative case and *den Brief* is in the accusative and this tells you that *dem Mann* is the indirect and *den Brief* the direct object of the verb *gab*. In English, *the* does not have different endings; we can tell that *the man* is indirect and *the letter* direct object in the following sentence, which is the English equivalent of (35), by word order and semantics:

(36) The woman gave the man the letter

One of the things which always strikes the second-language learner of German is that the word order is not important in determining the grammatical function of the elements in the sentence, as it is, for example, in English. For (35) we could equally well say:

(37)   Dem Mann gab die Frau den Brief

or

(38)   Den Brief gab die Frau dem Mann

But even though *the* in (36) cannot change, and its grammatical function is clearly determined by word order, it is nevertheless common in traditional, Latin-based grammar to say that *the man* in sentence (36) is in the dative case and *the letter* in the accusative case, even though there is no difference in any endings.

The conflict here arises from the difference between **abstract case** and **morphological case**. All languages have abstract case, that is, there are structural positions in the sentence which are related directly in various ways to other elements appearing in the sentence. Thus the presence of abstract case – it determines, for example, that the subject of a sentence is in the nominative case whether or not we can see that it is – is a matter of universal principle. All languages have abstract case, English just as much as German. How much morphological case languages show, on the other hand, is a question of parametric variation. German has far more than English, as examples (35), (36) and (38) show. Latin has more than German, and Chinese has none at all. There may also be variation within a language historically, as we shall show during the discussion of Old High German case endings on nouns in chapter 8.

In German there are the following four cases:

(39)   Nominative: der Mann
       Accusative: den Mann
       Genitive: des Mannes
       Dative: dem Mann(e)

and the endings are seen in most cases on the article (*der, den, des, dem*), or an adjective which precedes the noun, as in *der alte Mann*, or, as in *des Mannes*, on the noun itself. In some instances, the case is not so clearly visible as an ending:

(40)   Nominative: die Frau
       Accusative: die Frau
       Genitive: der Frau
       Dative: der Frau

Here, the nominative and accusative share the same form of the article, as do genitive and dative, and all four cases of the noun have the same ending. Nevertheless, we assume that these four forms of the lexical item *Frau* (in 40) represent the same four abstract cases as the four forms of *Mann* in (39), even though its morphological realizations give no such signals.

Intuitively, it appears that the freedom of word order in any particular language ought to be linked to the amount of overt, morphological case in that language. English, for example, does not have much in the way of obvious case endings and its word order is fairly fixed. We cannot say, corresponding to (37):

(41)   The man gave the woman a letter

and mean exactly the same as (37), that is

(42)   The woman gave the man a letter

though the two corresponding German sentences (37) and (35) do mean the same.

In fact, studies by linguists have suggested that it is actually the way abstract, underlying case is assigned which largely determines word order in a language. We shall not worry about this here, though the interested reader may consult books such as Felix and Fanselow (1987) or von Stechow and Sternefeld (1988). The observation that overt, that is, morphological, case corresponds to free word order is indeed a valid one.

When we consider abstract as opposed to morphological case, we speak of case being assigned by one element in a phrase structure to another. NPs are assigned case by verbs and prepositions, and recent linguistic research indicates that all NPs must actually be assigned case, whether or not we can see it. In the following example

(43)   Ich helfe dem Mann(e)
       I help the man

we say that the verb *helfen* assigns dative case to its object. We can illustrate this in a tree-diagram like this:

(44)

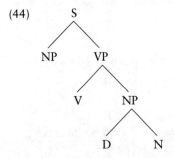

Ich   helfe   dem   Mann

where the arrow indicates the assignment of case by the verb to the NP. In the terms familiar from German grammar lessons, *helfen* 'takes' the dative. Prepositions also assign case, for example, the preposition *angesichts* assigns the genitive:

(45) angesichts des schlechten Wetters
      because of the bad weather

Again, learners of German are familiar with lists of prepositions and the cases they 'take'. But it is not only verbs and prepositions which assign case. In German, adjectives do too, as the following examples show:

(46) a. Sie war ihren Idealen treu
          She was faithful to her ideals

      b. Er war sich der Tatsache bewusst
          He was aware of the fact

      c. Ich bin dir dankbar
          I am thankful to you

It would be most helpful to learners of German grammar if particular adjectives were more explicitly given as 'taking' particular cases, just as verbs and prepositions are. This is not, of course, true of all adjectives; words like *gelb, alt, klein* do not assign case at all. (Note that the corresponding adjectives in English to those in (46) have to be followed by a preposition: *faithful to, aware of, thankful to*, and it is the preposition which assigns the case, not the adjective.) In the examples in (46), the adjectives *treu, bewusst* and *dankbar* assign dative and genitive case respectively to the preceding nouns. All languages assign case, even if it is not visible, as in Chinese. So we can assume that case assignment is a universal principle. It appears, however, that the direction in which case is assigned is a matter of parametric variation. Let us assume for a moment that the German subordinate clause represents the underlying word order in German, an assumption we shall return to in 2.4, but will simply take as given here. Consider the following examples, where the relevant phrasal categories are marked and arrows indicate the direction of case assignment:

(47) a. Peter meinte, dass er [seinem Vater]$_{NP}$ [geholfen habe]$_{VP}$

          Peter thought that he had helped his father

      b. *Peter meinte, dass er [geholfen habe]$_{VP}$ [seinem Vater]$_{NP}$

The second sentence, (47b), is not an acceptable sentence of German. This fact, together with examples such as those in (46), has led linguists working with German to assume that in German case is generally assigned to the left, though the observant reader will have noticed that prepositions (as in 45) appear to do it the other way round, with a few exceptions, such as:

(48)   a.   der Straße entlang
            along the street

       b.   entlang der Straße

where either word order (and hence either direction of case-assignment) is possible. In English, however, case is always assigned to the right. Compare:

(49)   a.   The woman [wrote]$_{VP}$ [the letter]$_{NP}$

       b.   I walked [along]$_{PP}$ [the street]$_{NP}$

with

(50)   a.   *The woman [the letter]$_{NP}$ [wrote]$_{VP}$

            *I walked [the street]$_{NP}$ [along]$_{PP}$

It is generally assumed that the direction in which case is assigned in a particular language is directly linked to the underlying word order in sentences. Thus languages like German or Japanese which assign case to the left will have a basic subject–object–verb (SOV) order, and those like English and French, which assign case to the right, will have an SVO order. Broadly speaking, then, the verb will be in the appropriate position in relation to its object in which it needs to be to assign case to the object. However, though this apparent common pattern of case assignment to the left in German is one reason for assuming that it has a basic SOV order, the issue if far from clear, as the discussion in the next section shows.

2.4   The Position of the German Verb

In the view of German we are putting forward here, broadly a principles and parameters view, the variation in whether the head of a phrase precedes or follows its specifier and complement is determined by the parametrization of this order. But this is not only a consideration in principles and parameters theory. German has traditionally been considered problematic because of the position of its verb, which is at the end in a subordinate clause such as *weil es heiß ist* ('because it is hot') but in second position in main clauses. We shall consider this instance first. The following examples show the main verb (or finite verb; that is, that part of the verb which is marked for person, number and tense) in second position in a sentence or main clause:

(51) a. Hans *hat* gestern den Kuchen gegessen
Hans ate the cake yesterday

b. Gestern *wollte* Hans den Kuchen essen
Yesterday Hans intended to eat the cake

c. Bis ich komme, *wird* Hans den Kuchen gegessen haben
By the time I arrive, Hans will have eaten the cake

This constraint has been known for a very long time to scholars working on the German language. Steinbach (1724; mentioned in Scaglione 1981) and Erdmann (1886–98), for example, discuss it. This apparently central feature of main clauses, that the finite verb occupies second place, can be seen to apply whatever is in first position; as the three examples in (51) show. When the verb has more than one part, the second part is at the end of the clause, as example (51c) indicates. This is the phenomenon sometimes referred to as the 'Zweiteilung des Prädikats' (division of the verb into two). As the following examples show, the finite verb, traditionally referred to as P1 (the first part of the predicator), is a single element, but the other part of the verb, sometimes called P2, may consist of several words, shown in bold:

	P1	P2
(52) a.	Gestern **wollte** Hans den Kuchen **essen**	

Yesterday Hans intended to eat the cake

	P1	P2
b.	Gestern **hat** Hans den Kuchen **essen wollen**	

Yesterday Hans intended to eat the cake

	P1	P2
c.	Bis ich ankomme, **wird** der Kuchen noch nicht ganz **gegessen worden sein können**	

By the time I arrive, the cake won't have been able to be completely eaten

The type of structure in (52c) is very typically German, and is something many learners of German find difficult. And yet if learners remember that the finite part of the verb is always in second position in the sentence and all the other parts at the end, the only real room for error is in the order of those parts at the end. The structure which arises from this two-part division of the verbal elements is referred to in traditional grammar as the **Satzklammer** (sentence bracket); Fox (1990: 248) calls this the 'frame or bracket construction'. The *Satzklammer* contains the **Mittelfeld** or central field of the sentence; to the left of this is the **Vorfeld** or first field and to the right the **Nachfeld** or final field. For sentence (52a) above, the division would thus be as follows:

(53) Vorfeld   P1   Mittelfeld   P2   Nachfeld
      Gestern   wollte   Hans den Kuchen   essen   ——

In this sentence the *Nachfeld* is empty, but it could contain a number of elements, such as, for example, a causal clause:

                                                      Nachfeld
(54) Gestern wollte Hans den Kuchen essen, **weil er Hunger hatte**
      Yesterday Hans intended to eat the cake, as he was hungry

Here, the phrase *weil er Hunger hatte* occupies the *Nachfeld*; other possible phrases here are *glaube ich*, *komischerweise*, or, colloquially, *trotzdem*.

   Although the verbal elements in the sentence have a fixed position, with the finite part in second place and the rest at the end, there are apparent variations in the second-place position of the finite verb (V2). Both traditional descriptions and those within the framework of generative grammar pay particular attention to the position of the verb. If the *Vorfeld* is not occupied, the verb will be in the initial position; this will be what is called a verb-initial (V1) sentence. If, on the other hand, the main verb is in P2 rather than P1, as in (47a), the sentence will be verb-final (Vf). These various possibilities give rise to the main types of word-order in German, and have been extensively documented; see section 2.6 of this chapter for details. They are as follows.

1. V1 clauses
These are questions such as:

(55) **Hat** Hans den Kuchen gegessen?
      Did Hans eat the cake?

imperatives:

(56) **Iss** den Kuchen!
      Eat the cake!

subordinate clauses without a conjunction:

(57)   **Regnet** es (so bleibe ich zu Hause)
       If it rains (I'll stay at home)

and occasional constructions of the type found in ballads, such as:

(58)   **Sah** ein Knab ein Röslein . . .
       Once a boy beheld a rose

(Goethe; Conrady 1977: 238)

2. V2 clauses

These are all declarative sentences (sentences making a statement) of the type given in (51) above (*Hans hat gestern den Kuchen gegessen*), as well as occasional relative clauses, common in Middle High German and also found in the style of German used in ballads and fables:

(59)   (Es war einmal ein kleines Mädchen,) das **hatte** nichts zu essen
       (*Once upon a time there was a litle girl;*) *she had nothing to eat*

where nowadays one would expect the verb to be at the end (*das nichts zu essen hatte*), and questions introduced by a question word:

(60)   Wer **hat** den Kuchen gegessen?
       Who ate the cake?

3. Vf clauses

These include subordinate clauses introduced by a conjunction, such as:

(61)   Peter sah, wie Hans den Kuchen **aß**
       Peter saw Hans eating the cake

These are the basic three patterns of word-order as determined by the position of the verb. If we consider the second, most common type, V2 clauses, we see that stylistic variation is possible in the elements around the *Satzklammer*. Thus phrases can be moved to the front of the sentence to give emphasis. The difference between (62a), (b) and (c) below is clearly of this type:

(62)   a.   Hans hat den Kuchen gegessen

       b.   Den Kuchen hat Hans gegessen

       c.   Gegessen hat Hans den Kuchen

Notice that the finite verb form *hat* remains in V2 position whatever is put at the front:

(63)

Vorfeld	P1	Mittelfeld	P2	(Nachfeld)
Hans	hat	den Kuchen	gegessen	——
Den Kuchen	hat	Hans	gegessen	——
Gegessen	hat	Hans	den Kuchen	——

In (62a) it is *Hans* who is being emphasized, in (62b) *den Kuchen* and in (62c) *gegessen*. The sentences in (62) may also be seen as answers to particular questions:

(64) a. Wer hat den Kuchen gegessen?   Hans hat den Kuchen gegessen
        Who has eaten the cake?   *Hans has eaten the cake*

      b. Was hat Hans gegessen?   Den Kuchen hat Hans gegessen
        What has Hans eaten?   *The cake is what Hans has eaten*

      c. Was hat Hans mit dem Kuchen   Gegessen hat Hans den Kuchen
        gemacht?   *Eaten it, that's what Hans has*
        What has Hans done with the cake? *done with the cake*

Here it is the element being asked about which is given precedence in the answer and is therefore placed at the beginning, something which, as the equivalent English sentences in (64) show, cannot be done so simply in English.

    Traditional descriptions of German word order are concerned to show what orders are possible and some of them assume as a matter of intuition that the main clause order, that is, the most common type which has the verb in second position, is the basic or underlying one; in other words, they assume German is a 'V2 language', or an SVO (subject–verb–object) language. It is often said that, for example, when a finite auxiliary takes the place of the main verb, this verb must then move to the end. Take the following sentence:

(65) Hans isst den Kuchen
     Hans is eating the cake

If this is put into the perfect tense, *hat* replaces *isst* and the main verb, in the traditional view, is sent to the end:

(66) Hans **hat** den Kuchen **gegessen**
     Hans ate the cake

This can be expressed like this:

(67) | Vorfeld | P1 | Mittelfeld | P2 | (Nachfeld) |
|---|---|---|---|---|
| Hans | isst | den Kuchen | —— | —— |
| Hans | hat | den Kuchen | gegessen | —— |

Similarly, it is said that a conjunction such as *dass* can take the place of P1, whereby the introductory phrase such as *Peter sagt* is in initial position and the replacement of P1 by *dass* will send P1 into P2; so (66) becomes:

(68) **dass** Hans den Kuchen **gegessen hat**
       that Hans ate the cake

We can see this 'displacement' if we again look at the *Satzklammer* structure of (66) and (68):

(69) | Vorfeld | P1 | Mittelfeld | P2 | (Nachfeld) |
|---|---|---|---|---|
| Hans | hat | den Kuchen | gegessen | —— |
| Peter sagt | dass | Hans den Kuchen | gegessen hat | —— |

In fact there is some evidence (as given in Scaglione 1981: 120) that there is a historical basis for this assumption: it appears that in Old High German the word *thaz* (the forerunner of *dass* in Modern German) was placed at the end of a main clause to signal that a subordinate clause was to follow. It then moved to the first position in the subordinate clause and, around the sixteenth century, the end position for verbs in subordinate clauses became fixed.

But notice that such notions in traditional grammar as 'underlying' and 'sends the verb to the end' do not necessarily relate to similar notions employed later in generative grammar. In traditional descriptions, such formulations are sometimes useful metaphors, meant to represent native speaker intuitions, and sometimes attempts to represent historical changes, so that terms like 'underlying' and 'basic' mean 'historically earlier'. In generative grammar, the notion of 'underlying' can be used to refer to a lower level of syntax, the deep structure or D-structure, and such notions as 'sending something somewhere' are usually related to transformational movement operations, which are simply operations which move phrases from their original position in D-structure to the final S-structure position, or, in more recent versions of generative theory, provide a link between related structures. However, generative grammar is not free from confusion between the synchronic (to do with the present state of the language, representing a speaker's knowledge as it is now assumed to be) and the diachronic (to do with historical development). Reading some of the vast literature on the word order of German (for examples of which, see section 2.6) one gets the impression that the processes of historical change have sometimes influenced the synchronic view of what is, in the sense of levels of syntax, underlying. Thus, although in generative grammar, and in the view we subscribe to, the assumptions made about the structure of sentences or clauses such as (65), (66) and (68) above are very different from traditional ones, assuming in fact that the underlying or basic order is the verb final order (Vf), as exemplified in (68), it is important not to forget that evidence is not conclusive. So what is the evidence for assuming that a sentence such as:

(70)   Hans hat den Kuchen gegessen

is derived from something like

(71)   Hans den Kuchen gegessen hat

which, as noted above, is the word order we find in a subordinate clause like (68)? In most modern generative studies the assumption is made that not only V2 but also V1 structures are obtained by movement of the verb from its original clause-final position. There have been numerous studies which have put forward evidence for this view, in particular Bierwisch (1963) and Traugott (1969) and, more recently, Edmondson (1982). Those who have argued against it include especially Weinrich (1964), who argues for SVO order, and Haiman (1974) who proposes VSO. It is not possible to go through all the arguments for our chosen view here, and they are given in great detail in the 'pro-SOV' works mentioned above and in section 2.6, but we shall give what we consider to be one of the most convincing arguments for adopting this view. This is the observation (made by Clahsen and Smolka 1986) that compound verbs such as *anstellen* ('to do/to place/to behave'), *aufgeben* ('to give up') and *ankommen* ('to arrive') must be inserted into phrase structures with their two parts together, and the only way this can happen is if they are, at that underlying stage, at the end of the sentence or clause, as the following examples illustrate:

(72)   a.   Sie wollte nicht aufgeben
            She did not want to give up

       b.   Sie gab nicht auf
            She did not give up

so that a sentence such as (72b), with the first part of the verb in second position, is derived from a structure with the whole verb at the end, in the position in which it occurs in sentences such as (72a). On this basis, it seems reasonable to assume that the underlying structure is the Vf one, and that German is thus an SOV language. This ties in interestingly with the historical evidence put forward by writers like Delbrück (1878) that all Indo-European languages at one time exhibited SOV order, which coincided with particularly strong patterns of inflection. The verb then tended to be moved to a position between subject and object (thus SVO) as the number of inflections decreased, a process completed in English but only partially carried through in German, leaving a mixture of SVO in main clauses and SOV in subordinate clauses. As we mentioned above, there seem no obvious reasons why the historical development should mirror the synchronic state of the grammar, and we should merely note it as an interesting correspondence, unless there are any reasonable grounds for assuming (as does Hopper 1975) that there is a link.

Most views of how the V2 order is derived are like the one we are suggesting here, assuming that the verb has been moved from its underlying final position to second position and that some other constituent fills the initial position. The elements that can occur in the initial position in a main clause (see Haider 1986) apart from the subject NP as in (66) are:

an interrogative phrase:

(73)   **Wann** hat Hans den Kuchen gegessen?
        When did Hans eat the cake?

a non-interrogative adverbial phrase:

(74)   **Gestern** hat Hans den Kuchen gegessen
        Yesterday Hans ate the cake

the expletive *es*:

(75)   **Es** hat gestern einer den Kuchen gegessen
        Someone ate the cake yesterday

(Because German is a so-called 'non-Pro-drop' language, the subject position, that is, the position before the verb, must be filled with some element. This is not true of all languages, as discussed in chapter 1.) It has frequently been observed by recent writers (for examples, see section 2.6) that, as traditional accounts have often noted, the complementizer *dass* is in complementary distribution with the V2 phenomenon. That is, when *dass* is present, the verb is at the end and when *dass* is not present, the verb is in second position. Thus the sentence:

(76)   Maria glaubt, dass Hans den Kuchen gegessen hat
        Maria believes that Hans has eaten the cake

is Vf, whereas

(77)   Maria glaubt, Hans habe den Kuchen gegessen
       Maria believes Hans has eaten the cake

is V2, even though it is an embedded clause. Note that the verb in such embedded V2 clauses without *dass* is usually subjunctive. This can be seen as evidence that the second position, occupied by the verb in main V2 clauses, is the same position as that otherwise occupied by the complementizer *dass*:

(78)   Vorfeld   P1   Mittelfeld   P2   (Nachfeld)

       Hans   hat   den Kuchen   gegessen   ——
       Hans   habe   den Kuchen   gegessen   ——
       Maria glaubt   dass   Hans den Kuchen   gegessen hat   ——

Though it might seem unimportant whether V2 or Vf is the underlying order in German sentences, these investigations in fact are attempts to say something about the native German speaker's knowledge of German syntax. Where most traditional studies are not concerned with reasons for changes in sentence order nor do they make any attempt to relate these to other aspects of German or to phenomena in other languages, generative grammar tries to posit reasons for assuming that Vf is the underlying structure which can be derived from other aspects of grammar, as example (72) illustrates. There is also some evidence from language acquisition by German children (see Clahsen and Smolka 1986) suggesting, though by no means conclusively proving, that the view of generative grammar does in fact reflect native speaker knowledge.

2.5   Syntactic Processes

In the previous sections we looked at how the phrase structures generated by the syntax of German interact with other areas of syntax such as case-marking to determine word order (or, to be more precise, phrase order) within a sentence. We saw that position, case-marking and the agreement of verbs all help to determine the relationships between the various elements of the sentence.

But native speakers of any language – and German is no exception – have intuitions that certain sentences with different word order are related. In this section we will look at two such instances, that of passive and active sentences, and, more briefly, the formation of questions. We saw in section 2.4 how sentences such as

(78) Der junge Mann hat den Kuchen gegessen
      The young man has eaten the cake

and

(79) Den Kuchen hat der junge Mann gegessen

are only stylistically different; the emphasis is placed on the first element in the sentence. But sometimes the difference in position is not just one of style or emphasis. Consider the following two sentences

(80) Der junge Mann aß den Kuchen
      The young man ate the cake

(81) Der Kuchen wurde (vom jungen Mann) gegessen
      The cake was eaten by the young man

These two sentences are related by passivization; (81) is the passive of (80). Intuitively, these do not mean the same thing so the difference is not one of style. We can observe certain things about the relationship between (80) and (81) which apply to all such pairs of sentences. Firstly, the object of the verb, *den Kuchen* in (80), has not only moved to subject position in (81), but has also taken the nominative case. (This is also of course true of passive sentences in English; we would not be able to see this with NPs, but a pronoun in object position in an active sentence such as *she saw him* will clearly change to nominative in the passive *he was seen by her*.) Furthermore, the subject of (80), *der junge Mann*, has become optional in (81), and for this reason is in brackets. If it is expressed, it is inside a PP, *vom jungen Mann*. The third change that has taken place between (80) and (81) is that the verb *essen* has changed from active third person singular present *aß* to passive *wurde gegessen*, consisting of the third person singular of the verb *werden* and the past participle of the original verb *essen*. To some extent this also involves a change of emphasis, just as in the sentences in (78) and (79). There the emphasis in (78) was on the agent, the person performing the action (see chapter 6), expressed in the subject, and in (79) on the theme, that which is directly affected by the action, expressed in the direct object. Similarly in (81), the emphasis is clearly no longer on the agent, *der junge Mann*, which is optional. The fact that some elements of (81) are the same as in (80) also suggests that in some sense the same content with different emphasis is involved. Notice, for example, that the tense of the verb *essen*, imperfect in (80), is preserved in the auxiliary *wurde* in (81), which is also in the imperfect tense, and that other elements such as number and person of the verb are maintained;

Kuchen remains singular and the article *der* remains definite. In fact, it is
a commonplace of so-called passive transformation exercises of the sort
students of German have to perform in tests that such elements as number,
gender, person and tense have to be preserved. The only differences,
then, lie in the fact that the agent, the person performing the action,
moves from subject position to an optional PP, the theme changes from
object to subject, and the verb to its passive form. Passive is thus to some
extent a way of giving a different emphasis. But the changed form of
subject, object and verb mean that it is a syntactic change, not just a
stylistic one.

But let's look at what happens in more complex sentences, those containing an indirect object:

(82)   a.   Der junge Mann gab der alten Frau einen Kuchen
            The young man gave the old woman a cake

       b.   Ein Kuchen wurde der alten Frau vom jungen Mann gegeben
            A cake was given the old woman by the young man

As we have already seen, the direct object, *einen Kuchen* in (82a), can
move to subject position, *ein Kuchen* in (82b). But in both English
and German, and in many other languages, it is also possible to put
the indirect object into the subject position. In an English sentence corresponding to (82a)

(83)   The young man gave the old woman a cake

this results in

(84)   The old woman was given a cake by the young man

where the phrase *the old woman* appears to have become the subject.
But in German there is a difference. (82a) becomes in the passive:

(85)   Der alten Frau wurde ein Kuchen (vom jungen Mann) gegeben

where the NP *der alten Frau*, which was the dative indirect object in
(82a), remains in the dative. One way of describing what happens in
changing (82a) to (85) is to say that, in German, as opposed to English,
only a direct object can become the subject of the sentence, and an
indirect object (*der alten Frau*), though it moves to the first position,
remains the indirect object in the dative case. However, if we compare (85) with other possible passive sentences in German, we can see
similarities:

(86)   Es wird im Bahnhof nicht geraucht
       There is no smoking in the station

(87)   Im Bahnhof wird nicht geraucht

(88)   Es wird behauptet, dass Frauen klüger seien als Männer
       It's said that women are cleverer than men

(89)   Behauptet wird, dass Frauen klüger seien als Männer

None of these sentences has a subject; they are called impersonal passives. Note that in (86) and (87), the intransitive verb *rauchen* is passive. This is clearly not possible in English, as attempts at translations of (86) and (87) such as *It cannot be smoked* will show. There are, however, equivalent sentences to (88) beginning *It is said . . .* , *It is maintained*, and so on, so the impersonal passive structure is clearly sometimes possible. Sentences like (85) are sometimes also referred to as impersonal passives in German (see Felix and Fanselow 1987: 95), because they do not have to have an agent; note that the agent *vom jungen Mann* is optional. What this suggests is this: the fact that *der alten Frau* has taken the first position in (85) has nothing whatever to do with the passive construction, but merely results from the freedom of German word-order, which is observed in the active, too. Thus we can compare (85) with two possible variants:

(90)   Vom jungen Mann wurde der alten Frau ein Kuchen gegeben

(whereby *vom jungen Mann* can be replaced by *es*, but the subject position cannot be left empty) and

(91)   Ein Kuchen wurde der alten Frau (vom jungen Mann) gegeben

The three sentences in (85), (90) and (91) are stylistic variants like those we saw earlier in (62). It is more useful to see (85) as a stylistic variant of (90) and (91) than as a passive version of (82), repeated here as (92):

(92)   Der junge Mann gab der alten Frau einen Kuchen

What this means is that in fact only the direct object (*einen Kuchen* in 82a) can become the subject of a passivized sentence (*ein Kuchen* in 91) and it moves to the subject position to do so. The indirect object (*der alten Frau* in 82a) cannot become the subject and it only moves to the first position in the same sort of stylistic variation as is possible between active sentences.

   It is important to note here that we are speaking of what is usually regarded as a different sort of movement from that sometimes assumed in traditional grammar to explain contrasts like those between (78) and (79) or between present and perfect in the examples in (65) and (66), repeated here:

(93)   Hans isst den Kuchen

(94)   Hans hat den Kuchen gegessen

where *hat* is sometimes said to displace *isst*, sending the verb *essen*, now in its participle form, to the end. The sort of movement we are describing in this section is assumed to be a representation of what we know about the relationship between sentences; we know that a syntactic operation has taken place whose effects can still be seen in the resulting structure. But this is not a straightforward matter, and a further elaboration of the word 'know' is required here. We are assuming that to know something in a grammatical sense means that it is (perhaps passively) part of our grammatical knowledge and it enables us to do certain things based on that knowledge. It is not to be confused with a conscious ability to explain phenomena. So to say that a sentence such as (82b) is a passive version of (82a) is to say that a German speaker's grammar holds information about this relationship, not that either he or she, in real time, has to begin with (82a) before producing (82b), nor that he or she can necessarily explain the connection. So to say that movement has taken place is to say that our grammar has an account of where an element was at a lower level of grammar (this is usually called a **trace** and will not concern us here) and that this fact has consequences for what is and is not a possible structure of German. Traditional views of movement or displacement were different in that they were rarely based on the notion of an internalized grammar; this made the distinction between historical change and grammatical operations difficult to maintain, as we saw in section 2.4 for questions about word order.

Another type of movement, mentioned briefly in section 2.4, and called wh-movement, is responsible for the formation of questions. Consider the change that has taken place between the next two sentences:

(95)   Hans hat den Jungen gesehen
       Hans has seen the boy

(96)   Wen hat Hans gesehen?
       Who has Hans seen?

The assumption here is that *den Jungen* can be converted to *wen*, the corresponding wh-word, which is also in the accusative case (as in *Hans hat wen gesehen?*, a perfectly possible question with the correct intonation) and that this word *wen* is moved to the first position in the sentence, where, as we saw in 2.4, interrogative elements usually go, whatever case they are in, for example:

(97)   **Wer** hat den Kuchen gegessen?

(98)   **Mit wem** bist du befreundet?
       Who are you friends with?

(99)   **Als was** wirst du dich verkleiden?
       What will you disguise yourself as?

and so on.

Today, many linguists would argue that the sort of movement we see in passivization and the formation of wh-questions and other operations (see Felix and Fanselow 1987) are not entirely separate operations, but that there is a generalized movement operation, which simply applies whenever a particular element for whatever reason cannot remain where it is in the structure (cf. Ouhalla 1994: 236). Traditionally, though, and almost certainly in terms of the intuitions of German native speakers, an active sentence can be passivized in one sort of syntactic process and, in another, a question can be asked about a particular element of a sentence, as in (96) it is asked about the person whom Hans has seen.

In this chapter we have seen how structures are generated and also moved within a sentence. It will have been noted that, when something happens to create movement in the syntax, the elements themselves change their form. Thus, in passive formation, the subject (*der junge Mann* in (78), for example) changes to a prepositional object in *vom jungen Mann* in (81). This is not just a change of position from before the verb to after it or of grammatical function from subject to prepositional object, but it is also a change in the actual form of the words: *junge* to *jungen*. It is with such changes to words, as opposed to changes within sentence structure, that the area of grammar called morphology is concerned, and this is the topic of the next chapter.

2.6   Further Reading

For a detailed description of what is covered by syntax, see Jacobs et al. (1993), especially chapter 1. Ouhalla (1994) provides general linguistic background on many concepts discussed here, as does Part 3 of Radford et al. (1999).

There is a vast literature on child language acquisition. Some useful sources are given in section 2.1. Hornstein and Lightfoot (1981) give a useful survey of the arguments put forward to suggest that universal syntactic principles are innate, as do Felix and Fanselow (1987: 65ff) and Stechow and Sternefeld (1988: 30f). Newton (2001) is a (non-linguistic) study of children isolated from language input.

Readers who would like to know more about the way syntactic theory has developed should consult Felix and Fanselow (1987), Radford (1988) or van Riemsdijk and Williams (1986) for the prevailing view in the 1980s and Chomsky (1993) or Roberts (1997) for the latest version of the theory. Both van Riemsdijk and Williams (1986) and Ouhalla (1994) discuss the developments and changes in syntactic theory.

For information on the reasons for using the term 'determiner phrase', or DP, for what we have here called an NP, read Roberts (1997: 22f), Ouhalla (1994: 179ff) or Abney (1987).

There is a useful overview of the development of phrase-structure rules in Ouhalla (1994: ch. 4). See also Felix and Fanselow (1987) or von Stechow and Sternefeld (1988) for specific reference to German.

On the inconsistency of the head-position, see Roberts (1997). On word order, see den Besten (1984) and Felix and Fanselow (1987: 65ff), and, with special reference to the position of the German verb, Wackernagel (1892), Fourquet (1974), Behagel (1929, 1930), Delbrück (1920), Greenberg (1961), Bach (1962), Weinrich (1964), Olsen (1984), Beckman (1980) and Clahsen and Smolka (1986). In particular, on the assumption made in generative grammar that the basic order of the German sentence is verb-final, see Bach (1962), Bierwisch (1963), Traugott (1969), Thiersch (1978), Lenerz (1981), Edmondson (1982), Lehmann (1971) and Clahsen and Smolka (1986). Koster (1975) is a discussion of verbal-final order in Dutch.

Haider and Prinzhorn (1986) contains studies of the V2 constraint in Yiddish, Frisian, Swedish and Icelandic as well as German. Roberts (1997: 153) and Lenerz (1984) discuss the absence of sentences with unfilled subject positions in V2 languages and, besides Haider (1986), others who discuss the distribution of *dass* are den Besten (1983), Vikner (1990), Haider (1984) and Olsen (1984); see also Ouhalla (1994: 286) on this question.

EXERCISES

1   Ask any German speakers you know (use the internet if necessary) for other adjectives, besides those in (46), which assign case. Remember that native speakers' knowledge of language is passive, and you will probably have to explain what you mean! Find five such adjectives with the cases they assign.

2 Draw tree-diagrams like that in (20), using the categories given in (21), for the following three sentences:

Peter geht in die Stadt.

Die Kinder schwimmen in diesem See.

Das Mädchen malt Blumen in ihrem Klassenzimmer.

3 Divide the following three sentences up into Vorfeld, P1, Mittelfeld, P2 and Nachfeld, as in example (53):

Am Sonntag kommt der Zug am Bahnhof später an.
(Remember that *an* is part of the verb.)

Glücklicherweise hatte Paul den Termin nicht vergessen, wie er es manchmal tut.

Manchmal wollte ich wegfahren, aber ich konnte nicht.

4 Using a modern German novel (begged or borrowed from a friend if necessary), find six examples of V1 clauses (which may be complete sentences). Read section 2.4 again first if necessary.

5 Give English translations – not word-for-word literals but good, idiomatic equivalents – for the following sentences:

Hier wird nicht getanzt.

Gesagt wird manchmal schon, dass Deutsche keinen Humor haben.

Dieses Geschenk wurde der Frau von ihren Töchtern gegeben.

CHAPTER THREE

Morphology

3.1 Morphemes and Morphology

In chapter 2 we saw how words are put together to form sentences of German, and in this chapter we will examine the internal structure of the words themselves, and observe how they, too, are put together from smaller units of the language. This type of knowledge about words is part of a German native speaker's knowledge of the language, along with the ability to construct and understand sentences. This means that he or she can form new German words according to strict rules, many of which will reflect universal principles of word-formation.

For example, the word *gehen* ('to go', 'to walk') can be seen to consist of two parts: *geh* and *en*, a structure we can represent as *geh + en*, and it is clear to a German speaker that the word should be split up thus and not as, say, *g + ehen* or *gehe + n*, because *geh* is the part of the word also in evidence in *geht*, *gehst* and *Gehweg*, and *en* is the part we see in other verbs such as *waschen*, *raten* and *sparen*.

We refer to the parts of the word *geh* and *en* as **morphemes**. Very roughly speaking, morphemes can be defined as the smallest meaningful elements of grammar, whereby 'meaningful' can also be taken to encompass grammatical function: the *t* of *geht* is a morpheme which indicates third-person present and this is not perhaps what we would usually want to describe as meaning.

Though this definition is a useful starting point, simply observing that a sequence of sounds appears meaningful in some circumstances does not necessarily lead us to call it a morpheme in all circumstances. For example, *un-* has the function of rendering negative the meaning of adjectives:

(1) un + ordentlich
     un   *tidy*

un + klug
not   clever

un + fair
un   fair

but this does not mean that *un-* is a morpheme in words such as *unter* ('under') and *und* ('and'). It just happens to have the same sequence of sounds as the initial part of these words.

In other cases the function or meaning of part of a word is difficult to assess because it occurs so rarely (see Motsch 1988: 17). For example, in:

(2)   Dickicht   Kehricht
      thicket   *sweepings up*

      Zierde   Begierde
      ornament   *desire*

we can guess that *-icht* suggests something like a collection of things or that *-de* is a reifying morpheme, a little like *-ion*, as in *decorate, decoration* in English. But because so few examples of such words occur in German, it is difficult to be sure of the meaning of these morphemes.

Sometimes a part of the word which may appear to be a morpheme turns out on further reflection not to be one at all, as in:

(3)   Stragula
      linoleum

This word may intuitively appear to be analysable as *stra + gula* whereby the final 'morpheme' is a diminutive ending similar to that in *Molekül* or *Dracula*, both of which contain the modern German equivalent of the Latin diminutive *-ulus* or *-culus*. In fact, *Stragula* does not contain a diminutive ending at all, but is derived from Latin *stragulum*, meaning 'that which is spread out', possibly related to English *straggle*.

This suggests that a decision as to what constitutes morphemes can only be taken when words are seen in contrast to one another. The ending *-en* in our first example *gehen* relates to the *-en* in other words but contrasts with the *-st* or *-t* endings which can appear in the same lexical item. (Note that we say 'lexical item' rather than word. This is because, though in one sense *gehen, gehst, geht* are obviously different words, in another sense they are forms of the same word and would not have separate entries in a dictionary of German. The distinction between individual words and the lexical item with different forms is further discussed in chapter 6, but for now we shall assume that it is intuitively clear.) To return to our example of *geh + en*: we would want to see both of these, in the contrastive sense just given, as morphemes. Now consider the following examples:

(4) a. gehen

    b. Geh ins Bett!
       go to bed

In (4a) the morpheme *geh* is clearly one which can appear alone as it does in sentence (4b), and it is therefore referred to as a **free morpheme**; other examples are *gang* (as in *der Gang*, 'gait'), *schuh* (*der Schuh*, 'shoe'), *ich* ('I'), *rot* ('red'). But the morpheme *-en* in (4a) cannot occur alone; this is a **bound morpheme**. Bound morphemes are often written with a hyphen in linguistics.

    The same morpheme may be realized differently. In the various tenses of the verb *gehen*, for example, we find the forms:

(5) gehst
    gingst
    (bist) gegangen

If we remove those morphemes indicating different grammatical functions from each example, we are left with

(6) geh
    ging
    gang

These are regarded as being simply different realizations of the same morpheme *geh* and are called **allomorphs**. Allomorphs are commonly found in strong verbs such as *gehen*, *stehen* ('to stand'), whose past tense is *stand*, *waschen* ('to wash'), with past tense *wusch*, or *backen* ('to bake') with past tense *buk*. Another example is the plural morpheme, which has several allomorphs, as illustrated in the following words:

(7) Autos
    cars

    Tage
    days

    Frauen
    women

Eier
eggs

Schemata
schemes

Assuming that *geh* is the basic form for the allomorphs *ging* and *gang*, it is clear that this morpheme differs in nature from morphemes such as *ge-*, *-en* and *-t*. It is found in different categories in the **lexicon**, the inventory of words and morphemes of German (see chapter 6):

(8) er geht (V)
     he walks

     der Gehweg (N)
     the path

     begehbar (A)
     '*walkable on*'

and appears to be the basic element of a word, to which affixes are added. This type of morpheme, a **root**, may be free, as is *geh*, or it may be bound, as is *mög-*, which occurs in words like *möglich* and *Vermögen*. If the root is a free morpheme, it is often referred to as the **base word**.

To return to example (6), the first morpheme in *gegangen*, *ge-*, is a **prefix**, coming before the root, and the *-en* is a **suffix**; it follows the root. Prefixes and suffixes are classed together as **affixes**. Some morphemes, as can be seen from this example, are **discontinuous**. Because *ge-* and *-en* together indicate that this is the past participle of *gehen*, we do not speak of two separate morphemes here but of one which consists of both a prefix and a suffix, and it is discontinuous in the sense that *gang* intervenes. If *ge – en* is a past participle morpheme, so is *ge – t* as in *gebracht* or *gehabt*. The past participle morpheme thus has two allomorphs, both discontinuous: *ge – en* and *ge – t*.

For further illustration, in the examples which follow, all the roots and affixes (**pre** stands for 'prefix' and **suf** for 'suffix') are marked:

(9) geh en   geh st   be geh bar
     root suf   root suf   pre root suf

     Geh weg   geh   ver gäng lich
     root root   root   pre root suf

     ver geh st   geh bereit   unter geh en
     pre root suf   root root   root root suf

In these examples, we see that roots can be combined to form compounds
(*Gehweg*), an issue which will be discussed later in this chapter, and also
that there is yet another allomorph, *gäng*, of the *geh* morpheme.

Sometimes it is useful in morphology to speak of the word without its
inflectional affixes. The resulting part of the word is called a **stem**. In the
examples above, the stems are, respectively, *geh, geh, begehbar, Gehweg,
geh, vergänglich, vergeh, gehbereit, untergeh*. To all these stems can be
added inflectional affixes as illustrated by the italicized endings in the
examples below:

(10) geh: geh*st*   geh*en*   geh*t*
      begehbar: begehbar*e*   begehbar*en*   begehbar*ste*
      Gehweg: Gehweg*e*   Gehweg*s*
      vergänglich: vergänglich*e*   vergänglich*en* vergänglich*er*
      transient

At this point, the notion of inflection has not been introduced and so we
are using it in a very intuitive sense, to mean the endings that are added
to words to enable them to fit in with the syntax of the sentence. It will
shortly be discussed in detail.

Morphology, then, is that area of the grammar which covers all these
aspects of the way words are structured. In a modularly organized model
of our knowledge of grammar, as described in chapter 1, it might be
tempting to regard morphology as a module of the grammar, along with
the other traditional areas of grammar such as phonology, syntax and
semantics. However, as explained in chapter 1, because modules are sets
of principles, we are assuming that areas of the language such as morphology or syntax are not necessarily to be understood as modules in the
sense of autonomous areas of grammatical knowledge. 'Morphology' is
just a convenient label for an area of the grammar which may itself be
made up of elements from different modules such as X-bar theory (see
section 2.2) and case theory (see 2.3), both discussed in chapter 2 in
relation to syntax, and which is concerned with the structure of the
words of the language.

3.2   Morphology and Word-Formation

As discussed in section 3.1, words can be described and analysed as
consisting of different morphemes. Descriptive studies of German
morphology such as Henzen (1965), Fleischer (1975) and Erben (1975)
attempt to describe all the existing types of words in the German language. But morphology is not simply a linguistic level at which analytical
observation can be carried out. It is also possible to extract from such

descriptions productive morphological processes, which alter the form of words and also create new ones. This latter aspect of morphology is sometimes referred to as **word-formation**, because it is largely concerned with how new words come into being. Another distinction which is sometimes made is to say that rules of word-formation include only rules which actually make new words like *Gehweg* and *begehbar*, whereas rules of morphology include in addition rules for the inflection of words, producing such forms as *gehst*, *gehen*, as well as rules for unproductive processes such as Umlaut, which occurs in forms such as *fährst* ('drive', V), *Köche* ('cooks', N) or *kürzer* ('shorter'). All these processes are discussed in this chapter. The term word-formation is also frequently associated with the view that new words are formed within the lexicon (see chapter 6), the list of words of the language, as opposed to processes such as inflection, which are sometimes considered the province of syntax. Whatever view of the lexicon is taken, however, a distinction can be made between earlier descriptive studies of morphology such as those mentioned above, and later ones which concentrate more on explaining systematically how words are analysed and how new words can be formed. Such studies describe the potential rather than simply the existing words of German, and are sometimes referred to as theoretical studies to distinguish them from descriptive studies. Examples are Olsen (1986b) and Toman (1983).

It is generally considered that there are four productive morphological processes. These, with an example in each case of a word formed in this way, are:

(11) inflection   (gehst)
      derivation   (begehen)
      compounding   (Gehweg)
      conversion   (schulen, *to school*)

We shall now look at each of these in turn in order to see what the process involves in German.

3.2.1 *Inflection*

Inflection involves the attaching of an affix to a stem (which may also be a root, as is the case with *geh*; remember that a stem is that part of a word, whether a root or not, which has no inflectional endings). Inflection does not alter the category of the word which forms the stem:

(12) geh en
      geh st
      geh t

Frau (*woman*)
Frau en

rot (*red*)
rot e
rot es

Here the affixes -*en*, -*st*, -*t* indicate person, number and tense of the verb *gehen*, but they do not alter its category. It still remains a verb; *Frauen*, like *Frau*, is an N and the various forms of *rot* with their respective endings are all As. In each case they retain the same basic meaning; inflectional endings simply change their grammatical function. It is important to be aware that the infinitive -*en* ending of verbs is not universally regarded as an inflectional affix. Fleischer (1975) regards it as a derivational ending. However, it is not clear what a verb such as *gehen* could be derived from, and furthermore it seems intuitively evident from the contrasts in (12) that -*en* is an inflectional affix just like -*st* and -*t*. In common with most recent views of German word-formation (for example Olsen 1986b or Fox 1990: 107) we are here assuming therefore that infinitival -*en* is an inflectional affix.

It should now be clear that the distinction we made earlier in saying that the syntax was concerned with the structure of sentences, whereas the morphology was concerned with the structure of words, is perhaps not as clear-cut as might at first have appeared, because in fact inflection is concerned with how syntax affects words. Whether or not inflection is separated from what is regarded as word-formation proper, that is, the processes of derivation, compounding and conversion, it seems that it represents an area of potential overlap between syntax and morphology.

Inflectional affixes (sometimes in conjunction with other structural markers) indicate a number of grammatical functions, as the following examples illustrate:

(13)	*Function*	*What is indicated*	*Which categories*	*Examples*
	number	singular or plural	V	geht, gehen
			N	Weg, Wege
			A	rote, roten
	person	first, second or third	V	gehe, gehst, geht
	gender	masculine, feminine neuter	A	rote, roter rotes

tense	present, past	V	sage, sagte
mood	indicative or subjunctive	V	geht, gehe
voice	active or passive	V	sehe, gesehen

Note that inflectional morphemes can have multiple functions: *-t*, for example, can indicate person, number and mood among other things. Inflectional affixes apply to all words in a particular class. Thus the *-st* ending for second person singular applies to any verb, and *-en* indicates the infinitive of any verb. Although the plural morpheme for nouns, as observed above, may manifest itself in different allomorphs it can be added, in one of its forms, to almost any noun. The only exceptions are those which do not have a plural form for semantic reasons, such as

(14) a. Gemüse   Käse   Zucker   Wasser
         vegetables   *cheese*   *sugar*   *water*

      b. Ehrlichkeit   Musik   Evidenz
         honesty   *music*   *evidence*

The examples in (14a) represent collective nouns which have no plural. If we wish to speak of a plural of the collective concept, we have to resort to compounds such as *Gemüsearten* ('types of vegetable'), *Käsesorten* ('types of cheese'), *Zuckerarten* ('types of sugar'), or *Wassertypen* ('types of water'). Sometimes one even finds invented plural forms such as *Wässer* or *Käsen*, formed using common ways of marking plurals; *Käsen* is analogous to words like *Affe – Affen* ('ape – apes') and *Wässer* to words like *Garten – Gärten* ('garden – gardens'). Of course, it is rather difficult to establish whether such forms are 'invented' or 'real'. In the case of *Käsen* and *Wässer*, many speakers regard them as unacceptable and one would be unlikely to find them in a dictionary. Note that the English words *vegetables* and *cheese*, which correspond to the nouns in (14a) are not, morphologically speaking, collective nouns. *Sugar*, though, is a collective noun in English, too, and cannot have a plural. The examples in (14b) represent abstract nouns which are non-countable; their counterparts in English – *honesty, music, evidence* – behave similarly. But unless there is a semantic reason for the absence of a plural form, some allomorph of the plural morpheme will attach to any member of the class of nouns.

3.2.2 Derivation

Derivation differs from inflection in that it creates a new word, frequently of a different category, with a different meaning, rather than merely a different grammatical function, from the base word, though in fact the meaning of the base word itself does not change but is supplemented with additional semantic characteristics.

Thus in the following examples:

(15)   Gift   giftig
       poison   *poisonous*

       Eis   eisig
       ice   *icy*

       Holz   holzig
       wood   *woody*

an adjective is formed from a noun by the addition of the suffix -*ig*, along with additional semantic characteristics appropriate to the meaning of an adjective. Sometimes the new word is not of a different category. In

(16)   giftig   ungiftig
       poisonous   *non-poisonous*

       klar   unklar
       clear   *unclear*

       klug   unklug
       clever   *stupid*

both words are adjectives, though the second is derived by the addition of the negative prefix *un-* from the first, along with the semantic aspect 'not'.

Derivation, then, is the process by which affixes (prefixes or suffixes) are added to roots to produce new words. The addition of a particular affix is a **productive** process if it occurs frequently and with few restrictions. Sometimes we also describe the affix in question itself, rather than the process, as productive. The -*er* ending added to a verbal root in German is a case in point.

(17)   a.   Lehrer   Fahrer   Leser   Anrufer
            teacher   *driver*   *reader*   *caller* (on the
                                                        telephone)

       b.   Wecker   Locher   Verteiler
            alarm clock   *hole-puncher* *distributor*

Those in (17a) represent the agent of the action to which the base verb refers, while those in (17b) refer to the instrument with which the action is performed. Many *-er* derivations in German, as in English, are ambiguous as regards agentive and instrumental readings. Consider the following derived nouns:

(18) Empfänger
      Schreiber
      Spieler

Empfänger can be an agent as in *Sozialhilfeempfänger* ('recipient of social security') or it can be an instrument, as in *Fernsehempfänger* ('television receiver'). The same applies to *Schreiber* and *Spieler*: *Berichtschreiber* ('report-writer') and *Klavierspieler* ('piano-player') which are persons, whereas *Wehenschreiber* ('toko-dynamometer') and *Plattenspieler* ('record-player') are inanimate objects. It thus seems reasonable to assume that the ending *-er* has a semantic characterization as agent or instrument. The semantic component becomes clearer if we try to add *-er* to a root that does not indicate an action, such as *sei-* from the verb *sein* or *werd-* from the verb *werden*. The forms **Seier* and **Werder* are not possible. When a derived noun formed by affixing it to a verbal root has become lexicalized, that is, when it has become part of the inventory of words which makes up part of our knowledge of German, it is lexicalized with either an agentive or an instrumental meaning or both. As Olsen (1986b) points out, *-er* can also be added to nouns to form further nouns such as *Musiker*, but this *-er* affix is unproductive.

Another productive suffix is *-bar*, attached to the verbal root of transitive verbs to form adjectives as follows:

(19) lesbar   essbar   fassbar
      readable *eatable*   *graspable* (comprehensible)

We could also form new adjectives of this type, such as *nähbar* ('sewable'), *besitzbar* ('possessable'), *kaufbar* ('buyable'), and so we would want to regard this suffix as productive. An example of a productive prefix is *ent-*, as in the following examples:

(20) falten (V)   entfalten
      fold   *unfold*

      Gift   (N)   entgiften
      poison   *detoxify*

      mutig   (A)   entmutigen
      courageous   *discourage*

Note that *entgiften* is not formed from a verb **giften*; *ent-* is added to the root *gift*, to give *entgift-*, which then takes the inflectional endings of the verb: *entgiften*, *entgiftest*, *entgiftete*, and so on. It is frequently not clear what the category of the root is: for example, is *enthüllen* made up of *ent-* plus the verb *hüllen* or *ent-* plus the noun *Hülle* plus verbal endings? For this reason it might be considered easier not to categorize the root at all if it is not free. We shall return to this question below, for the moment assuming that roots do belong to particular categories.

Rather than saying that an affix attaches to a root to produce derived forms of a particular category, we could equally well say that the affix itself belongs to a particular category. An *-er* affix, for example, could be labelled as belonging to the category of noun. This information, along with the information about the type of root it attaches to, is part of a German speaker's knowledge of the language which is stored in the lexicon in what is called a **lexical entry**. Lexical entries for the suffixes *-er* and *-ig* will thus include the following information:

(21)   a.   **-er**

category:	N
phonological representation:	/-ər/
attaches to:	root$_v$
semantic characterization:	agent/instrument performing V

(21)   b.   **-ig**

category:	A
phonological representation:	/ɪg/
attaches to:	root$_N$
semantic characterization:	quality bearing characteristics of N

In these simplified examples of lexical entries, besides information on phonological representation which will not concern us here (though note that the different possible pronunciations of *-ig* are not given in the lexical entry; see chapter 5), (21a) tells us that *-er* attaches to a verbal root. The option of it attaching to a nominal root, as in the example of *Musiker* mentioned above, is assumed not to be part of our lexical information, as it is not possible to form new words in this way. (21b) indicates that *-ig* attaches to nominal roots, like those given in (15). The 'semantic characterizations' given are a first attempt at suggesting what sort of information we may store in our lexicon about the meaning of the resulting word. This will be discussed in more detail when lexical entries are considered again in chapter 6. For the moment it is sufficient to note that many affixes in German are productive, and it is then generally possible to give a rough equivalent for their meaning in English. For example, *-er* means 'person or thing performing the action expressed in the verbal root' , -*bar* means '-able', *ent-* means 'de-'. These are of course only rough characterizations of meaning, and should not be confused with appropriate *translations* of the prefix into English. We saw from the example above that *fassbar* may be translated as 'comprehensible' or even 'clear', and a word like *entkommen* is not, in English, to 'de-come' but to 'escape'. Nevertheless, the meaning that we associate with *ent-* in *entkommen* remains the same, that of doing the opposite. Other productive affixes are -*lich*, '-ish/-y/-ly' as in *süßlich*, 'sweetish', *sommerlich*, 'summery', *fraulich*, 'womanly'; -*en*, 'made of', as in *metallen*, 'made of metal', *seiden*, 'made of silk', *ledern*, 'made of leather'; -*in*, 'woman', as in *Lehrerin*, 'woman teacher', *Autorin*, 'female author', *Technikerin*, 'female technician'. Note that these latter words are considered politically correct in German, whereas in English the situation is quite different. It is unacceptable in German nowadays to speak of *Studenten* or *Linguisten* collectively; they must be *Studenten und Studentinnen* and *Linguisten und Linguistinnen*. A possible alternative, but only for written German, is *StudentInnen* and *LinguistInnen*. In English the opposite is true: many women find forms such as *actress* offensive, and words such as *authoress* and *poetess* have practically disappeared. Note, too, that the derivational affix -*lich* also sometimes changes the root vowel by the addition of an Umlaut (discussed later in section 3.2.5). Examples are *grünlich*, 'greenish', *östlich*, 'east(erly)', *nächtlich*, 'nightly/at night'. Words in -*lich* do not always take an Umlaut, though: *sommerlich* and *fraulich*, given above, do not (*süß* already has one), and sometimes the presence or absence of an Umlaut can indicate variation in meaning: *vertraglich*, derived from *Vertrag*, 'contract', means 'contractual', but *verträglich*, from the verb *vertragen*, 'to bear', means 'bearable'.

Though we have said that we can usually give the 'meaning' (as opposed to translation) of an affix, this is not always the case. A suffix such as -*ung*, as in *Wohnung*, 'flat', 'house', *Zeitung*, 'newspaper' or *Bedeutung*, 'meaning', does not seem to have any common semantic characteristics, but only functional ones: it forms nouns. The same applies to many other productive suffixes, for example -*tät* (*Universität*, 'university', *Majestät*, 'majesty', *Varietät*, 'variety'), which has an English equivalent -*y* but no apparent semantics, or -*nis* (*Bedürfnis*, 'need', *Bekenntnis*, 'confession', *Behältnis*, 'container').

It is typical of productive affixes, especially suffixes, that they are used by speakers of German to form new words, often facetiously, where there appears to be a lack of a suitable word. Forms such as *obstig* ('fruity'), *keksig* ('biscuity'), *bierig* ('beery'), though not lexicalized like their English counterparts, and certainly not to be found in a German dictionary, can nevertheless be heard.

Some affixes are not at all productive. They cannot be used to make new forms and the range of lexicalized existing words formed by their attachment is very limited. An example is the *-e* suffix with which nouns are formed from adjectives, with or without an Umlaut:

(22)   tief   Tiefe
        deep   *depth*

        gut   Güte
        good   *goodness*

        hoch   Höhe
        high   *height*

But no new words can be formed thus, and speakers of German would not try, even in fun, to do so; the process is completely unproductive. Other unproductive affixes are, for example, *-icht* as in *Dickicht*, 'thicket', *Kehricht*, 'sweepings up', mentioned above; *-sal* as in *Scheusal*, 'horrible person', *Drangsal*, 'suffering', *Schicksal*, 'fate'; *-at* as in *Plagiat*, 'plagiarism', *Kommissariat*, 'police inspection', *Internat*, 'boarding school'; or *-lings*, as in the adverbs *bäuchlings*, 'on the stomach', *rücklings*, 'on the back/backwards', and *blindlings*, 'blindly'. It is important to note that affixes, especially suffixes, may attach to roots which do not appear elsewhere or appear rarely. This is not the same as saying that they attach to bound roots: *möglich* consists of a productive affix *-lich* attached to a bound root *mög-*, which, however, also occurs in the verb *mögen*, 'to like', or the noun *Vermögen*, 'fortune/ability'. But *glimpflich*, 'without serious consequence', for example, consists of the productive suffix *-lich* attached to a bound root *glimpf-*, to which a native speaker would find it difficult to attach any sort of meaning, although it does also occur in *Verunglimpfung* 'disparagement', and in the rare word *Unglimpf*, 'wrong'. Other morphemes, both affixes and roots, occur even less frequently, perhaps just in one word. Examples are the morphemes *him-* in *Himbeere*, 'raspberry' or *preisel-* in *Preiselbeere*, 'cranberry'. These seem to be in contrast to the morphemes *Blau-* in *Blaubeere*, 'blueberry/bilberry' or *Erd-* in *Erdbeere*, 'strawberry', but, like their English counterparts, to have no meaning nor any distribution beyond this one word. Such morphemes are referred to as **cranberry morphemes**, after the English example of *cran-* in *cranberry*. *Glimpf* is not quite a cranberry morpheme, but it is very rare. Note that this is not the same case as that illustrated by *Stragula*, 'linoleum', given in (3) above. There the ending *-gula* was not an ending at all, whereas *-lich*, in *glimpflich*, clearly is.

Though it might seem obvious that derivation differs significantly from inflection in that the former gives rise to new words and the latter merely to different grammatical forms of the same word, this distinction is not always completely clear; it could be maintained that there is no basic difference between the two processes, as all devices available to derivation are available to inflection and affixes differ not in form but merely in that those we call inflectional have more syntactic consequences. In terms of information stored in the lexicon, it could be supposed that inflectional endings are stored there with the relevant information about their category and semantics and the category of the word they attach to, just as derivational affixes may be, or a strict division could be made between derivation, which is seen as taking place in the lexicon and thus as a morphological process, and inflection, which is seen as located in the syntax and thus as a syntactic process (see Anderson 1982). One difference is that, whereas the semantics of the stem does not matter for the inflectional processes – the *-st* in the second-person singular present attaches to all verb stems regardless of meaning – the attaching of affixes to roots in derivation does depend upon the semantic properties of the root. As was pointed out earlier, words such as *Seier* and *Werder*, as well as *Sitzer* and *Lieger*, cannot be formed by *-er* derivation, because roots whose meaning does not contain the notion of action cannot function as the base for derived forms in *-er*.

Even if a clear division can be made between the processes of derivation and inflection, there are some instances of affixation in German which cannot clearly be assigned to the one or the other. It is unclear, for example, whether the suffixes *-(e)r* and *-(e)st* in the following comparative and superlative forms of adjectives are derivational or inflectional:

(23) klein   kleiner   kleinst-
      small   *smaller*   *smallest*

      groß   größer   größt-
      big   *bigger*   *biggest*

      spät   später   spätest-
      late   *later*   *latest*

If they are derivational affixes, then the comparative and superlative forms *kleiner* and *kleinst-*, for example, are different lexical items and both are separate from *klein*. If they are inflectional, then these are simply different forms of the same lexical item. This sort of lack of clarity about how to classify particular affixes might be seen as a further reason not to make a strict division between derivational and inflectional affixes and the two affixation processes.

At the beginning of section 3.2.1, we said that inflection involves the attaching of an affix to a stem, which may or may not be a root, and at the beginning of this section we noted that derivation involves the attaching of an affix to a root. Looked at another way, this means that derivations can be inflected, but inflected forms cannot be subject to processes of derivation. In other words, (24a) contains possible examples but (24b) contains impossible ones:

(24)   a.   giftige   b.   *riesenig
            poisonous

            essbaren   *essenbar
            edible

            Schreibers   *Schreibster
            writer (genitive)

The adjective *giftige*, as in *giftige Pflanzen*, 'poisonous plants', is an inflected form of *giftig*, itself derived from *Gift*, 'poison'; *essbaren*, as in *die essbaren Pflanzen*, is an inflected form of *essbar*, derived from *ess-*, 'eat'; and *Schreibers* is the genitive form of *Schreiber*, itself derived from the root of the verb *schreiben*, 'write'. The examples in (24b) all contain an inflected element to which a derivational suffix has been added: to *Riesen*, plural of *Riese*, 'giant', the derivational ending *-ig* has been attached, to the infinitive form *essen* with *-en* inflection, the derivational suffix *-bar* has been added, and to the second person form *schreibst* an *-er* ending has been added.

In purely functional terms, it is not surprising that the inflectional endings should come after the derivational ones, because the former are, as mentioned above in section 3.2.1, the elements that must interact with the syntax of the sentence, and must thus be 'visible' to it.

3.2.3   Compounding

In the process of **compounding**, two stems are joined to form a new word. In theory, compounds could be formed from all major categories, that is, from any combination of V, N, A and P, but in fact many types do not exist at all and others are extremely unproductive.

Many types can be ruled out on the grounds of semantic incompatibilities. Thus VV compounds are generally impossible because verbs always require mention of the instrument, agent, or, if transitive, of the theme, the role realized in the object, and this is true whether the verb occurs alone in a syntactic construction or as one element in a compound. A second verb cannot fulfil either of these roles. (See chapter 6 for a discussion of semantic roles.) So whereas *Kochapfel*, 'cooking apple', realizes the theme of *kochen* within the compound, a compound such as **kochschreiben* would be meaningless, as *schreiben*, 'to write', could not stand in a relationship of agent, theme, instrument, location or any other such relation to the verb *kochen*. Some of the restrictions on these and other types of compound are discussed in Boase-Beier (1987a) and Boase-Beier and Toman (1986). Some categories of words can be assumed to constitute **closed classes,** that is, classes or categories of words to which new ones cannot be added. Prepositions are a case in point. It is presumably for semantic reasons that we cannot form new prepositions – there are simply no new relationships of the type expressed by prepositions which are not already encoded in the language. Thus new compound prepositions of any type are impossible.

One of the most productive types of compound in German is that formed from two nouns. These are referred to as N+N or simply NN compounds. These have been described variously in earlier studies as having a relationship of possession between the elements, as in Henzen (1965). Sometimes this would seem to be indicated by the presence of an -*s* on the first element, as in

(25)	Landsmann	Kindesmisshandlung	Amtsdeutsch
	native	*child abuse*	*official German*

But this -*s*, known as the *Fugen* -*s*, or linking -*s*, is not always a clear indication of a genitive form. Note that it can occur on feminine nouns, which do not take an -*s* in the genitive:

(26)	Liebesgedicht	Geschichtsbuch	Übersetzungskurs
	love-poem	*history book*	*translation course*

For this reason it is usually suggested that the linking -*s* or some other link (for example -*n* as in *Kronenräuber*, 'usurper', where the -*n*- is unlikely to indicate a plural) is determined by a number of factors, some phonological, some merely conventional.

A more useful way of describing the relationship between the elements of an NN compound is to classify possible relations according to type, such as:

(27)	locality	Stadthaus *town house*	(Haus **in** der Stadt)
	material	Holztisch *wooden table*	(Tisch **aus** Holz)
	similarity	Butterblume *buttercup*	(Blume, die Butter **ähnlich ist**)

This is basically the type of classification given by Lieber (1983) for English compounds, and Fanselow (1981) for German compounds.

Fanselow suggests that the relationship between the two elements of a compound in many cases depends crucially on the semantics of the elements. He employs the term **stereotype** to indicate an aspect of meaning which is typically associated with the element in question and can therefore be assumed to form part of a native speaker of German's lexical knowledge. Thus a compound such as *Bücherregal* can be interpreted with the help of a stereotypical relation which can be characterized as something like 'put things in/on'. This relation, which is discussed in chapter 6, can be extracted from the meaning of *Regal*: its theme is *Bücher*. If one takes this view, then many types of compound can be interpreted without recourse to anything extrinsic to their elements. Thus new and unusual compounds can be formed and interpreted in this way: *Bären-Geschäft* is a shop selling only (toy) bears, *Peitschenschrank* is a cupboard full of whips and *Salatklasse* is a cookery class on making salads. Many NN compounds, though, are not interpretable on the basis of stereotypes; these include, for example, **copulative compounds**, so called because the two elements are conjoined in an additive, or copulative, relationship; the relation between them can roughly be expressed as 'and'. Examples of this type include

(28)   Ökonom-Ökologe
       economist-ecologist

       Priester-Dichter
       priest-poet

       Baden-Württemberg

Note that there is commonly a hyphen in the spelling of such compounds. Fanselow (1984: 116ff.) has pointed out that it is, semantically speaking, not always quite the same 'and' which conjoins the elements of these compounds, but we shall not be concerned with the differences here. Also not interpretable by stereotypes are compounds with relations of locality, similarity or materials, such as those given in (27). Further examples are:

(29)   a.   Tischlampe   Küstenstadt   Wohnzimmerschrank
            table-lamp   *coastal town*   *living room cupboard*

       b.   Blechdose   Seidenstrumpf   Glastisch
            tin   *silk stocking*   *glass table*

       c.   Samtstimme   Schneetulpe   Leinenhaare
            velvet voice   *snowy tulip*   *flaxen hair*

Those in (29a) are interpreted such that the first element expresses the location of the second, those in (29b) such that the first element is the material of which the second is made and those in (29c) contain a relation 'similar to'; in *Samtstimme* the voice is being compared to velvet on the basis of a perceived quality, smoothness, which both have in common, in *Schneetulpe* the tulip is compared to snow in colour and hair in *Leinenhaare* is compared to linen (or flax) in either colour or texture or both. Note that the qualities forming the basis of the comparison are again the stereotypes mentioned above. *Schnee*, for example, is stereotypically white, though it may not actually be so, and so on.

Other NN compounds can be interpreted using the overt, as opposed to stereotypical, relation which one of them contains. These so-called **relational compounds** include examples such as the following:

(30) Autoverkauf   Arztmutter   Wortuntersuchung
       car sale   *doctor's mother* *word-study*

Verkauf and *Untersuchung* are deverbal nouns, that is, they are derived from verbs, and the relation expressed in the verb can be used to interpret the compound: '*der Verkauf von Autos*', semantically identical to 'act by which someone sells cars', where *cars* is the theme of *sells*, '*die Untersuchung des Wortes/der Wörter*', semantically 'act by which someone studies words', where 'words' is the theme of 'studies'. *Mutter* is what Brekle et al. (1983–5) describe as a relational noun, that is, a mother is the mother *of* someone, and this relation is fulfilled by the noun *Arzt* in (30). NN compounds are the most productive type, but others are also common, for example:

(31) NA   schneeweiß   grasgrün   pechschwarz
            snow-white   *grass-green* *pitch-black*

      AA   blaugrün   tiefblau   pragmatisch-semantisch
            blue-green   *deep blue*   *pragmatic and semantic*

AA compounds are in general much more common in German than in English, especially those like *pragmatisch-semantisch*, frequently found in the titles of linguistics books, and regarded as very clumsy in English, where they would usually be rendered by phrases. Other examples are *naiv-romantisch*, 'naively romantic', *winterlich-schön*, 'beautiful and wintry', and *sprachlich-sozial*, 'social and linguistic'. Many compound types are less productive, though, for example:

(32) AN   Edelmann   Vollmond   Altpapier
            nobleman   *full moon*   *recycled paper*

PV   aufgeben   untersuchen   nachforschen
        give up   *examine*   *look into*

Sometimes what appear to be compounds are formed from complete or partial phrases:

(33)   Vergißmeinnicht   Taugenichts   Hin-und-her-Gehen
       forget-me-not   *good-for-nothing*   *to-ing and fro-ing*

and although these are frequently referred to as phrasal compounds (see, for example, Henzen 1965), it may be better to think of them as phrases which have undergone a process of conversion to become nouns (see section 3.2.4). It is important not to confuse these with two other types of compound. Firstly, there are compounds consisting of a phrase and a noun, that is, these are not phrases converted to nouns but phrases conjoined with nouns. Examples are *Oben-ohne-Baden*, 'topless bathing', *Wegwerf-Gesellschaft*, 'throw-away society', *Getreide-und-Gemüse-Export*, 'cereal and vegetable export'. Secondly, there are multiple compounds, which involve several compounds conjoined to make another. Examples of this are *Müllverwertungsplatzzaun*, 'fence around recycling area', *Hochglanzvollmetallsicherheitsschnellkochtopf*, 'high-gloss, all-metal safety pressure cooker', or *Eisenbahnschienen-legegeräteschuppen*, 'shed for tools used in laying railway lines'. Each of these compounds can be analysed as a series of compounds, for example:

(34)   [Müllverwertungsplatz]ₙ   [zaun]ₙ
       rubbish recycling area   *fence*

       [Müllverwertungs]ₙ [platz]ₙ   zaun
       rubbish recycling   area   *fence*

       [Müll]ₙ [verwertungs]ₙ   platz   zaun
       rubbish recycling   *area*   *fence*

Square brackets, labelled N, indicate nouns, and it can be seen that in many cases the N is itself a compound consisting of other Ns.

What we said above with regard to the frequency of AA compounds in German also applies to phrasal and multiple compounds: they are much more common than in English. In fact, they are such a characteristic feature of German that they are the source of parodies of German style: most of the examples above, though all authentic, are of course not lexicalized compounds, but are formed on an *ad hoc* basis for use in a particular instance, and part of their impact is humorous. Such words are sometimes called **nonce formations**.

Sometimes two types of compound are distinguished according to whether they contain stems or words. Those which contain only stems are sometimes referred to as *echte Komposita*, that is, true compounds, and those which contain words are known as *unecht* (see Henzen 1965: 36f.), because they are felt not to be true compounds. Examples of the first type are

(35) Buchladen   Wortfeld   Buchstütze   Mannweib
     book shop   *word field*   *book end*   *masculine woman*

and of the second:

(36) Bücherregal   Wörterbuch   Bücherstütze   Männerhemd
     bookshelf   *dictionary*   *book end*   *man's shirt*

The *echte Komposita* are assumed to be an older type. *Unechte*, according to Henzen (1965:38) may contain not just plural inflection, but also genitive:

(37) segensreich   Tagesblatt   Liebesgeschichte
     beneficial   *daily paper*   *love-story*

This is the linking -*s* mentioned above, which, as discussed there, cannot unequivocally be taken to indicate a genitive ending. Note that some words, such as the two equivalents of 'book end', exist in both forms. There is no apparent semantic difference. The difference may, however, sometimes relate to the structure of the compound: *Fremdenzimmer*, 'hotel guest room', is an NN compound, whereas *Fremdarbeiter*, 'foreign worker', is an AN compound, as the English equivalents indicate. Because *Fremd-* in *Fremdarbeiter* (and in *Fremdsprache*, 'foreign language' and *Fremdwort*, 'loan word') is an adjective, it cannot have an optional plural or genitive ending; adjectives always occur as stems in compounds.

It might appear that there is a clear distinction between derivation and compounding: the former involves words and affixes while the latter involves only words (or, usually, stems). However, the difference is not always entirely clear-cut. Theories which suggest that affixes are listed in the lexicon like words will not necessarily make a distinction in theoretical terms between the two processes.

In a historical sense, the distinction between derivation and compounding is often blurred, too, as many suffixes are, historically speaking, formed from words:

(38) -*heit* from OHG   *heit*   meaning 'grade', 'rank'
     -*tum* from OHG   *tuom*   meaning 'state', 'condition'

Furthermore, many compounds are formed with second elements which are so productive as to be almost like suffixes:

(39)   *-werk* as in   Blattwerk   Kraftwerk   Sägewerk
                           foliage   *power*   *saw-mill*
                                            station

       -zeug as in   Werkzeug   Grünzeug   Waschzeug
                           tool   *greens*   *washing kit*

These can be attached to words of a particular category (in both the cases in (39) the elements attach to Ns, As and Vs) as freely as affixes, and do not carry a great deal of semantic weight, that is, their meaning tends to be less specific than their function.

It will have been noticed that a compound takes its category and gender and a large part of its meaning from its second element:

(40)   Schreib +   tisch =   Schreibtisch   (a type of *Tisch*)
       V   N   N; *desk*

       Tisch +   lampe =   Tischlampe   (a type of *Lampe*)
       N(m)   N(f)   N(f); *table lamp*

This could also be said to apply to derivation if it is assumed that derivational affixes are listed with categorial information in the lexicon:

(41)   Lehr   +   er   =   Lehrer
       root$_v$ N(m)   N(m)
                                           teacher

And if we assume that our knowledge of *-er* involves its being characterized semantically as an agent or instrument, then the meaning would also largely be derived from this: *Lehrer* is a type of agent, all persons in *-er* can be characterized as 'someone who Xs' where X is the action expressed in the root. This is a principle known as the head principle. We have discussed this in relation to the syntax in chapter 2, but in fact there is no reason to suppose this is merely a syntactic concept. Many linguists assume that words also have heads. (See suggestions for further reading about this in section 3.7.) In principle, the head in morphology is the same as the head in syntax: it carries the characteristics of the whole word, as a syntactic head carries those of the whole phrase containing it. (We shall discuss some consequences of this view in section 3.6.) In this sense, derivation and compounding can be seen as similar operations which conjoin two elements to make a third containing a head – in both German and English the right-hand element. The difficulty with this is that a prefix such as *ent-* appears, in terms of deciding function and category of the resulting word, to be the head, even though it is the left-hand element. Di Sciullo and Williams (1987: 26) introduce the notion of 'relativized head', and view *ent-* as the head only with respect to category; theories such as that put forward by Scalise (1984) assume that the process of affixation consists of rules which actually introduce the respective affixes, rather than being simply a process of concatenation connecting affixes which are listed, like words, in the lexicon. These are to some extent technical matters, but they do reflect different views of how our knowledge of morphology is organized, and can be pursued further using these references and those at the end of the chapter.

3.2.4 *Conversion*

Besides derivation and compounding, a further process known as **conversion** is used for creating new words without the addition of an affix. This is sometimes described as a process of derivation which conjoins an affix to a root as in any other type of derivation, with the difference that in this case the affix is not morphologically realized. If this view of the process is taken, it is frequently referred to as **zero-derivation** or **zero-affixation**, whereby a **zero-morpheme**, a morpheme which has no actual realization, is affixed to the root. The term conversion, used by Bauer (1983) and Olsen (1986b), on the other hand, is less explicit about what the process involves. It is generally assumed that it is not the combination of two elements but rather a change of category indicator. If we view conversion as the latter, then we are indeed saying that it is a further morphological process, quite distinct from derivation and compounding, whereas regarding it as zero-affixation suggests that it is simply a type of derivation and not a separate process at all.

Conversion always forms a word of a different category from the base word, thus from the word *Buch* ('book') can be derived by conversion the word *buchen* ('to book'). Remember that the *-en* ending is not a derivational affix but an inflectional affix indicating the infinitive: it can be replaced, in the appropriate circumstances, with the various other inflectional affixes such as *buchst, buchte, buchten*.

Some of the most common types of conversion are those which derive verbs from nouns as in the example above, or the formation of verbs from adjectives as in the examples below:

(42) weit   weiten
      wide   *widen*

locker   lockern
loose   *loosen*

kurz   kürzen
short   *shorten*

whereby, it should be noted, the verb may take an Umlaut. Nouns are also commonly formed from verbs, as in the following examples:

(43) treffen   Treff
      meet   *meeting-place*

      laufen   Lauf
      run   *race*

      stürzen   Sturz
      fall   *fall*

It is not always easy to say why the assumption is made that the conversion has proceeded in a particular direction. Why, for example, do we say that *buchen* is derived from *Buch* or *schulen* is derived from *Schule*, but *Treff* is derived from *treffen*?

Marchand (1964) gives a number of criteria for determining how the direction of conversion can be ascertained. These include the fact that the word whose presence in the language is attested earlier is assumed to be the base word, from which the later word is derived, though there is a problem here if we assume grammatical information to be the same as a native speaker's knowledge. Historical information is clearly not likely to be part of the latter, though it may be in some circumstances. The notion of added semantic characteristics is more useful here: usually the meaning of the derived word will include the meaning of the base word, but some characteristics will be added, so that the base word commonly appears in the definition of the derived word, but not vice versa. Thus *Treff* comes from *treffen*; we define *Treff* as '*Ort, an dem man sich trifft*' ('place where people meet') but we cannot define *treffen* as '*das, was man an einem Treff macht*' ('what you do at a *Treff*'). *Kürzen* means '*kurz machen*', 'to make short', that is, it has more semantic information than the adjective from which it is assumed to be derived, but we could not define *kurz* as '*das, was resultiert, wenn man etwas kürzt*', that is, as the result of shortening something.

Fleischer (1975) also includes nominalization of adjectives, verbs and participles, all of which are very common in German, under the heading of conversion. The following are examples:

(44) a. alt   der Alte   arm   die Armen
     old   *the old man*   *poor*   *the poor*

     b. bestehen   das Bestehen   singen   das Singen
     exist   *the existence*   *sing*   *the singing*

     c. angestellt   der Angestellte   geschrieben   das Geschriebene
     employed   *the employee*   *written*   *the written material*

Again, opinions among morphologists differ here; Olsen (1986b) explicitly rules such cases not to be morphological processes at all, but syntactic ones. The second type, verb to noun, exemplified in (44b), is the most productive process in German; any verb can be converted to a noun in this way: *das Sein*, 'being', *das Werden*, 'becoming', *das Buchstabieren*, 'spelling'.

While conversion is not as productive as compounding or derivation, it is, nevertheless, used to form new words. This applies particularly to the formation of verbs from nouns, and especially in areas of rapid technological expansion, in which there is need for new words, verbal equivalents to newly coined nouns are very common, for example:

(45) Ausdruck   ausdrucken
     print-out   *to print out*

which is not to be confused with *ausdrücken*, 'to express', with its corresponding noun *Ausdruck*, 'expression'.

Many verbal conversions of this type are formations on the basis of English nouns which have been taken over into the German language. Usually, though not always, the noun first became accepted as part of German vocabulary, and the verb then followed via conversion; examples include:

(46) e-mail   e-mailen
     e-mail   *to e-mail*

     Scanner   scannen
     scanner   *to scan*

     Puzzle   puzzeln
     jigsaw   *to do a jigsaw*

Sometimes the English noun has a German equivalent (thus *der Scanner* can also be called *das Ultraschallgerät*), but there is no obvious verbal equivalent, which is why the English term is used as a basis for conversion.

This is only possible if the English term lends itself phonologically to the process.

3.2.5 Other Morphological Processes

There are a number of other processes by which words have been formed historically but which are not today used productively.

Suppletion is a process by which gaps in the morphological system of a language are filled by the substitution of words which are related in function and meaning but historically have different sources and are thus not related in form. Examples are:

(47) gut   besser   best-
      good   *better*   *best*

      bin   sind   war
      am   *are*   *was*

      gern   lieber   am liebsten
      gladly   *preferably* *most preferably*

Just as affixes which are not necessarily formally related may be considered as allomorphs by function rather than by form, for example the plural affixes -er (*Kinder*), -e (*Tage*), -en (*Menschen*), so roots which are phonologically unrelated but functionally related by suppletion may also be considered allomorphs, as indeed they are, for example, by Fox (1990: 97). It is worth noting that often the same words tend to be involved in the processes of suppletion in related languages, as the following examples show:

(48) **German:**   bin   sind   war
      English: am   are   was
      French: suis   sommes   était
      Latin: sum   sumus   erat
      German: gut   besser   best-
      English: good   better   best
      French: bon   meilleur   le meilleur
      Latin: bonus   melior   optimus

Ablaut is the alternation of the stressed root vowel in different grammatical forms, either instead of or in addition to the presence of prefixes and suffixes. This is found in strong verbs in German:

(49) bleiben   blieb   geblieben
      stay   *stayed*   *stayed*

ziehen	zog	gezogen
pull	*pulled*	*pulled*

bewegen	bewog	bewogen
move	*moved*	*moved*

As examples such as *ziehen* indicate, the consonant may also change. This is the result of historical developments unrelated to Ablaut. There are also nouns which stand in a relationship of Ablaut to the base verb

(50)   gehen   Gang
       go   *gait*

       stehen   Stand
       stand   *stand*

       finden   Fund
       find   *find*

While there are certain regularities about the various forms of such lexical items, there are also a number of irregularities, so that the forms of strong verbs or of nouns derived by Ablaut cannot simply be determined on a regular phonological or morphological basis, but must be learned piecemeal, whether by native German speakers or by speakers of other languages learning German as a foreign language.

The direction of derivation for lexical items related by Ablaut is difficult to establish. In other words, is *Stand* derived from *stehen* or vice versa? A description of the types of Ablaut found in German is given in Lodge (1971).

Umlaut, as discussed in chapters 4 and 8, is the relationship between lexical items whose derivation involves an alternation between back and front vowels. Sometimes base forms exhibit historical Umlaut with no alternations:

(51)   grün   schön   Bühne   Bär
       green   *beautiful*   *stage*   *bear*

Usually, however, Umlaut relates functionally connected forms such as:

(52)   a.   singular – plural:

          Mann   Männer
          man   *men*

Koch   Köche
cook   *cooks*

Grab   Gräber
grave   *graves*

b. first, as opposed to second and third persons, singular present indicative of strong verbs:

fahre   fährst, fährt
go, drive

backe   bäckst, bäckt
bake

laufe   läufst, läuft
run

c. adjectives and their comparative and superlative forms:

lang   länger, längst
long   *longer, longest*

hoch   höher, höchst
high   *higher, highest*

kurz   kürzer, kürzest
short   *shorter, shortest*

d. past indicative and subjunctive II of strong verbs:

kam   käme
came

bot   böte
offer

las   läse
read

e. base and derived forms with particular suffixes such as *-chen* and *-lein*:

Haus   Häuschen
house   *small house*

Baum	Bäumlein
tree	*small tree*

Buch	Büchlein
book	*little book*

f. verbs formed by conversion from nouns and adjectives:

kurz	kürzen
short	*to shorten*

Sturm	stürmen
storm	*to storm*

Farbe	färben
colour	*to colour*

g. words of various categories formed by derivation:

groß	vergrößern
large	*enlarge*

gut	Güte
good	*goodness*

Farbe	verfärben
colour	*to colour*

These are some of the main instances of Umlaut, but in fact it is difficult to find absolute regularities. It is not the case that a particular root always takes Umlaut or that a particular affix always produces Umlaut in the root or stem to which it is attached. *Hund*, 'dog', takes an Umlaut in the feminine form *Hündin*, but not in the plural *Hunde*. And the feminine ending *-in* produces Umlaut in *Hündin* but not, for example, in *Professorin*, '(female) professor'. The diminutive *-chen* produces Umlaut in the root in all the examples given in (52e) above, but sometimes it does not, as in *Kuhchen*, 'little cow' or *Tantchen*, 'auntie'.

Yet other processes, besides being unproductive today, and therefore only important for the historical study of German, are also different from the morphological processes of derivation, compounding and conversion in that they cannot, like these, be regarded as the concatenation, or adjoining, of two elements, root and affix, as in derivation (a zero-affix for conversion), root and root, as in compounding, or indeed stem and inflectional ending. Sometimes these processes are therefore regarded as being peripheral to the morphology. One such process is **back-formation**

(German *Rückbildung*), which is even less common in German than in English. English examples are usually considered to include words such as the verb *edit*, from the noun *editor*, or *intuit* from *intuition*. Aronoff (1976) simply says they are examples of word-formation rules being applied backwards. Fleischer (1975) does give examples for German such as *Ruf* from *rufen*, but most of these could be considered normal types of conversion. An example of true back-formation, based on the example given by Bauer (1988a) for English, might be *surreal*, an adjective meaning the same as English 'surreal', from the noun *Surrealismus*. A further one is the verb *entsorgen* ('safely dispose of'), formed from the noun *Entsorgung* ('safe disposal'), which itself usually only occurs in compounds like *Atommüll-Entsorgung* ('safe disposal of nuclear waste') or *Asbest-Entsorgung* ('safe disposal of asbestos'). What appears to happen in back-formation is that native speakers analyse a word, often a new or loan word, as a derived form, and invent a 'base' form to complement it. Eventually such forms become lexicalized and the process is then indistinguishable from normal derivation, except in a historical sense.

Clipping is another process which is not strictly speaking part of the morphological component of the grammar. This is the process by which a word is simply shortened without change to category or meaning, though its stylistic value may change, making it more appropriate to a particular register (see chapter 9). *Sci-fi* (science-fiction) is an English example. Such words tend to be more informal than their unclipped counterparts. Examples in German are:

(53)   bi   (A: bisexuell)
                      bisexual

       Uni   (N: Universität)
                      university

       Klo   (N: Klosett)
                      lavatory

Though usually the beginning of the word is kept, it can also be the final part, as in:

(54)   Bus   (N: Omnibus)
       bus

       Tina   (proper N from names like Martina, Bettina)

       saugen   (V: staubsaugen)
       vacuum clean

Blends (this is not normally expressed as a process of 'blending') are words made up of bits of other words. Examples are

(55) jein   (Adv: ja + nein)
      yes and no

      Bilka   (Proper N: billig + kaufen)

      Azubi   (N: Auszubildende(r))
      apprentice

The only restriction on words of this type is that they must be pronounceable. That they may look outlandish is apparently no barrier, as is shown by the case of *Azubi*, which many German native speakers find ugly and strange.

Another process of this type is the formation of **acronyms**. Much-loved in English, as in *UEA* (University of East Anglia), *GBH* (grievous bodily harm) and many other instances, these are also fairly common in German:

(56) UKW   (N: Ultrakurzwelle)
      VHF   *very high frequency* (literally: very short wave)

      FCKW   (N: Fluorchlorkohlenwasserstoff)
      CFC   *chloro-fluoro-carbonate*

      DDR   (Proper N: Deutsche Demokratische Republik)
      GDR   *German Democratic Republic*

Note that some acronyms, when they are well established and pronounceable, are pronounced as normal words, as in the case of NATO (pronounced [náːto] in German; North Atlantic Treaty Organization).

Reduplication is a repetition of words or morphemes, which may not necessarily exist in the simple form. Adapting Fleischer (1975), we can distinguish three types:

(i)   simple reduplication, whereby both parts are identical

(57) Mama   Papa   Agar-Agar
      mummy   *daddy*   *agar*

(ii) rhyme reduplication, whereby initial consonants or consonant clusters or syllables vary

(58) Hokuspokus   Picknick   Tohuwabohu
      hocus-pocus   *picnic*   *chaos*

(iii)   assonance reduplication, whereby the vowels vary

(59)   wischywaschy   Krimskrams   Hickhack
        fuzzy, unclear   *bric-a-brac*   *squabble, muddle*

It is extremely difficult in these cases to distinguish between borrowings
from other languages and words which have been formed by reduplication within the German word-formation system; many of the examples
above (*Agar-Agar* from Malay, *Picknick* from French via English and
Tohuwabohu from Ancient Hebrew, which is used at the beginning of
Genesis) are not native German words. It is interesting to note in this
context that a further reason for wishing to exclude these processes from
those which are strictly morphological is that, at least in the case of
reduplication, it seems more likely that some version of a process of
repetition (discussed in chapter 7 as a stylistic principle) is at work, and
that it applies to syntactic constructions just as much as to words, as
indicated by the many lexicalized idioms such as:

(60)   er sagt einmal hü einmal hott
        he says first one thing, then the other

        Hinz und Kunz
        every Tom, Dick and Harry

        von Pontius zu Pilatus
        from pillar to post

3.3   The Relationship between Morphology
and Phonology

In some views of language, phonological alternations which are morphologically determined are separated from the morphology proper. Because
this view historically often involved the assumption that such morpho-
phonological rules are located in the lexicon (see Kiparsky 1982b), it is
frequently referred to as **lexical phonology**. Lexical phonology is to some
extent based on the concept of level-ordering in morphology, as proposed
by writers like Siegel (1979). This involves the view that the derivational
and inflectional processes of a language are organized in levels, each of
which is associated with phonological rules, and uses the phonological
information given in lexical entries (see section 3.2.2). Such phonological
processes are seen as quite distinct from phonology proper, which operates
after all morphological processes have occurred, without recourse to
morphological information. For example, the German voiceless stops

have aspirated allophones at the beginning of a stressed syllable, irrespective of the morphological structure of the word; this is a purely phonological matter.

The number of levels assumed in lexical phonology varies according to the arguments put forward by the analyst for distinguishing different types of morphology. Usually there are three or four. Example (61) is adapted from Bauer (1988a: 135), as applied to English, showing the order in which sets of rules apply within the lexicon; it should be read from top to bottom.

(61)

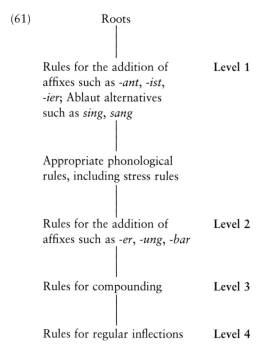

Roots	
Rules for the addition of affixes such as *-ant, -ist, -ier*; Ablaut alternatives such as *sing, sang*	Level 1
Appropriate phonological rules, including stress rules	
Rules for the addition of affixes such as *-er, -ung, -bar*	Level 2
Rules for compounding	Level 3
Rules for regular inflections	Level 4

The alternations of the voiceless and voiced obstruents that we mentioned in chapter 1 and will discuss in chapter 5 are dealt with as phonology proper, because they are phonologically motivated irrespective of morphological structure. The determining environment is the syllable boundary, a phonological trigger. This means that if we take the root form of *lieb-* to be /lib/ (see chapter 5), it will emerge from the lexicon, after level 4, still as /lib/. *Liebt* will be /lib+t/, until it is subject to the phonological rules of the separate, post-lexical component of the grammar, to give [liːpt].

The basic point we are making here is that the dividing line between phonology and morphology is not predetermined; it has to be decided on the basis of evidence. In German the evidence discussed often revolves around those lexical items which cause a change of stress placement, the learned vocabulary from Latin and Greek, where some unexpected alternations occur, for instance, *explodieren, explosiv*, and the status of Ablaut and Umlaut. Any phenomenon that can be shown to be lexically or morphologically determined will be handled in the lexicon, even though it may have direct and regular phonetic realizations, as in the case of Umlaut. It is not just that morphology interacts with phonology, but that the way information about the language is stored and categorized in these areas is the study of ongoing research. This is also true of the interaction between morphology and syntax, as we shall see in section 3.6.

3.4   Productivity

As noted above in section 3.2.2, words can be divided into lexicalized forms, which are stored in the lexicon and called forth as needed, and non-lexicalized forms which are created as and when they are required by the application of morphological operations. Lexicalized forms are words such as *Tisch, gehen, beschriftbar* and *Fahrer* (see chapter 6). Non-lexicalized ones are new creations such as *reduplizierbar* ('reduplicatable') and *Knöpfer* ('buttoner'). Both types can be the result of productive processes, but only productive affixes can give rise to non-lexicalized forms. The fact that new words can be created by attaching the affixes *-bar* and *-er* leads us to describe these affixes as productive. In other words, the *-er* suffix can be added to a root which can generally be supposed to be a verb stem, and the resulting word will be an agent (someone who performs the action described in the root) or an instrument (an object used for performing the action described in the root). The many unproductive affixes such as nominal *-tum*, as in *Reichtum*, *-icht* as in *Kehricht*, *-t* as in *Fahrt* or *–de* as in *Zierde* cannot be used to create new forms.

The fact that morphology is often productive, allowing the generation of new forms by the application of rules, might be seen as one reason to assume, as Fox (1990:125) points out, that syntax and morphology are not necessarily entirely distinct.

Productivity, however, as Fox (1990:124) also notes, is not an absolute phenomenon. Some affixes could be used to produce new words which are at least comprehensible, if unusual. Fox's example for this is *Buchtum*, which is certainly very odd. Perhaps this point is more clearly seen with nouns in *-tum* formed from nouns denoting groups of persons; *Sklaventum* and *Übersetzertum* are not lexicalized, but they are not particularly unusual, and many German native speakers would be uncertain as to whether they actually 'exist', in the sense of being accepted by a majority as part of the language and listed in German dictionaries, which purport accurately to reflect native speakers' know-ledge of the language.

It is unclear whether the productivity of an affix can be said to stand in an inverse relation to the number of restrictions governing its use. If it can, then -er could be said to be not completely productive because the verb to which it attaches must represent an action, and thus *Seier, *Haber and *Steher are ruled out. If productivity is regarded thus, then it is being viewed as a strictly grammatical notion, concerned with restrictions on the combination of roots and affixes.

It could, however, be seen as a less grammatical notion. Taking all grammatical restrictions on the root as given, a productive affix might be viewed as one which, within the framework of these restrictions, could be attached freely and an unproductive affix as one which could not. On this understanding of the notion of productivity, -er is a productive affix, whereas -tum is less so: there is no apparent reason for the absence of *Armtum, *Großtum or *Lehrertum as all obey restrictions on the combining of -tum with the base adjective or noun. The nominal -icht ending, mentioned at the beginning of this chapter, is even less product-ive, because apart from a handful of words such as *Dickicht* and *Kehricht*, no other words in -icht are formed.

The historical dimension of productivity causes further problems. Whereas the -t suffix in *Fahrt* is clear enough, is it still obvious to native speakers of German that *Saat* is related to *säen*, *Zucht* to *ziehen*, *Kunst* to *können* and *Macht* to *mögen*? Or would a modern speaker know that *Seuche* is related to *siechen* and *Menge* to *manch* via the -e suffix? Such questions are very difficult to answer. It is no use asking native speakers directly, because native speaker knowledge is subconscious and so aware-ness of linguistic relationships at a conscious level is largely haphazard, a product of untutored observation and explicit teaching, the latter being extremely variable across speakers. Some speakers may know that forms such as *Macht* and *mögen* are related because they have followed a course dealing with the history of their language, but that knowledge will not be available to all speakers and probably not to the majority. One way to approach the problem is to see whether their relatedness can be captured by a general rule, whereby we may have to refer to phono-logical, morphological or semantic information. For instance, we might be able to show that the phoneme sequence /-gt/ is realized as [xt] in words where Ablaut occurs. This would enable us to relate *Zug* and *Zucht*, *mag* and *Macht*, *Bucht* and *biegen*. *Flucht* poses yet another problem. On the basis of our suggested rule this word should be related to *fliegen* and *Flug*. It is not, however; it is the nominalized form of *fliehen*. Although historically we can explain this relationship quite easily, that does not help us with modern German. This also brings us to semantic considerations: *fliehen* and *Flucht* are related semantically to one another, but not to *fliegen*. (The fact that English has collapsed the two nominal forms into one, *flight*, makes it more difficult for English speakers to appreciate this.) On the other hand, another of the pairs, *Macht* and *mögen*, are no longer related semantically, even if we decide that the phonological rule is justified. *Mögen* has lost its earlier meaning of 'be able to/ have the power to' (expressed by the verb *vermögen*) which gave rise to the related noun *Macht*. (See chapter 8 on the question of historical change.) It seems unlikely that the relation between the two would be part of what a native speaker of modern German knows about the language. Given all these complications, we can see that the earlier productivity of -*t* has disappeared in modern German, and it is only marginally analysable. The question of analysability has a bearing on the matter of borrowings from other languages, which we consider next.

3.5   Borrowings from Other Languages

Loan words from other languages tend to be distinct in their phonological behaviour (see chapter 5) and may even contain foreign phonemes:

(62)   Appartement
     (pronounced [apaʀtəmáŋ], [apaʀtəmā̃], [apaʀtəmént] or [apaʀtəméŋ])

They may also use morphemes which are not part of the inventory of the German language. Some suffixes which were originally borrowed have now become so much part of the German language that they can be attached to native German roots. The suffix -*ier* was originally a verbal suffix from French, as in *blanchieren* ('to blanch') but is now attached to German roots such as *fund-* as in *fundieren* ('to found'). Many words which are borrowed from Latin have imported part of the Latin morphology:

(63) | Industrie | industriell | industrialisieren |
industry	*industrial*	*industrialize*
Suggestion	suggestiv	suggerieren
Suggestion	*suggestive*	*suggest*
Instruktion	instruktiv	instruieren
Instruction	*instructive*	*instruct*
Spekulant	Spekulation	spekulieren
speculator	*speculation*	*speculate*

Expression	expressiv	exprimieren
expression	*expressive*	*express*

All such loan words take German inflections, as in *ein instruktives Buch*, and many take German derivational suffixes, as in *die Industrialisierung der Landschaft*. In fact, foreign inflections are rare in German and are restricted to noun plural markers, some of which have German equivalents as well, for example *Schemata, Schemas, Schemen*.

The forms in (63) and many others like them can be analysed into morphemes, for instance *spekul-, -ant, -ation, -ativ, -ier*. Note too that there are vowel and consonant alternations in some cases, as in *-prim-, -press-*, just as there are in the German vocabulary, and general rules are as difficult to postulate for loan words as they are there. One suggestion that has been made for relating allomorphs which are not phonologically regular is to have rules in the lexicon which indicate the relationship, while giving the forms separately (see Lass 1984: 223–6). This suggests that German native speakers will have to make more effort to learn these relationships, if they are not straightforward in phonological terms. This would also be a solution for cases like *ziehen, Zug* discussed above. In fact, such an approach makes no distinction between alternations of this type and suppletion. The latter appears more distant because of the lack of any kind of phonological relatedness.

Even if we accept these analyses of the loan words, there is often a lack of clarity as to the meaning of morphemes in them, such as *instru-* or *sugger-*, and this relates to a distinction which can be made between opaque and transparent morphology (see Bauer 1988a: 189–91). Transparent morphological structure is easily understood by a native speaker whereas opaque structure remains obscure. Thus *Sprachwissenschaftler*, 'linguist', is analysable into *sprach + wissen + schaft + ler*, and each morpheme has a consistent and clearly expressible meaning. The Latinate equivalent *Linguist*, however, cannot be so readily analysed into morphemes: *-ist* appears in other loan words such as *Pazifist, Komponist* and indicates a person involved in a specialist area, although it is very restricted and has no easily recognizable semantic function. *Lingu-* appears in *Linguistik, linguistisch* but in this case there is no associated verb based on *lingu-*, as there is in the case of some other words ending in *-ist*, for instance *Komponist*, 'composer', and *komponieren*, and this may be a factor in making it difficult to comprehend. In a few cases words are related formally but not in their meanings. An example of this is *Ignoranz, ignorant* as opposed to *ignorieren*, which show the same difference of meaning as English *ignorance, ignorant* and *ignore*, respectively.

The fact that such vocabulary is opaque does not mean that Germans cannot use it, but it does mean that they have to learn it in specialized contexts. For this reason it is unevenly distributed among native speakers, and some speakers may indeed have difficulty with learned vocabulary, for instance, broad dialect speakers or those who have only a basic education. But it is often a matter of expertise, rather than educational attainment, which determines one's knowledge of specialist lexical terms. In (64) we give a few examples which will have very different distributions in the German-speaking population.

(64) rangieren   Chlornatrium   Tympanon
      shunt   *sodium chloride*   *tympanum*

      Sphragistik   deklinieren   Taxidermie
      sigillography   *decline (as a grammatical term)*   *taxidermy*

There are often pairs of words in German, one of which (65a) is of Germanic and one of which (65b) is of Latinate origin, which mean roughly the same:

(65) a. Sprachwissenschaftler   b.   Linguist
          linguist

          Fußpflege   Pediküre
          pedicure

          Briefumschlag   Kuvert
          envelope

          bequem   komfortabel
          comfortable

          zweideutig   ambig
          ambiguous

          entweihen   exsekrieren
          deconsecrate

However, there will generally be slight differences in the contexts in which the two words are used: *Linguist* may be a more theoretically orientated specialist of language than *Sprachwissenschaftler*, and it may also refer to someone who speaks foreign languages, just as the corresponding word in English may. *Exsekrieren* is used in strictly ecclesiastical contexts, whereas *entweihen* is more general. *Ambig* will be more likely to be used in scientific contexts, for example in philosophical or linguistics texts, whereas *zweideutig* is the more general word. *Pediküre* and *komfortabel* are typically used in advertising which aims to raise the status of the concepts referred to by using learned words. This is not always the case, however: (*Brief*)*umschlag* and *Kuvert* are used by different speakers – and sometimes even by the same speaker – to mean exactly the same thing.

One further problem is brought to light in particular with reference to loan vocabulary. A large number of the loan roots are bound and do not obviously belong to one particular grammatical category. For instance, *qual-* (as in *qualifizieren*, 'to qualify') and *spek-* (as in *spekulieren*, 'to speculate') can only occur with other morphemes and cannot be classified as verbs, nouns or anything else. This brings us back to the general problem of classifying morphemes on the basis of grammatical category. Related to this is the direction of derivation: can one grammatical category be considered basic, and other forms derived? It is usual to talk about derivation as a process which in many cases converts one grammatical category into another, as we have throughout this chapter. But if we consider a morpheme like *bau*, can we be certain that it actually belongs to a particular category? *Bau* is the stem of a noun and of a verb: *Bau* and *bau + en*. We therefore need to ask if it is necessary to classify roots according to grammatical category. At the level of the word, the basic unit of syntax, grammatical category is clearly relevant. At the level of roots, it is possible not to specify it and indeed to deem such specification unnecessary. In this way we could accommodate loan roots quite easily, without the need to try and ascertain category. The corollary of this would be that derivation was not seen as a process but as a relation between words. The trouble with this view, however, is that it does not really do justice to native speaker knowledge. Most native speakers would state unequivocally that *Bau*, 'building', comes from *bauen*, 'to build', and that *Kehricht*, 'sweepings up', comes from *kehren*, 'to sweep'. Even in the case of loan words, native speakers feel strongly that, for example, *Suggestion*, 'suggestion', comes from *suggerieren*, 'to suggest', and *instruktiv*, 'instructive', from *Instruktion*, 'instruction'. This aspect of native speaker knowledge can only be captured by assigning roots to particular categories, as indeed we have done in the lexical entries in (21). The failure to do this also causes difficulties with the interpretation of compounds of the type *Autoverkauf*, discussed in section 3.2.3 above, in which the verbal relation plays an essential role, and, as we shall see in the next section, it would cause difficulties for many other notions related to the structure of complex words.

3.6 The Relationship between Morphology and Syntax

We noted in section 3.2.3 above that the notion of head, which we had considered in chapter 2 in connection with syntax, is assumed by many researchers to be applicable to morphology. A fairly recent development in the study of morphology has been to examine whether morphology and syntax have so many characteristics in common that in fact it would be reasonable to assume that the same principles are at work in both areas. Such a view is aided by applying the concept of modularity, which views linguistic knowledge as a separate area or module of knowledge, to the grammar itself, as described in chapter 1. If morphology and syntax are not themselves modules, and if the principles linking them belong to a number of different modules, then conceptually there seems no reason why such principles should not cross traditional boundaries such as that between morphology and phonology, or between morphology and syntax. This would mean that it is the principles of grammar, rather than the areas into which it is traditionally subdivided, which are seen to reflect discrete, though interacting, areas of a native speaker's knowledge. Different writers have had different views on the actual organization of the morphological information, and though they sometimes do not explicitly link their view with the question of how knowledge is organized in the mind, the link is nevertheless there by implication. Studies such as Olsen (1986b), which is based on Selkirk (1982), place the processes of German word-formation, that is, all morphology except inflection, within the lexicon and view them as quite separate processes from the syntax, though they may (following a suggestion made by Chomsky 1970) be regarded as counterparts to syntactic phrase-structure rules. Though Jackendoff (1975) described lexical rules called redundancy rules which linked lexical entries, he did suggest that some lexical rules might not merely be rules of analysis but might perhaps be seen as capable of actually creating words. From such views developed two types of theory. One of these can roughly be characterized as lexicalist; for example, Olsen (1986b) formulated rules responsible for the production of German words in the lexicon, including the joining of roots and affixes in the ways we have discussed above. The other type of theory is exemplified by Toman (1983). Such theories, often described as **word-syntax** theories, are particularly concerned with the way word-formation parallels the formation of sentences.

Both types of theory assume that phrase-structure rules, following the X-bar schema described in chapter 2, are responsible for the formation of words. Most theories also assume that features can **percolate,** or move from the head of the word up to the next level. So, for example, in the compound *Blumentisch* ('flower table' in 66a), the fact that the whole word is masculine is explained as the result of the feature [masculine] being passed from *-tisch* to the compound. In a derived form (as in *Lesung* 'reading') in (66b), information percolates from the affix to the word. Percolation of features is often represented by an arrow thus:

(66) a.

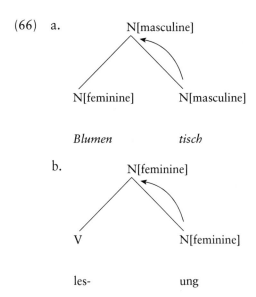

b.

Furthermore, the theory of thematic roles discussed in chapter 2, whereby lexical items such as verbs which express a relation have roles, for example agent or theme, attached to them, is also assumed in the theory of word-syntax to be relevant for word-formation. Just as characteristics such as [masculine] percolate to the overall word, or, to put it another way, are **inherited** by the word, so thematic structures are inherited. In a compound such as *Autofahrer*, 'car-driver', the thematic structure of *fahr-* could be said to be inherited by *fahrer* which thus, like the root *fahr*, requires a theme. This role is then filled by the element *Auto*. Note that if we adopt this view, then by implication roots such as *fahr-*, *bau-*, *sag-* cannot be left unspecified as to category, a possibility discussed in the previous section. Decisions of this kind thus depend upon theoretical considerations which aim, in the end, to find the best possible representation of native speaker knowledge. We tend towards the view that roots are marked by speakers of German for category and other information about semantic characteristics.

In various ways, then, it appears that the formation of words is similar to that of sentences. However, this view is not universally accepted. Di Sciullo and Williams (1987), while not disputing that some grammatical principles are relevant to both areas, nevertheless maintain that word-structure and sentence-structure are *per definitionem* separate things. Whether or not it can be maintained in the end that the same principles are at work in morphology and syntax, there is no doubt that the investigations attendant upon this idea have led to important refinements in the way word-structures are viewed, and thus to important insights as to how knowledge of such structures might be organized in the mind of a German speaker.

3.7   Further Reading

For general background reading on morphology and morphological theory, see Bauer (1988a), Katamba (1994), Spencer (1991), Scalise (1984) or Radford et al. (1999: part 2). Marchand (1969) is an older work concentrating on English word-formation, but it is fascinatingly detailed. Similar detail for German can be found in Fleischer (1975), and the other works mentioned in section 3.2, where there are also references for recent, more theoretical studies of German word-formation. Of these, Olsen (1986b) is the most accessible.

On the connection between inflection and derivation, Di Sciullo and Williams (1987), Lapointe (1981), Williams (1981) and Selkirk (1982) are helpful, though none of these deal specifically with German. Boase-Beier and Toman (1986) and Toman (1983) provide discussions of German, especially of derivation, and Boase-Beier and Toman (1986) also discuss compounding in German. Fanselow (1981), though not easy to read, has many interesting examples of German compounds and useful discussions of issues such as the *Fugen-s* and stereotypes. Brekle et al. (1983–5) is a microfiche publication which contains large amounts of authentic data collected during a research project on word-formation in German, and incorporates many of Fanselow's insights. Putnam (1975) is not concerned with morphology or word-formation at all, but provides useful background reading on the notion of 'stereotype'.

There are a number of works dealing in detail with the notion of 'head of a word'; some of the most important are Williams (1981), Selkirk (1982), Aronoff (1976) and Scalise (1984), as well as, specifically for German, Toman (1988), Boase-Beier and Toman (1986) and Olsen (1986b).

For discussions of conversion or zero-affixation, see Marchand (1964), who gives useful examples for English, French and German, or Bauer (1983) and Marchand (1969), who discuss this process in relation to English, and Toman (1983) and Olsen (1986b), who discuss it in relation to German.

Lexical phonology, discussed briefly in section 3.3 above, can be explored in more detail, though not with relation to German, in the works of Kiparsky (1982b, 1985), Mohanan (1986) and Durand (1990). Giegerich (1987) discusses level-ordering in German. Lieber (1981) discusses Umlaut in German.

Further discussion of percolation of features can be found in Spencer (1991) and in Toman (1988); the latter deals specifically with German, as do Toman (1983) and Olsen (1986b), which are referred to several times in section 3.6. Zwicky (1985) and Fanselow (1984, 1988a and 1988b) discuss the overlap between syntax and morphology.

EXERCISES

1 Mark the roots and affixes (prefixes and suffixes) in the following words, as in (9):

   unglaublich   Fernsehsessel   bespielbar

   unterhaltsam   Wohnung

2 Find a further 6 words, in addition to those in (14a) and (14b), which do not have a plural in German.

3 Write a lexical entry (using the ones in example (21) as a model) for the suffixes

   -bar
   -lich
   -in

4 What is the relation (see example 27) between the two elements of each of the following NN compounds:

   Glasfenster
   Sonntagsmaler
   Gartenhäuschen
   Eisblume
   Schneeglöckchen

5 Find 5 further examples of reduplicative compounds, like those in examples (57), (58) and (59).

CHAPTER FOUR

Phonetics

4.1 Introduction

This chapter is not intended to be a general introduction to phonetics: it is assumed that general phonetics requires a separate course – and certainly requires a separate coursebook. It is, rather, an introduction to the main points of articulatory phonetics, highlighting those articulations that are a characteristic of German pronunciation.

Speech is a continuous acoustic signal produced by the operation of the vocal organs in overlapping and simultaneous movements. It is not unlike a piece of orchestral music, where various parts are played on different instruments, each having its own part to play, to give the overall effect of the piece itself. As native speakers of our language we are, for the most part, completely unaware of the functioning of the vocal organs. However, as linguists we want to be able to discuss and analyse speech. To enable us to do this, we need to be able to describe what is going on during the production of speech and then to see how such physical characteristics of the speech continuum are organized into the higher, more abstract levels of the language. The latter is the task of phonology and will be the subject matter of chapter 5. For the purposes of the present book we shall restrict our investigations to articulatory phonetics, that is, a study of the way in which sounds are made by the speech organs.

As an example of a mechanism of speech production, let us consider the two German words *Tier* and *dir*. In the latter the vocal cords (see figure 1) are vibrating for nearly the whole duration of the word when spoken in isolation. In the former the vibration starts later, during the vowel. If we represent the vibration of the vocal cords as a straight line under the orthographical version of the word, we have a visual representation of the difference between the two words in (1).

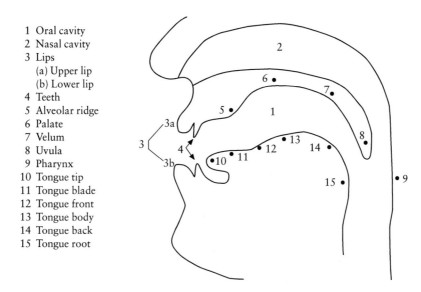

1 Oral cavity
2 Nasal cavity
3 Lips
  (a) Upper lip
  (b) Lower lip
4 Teeth
5 Alveolar ridge
6 Palate
7 Velum
8 Uvula
9 Pharynx
10 Tongue tip
11 Tongue blade
12 Tongue front
13 Tongue body
14 Tongue back
15 Tongue root

Figure 1 Cross-section of the nose, mouth and throat

(1) T<u>ier</u>   <u>dir</u>

This difference in vibration is crucial in German, as it distinguishes the initial consonants in each case and in a great many other pairs of words as well, e.g. *Pein, Bein*; *Tank, Dank*; *Kasse, Gasse*. This will be discussed further in chapter 5. For the time being this example is a simple demonstration of a mechanism of speech production. It is important to appreciate that, as observers of language (rather than as native speakers), we can separate out particular features of the speech continuum, such as the vibration in this case, and see them as independent features of speech, rather like the individual instruments in an orchestra.

As a basis for discussing articulation, let us start with the identification of the speech organs. These are given in figure 1, a cross-section of the nose, mouth and throat.

We can now go on to consider the major articulatory mechanisms in turn, as follows: air-stream type, state of the glottis, state of the velum, and the position of the oral articulators.

4.2 Air-stream Type

Although there are a number of possible sources of the air we use to produce speech, in German we only need to note that it is the air coming from the lungs which is used. This is generally referred to as egressive, pulmonic air.

4.3   State of the Glottis

The vocal cords are stretched across the glottal opening (glottis) in the larynx. These can be moved into different positions, so as to modify the flow of air through the glottis. The three positions which are of importance in German are:

(i)   **Closed,** thereby shutting off the flow of air, which can be released again by parting the cords, producing a glottal stop. The symbol for this is [ʔ] (see also the chart of IPA symbols at the beginning of the book). Since the rest of the vocal apparatus above the larynx can be used to produce separate articulations, it is possible to combine a glottal stop with some other articulation in the mouth, for instance, a closure at the alveolar ridge ([t]; see further sections 4.4 and 4.5). Such combined articulations are usually called **glottally reinforced;** in German they occur when [p], [t] or [k] precede another consonant, as in *tritt mal*. In English they occur in similar circumstances and also in utterance-final position, e.g. *get me* and *have a cup*.

(ii)   **Close together,** so that the air passing between them causes them to vibrate. This gives the feature of **voice** to any sound so produced, as discussed in the case of *Tier* and *dir* above. The rate at which the vibration occurs can be varied, which produces variation in the pitch of the sound: a slow rate of vibration gives a low pitch; the faster the rate, the higher the pitch. **Voiced** sounds are therefore singable.

(iii)   **Wide apart,** allowing air to flow through unimpeded. This gives the feature of **voicelessness** to any sound so produced. In contrast to the voiced sounds **voiceless** sounds are not singable. To test this distinction, try humming a tune with just a [z]-sound; then try humming with just [s]. You will find that you cannot change the pitch of the latter.

The term for this aspect of sound production generally is **phonation,** each state of the glottis producing a different type of phonation.

In German we find pairs of voiced and voiceless sounds, as in the medial consonants of the examples in (2). The relevant letter in the orthographic version is underlined and a phonetic transcription is given in each case.

(2)   Gru<u>pp</u>e [gʀʊpə]   Lei<u>t</u>er [laɪtʌ]   A<u>ck</u>er [akʌ]   rei<u>ß</u>e [ʀaɪsə]
        Kra<u>bb</u>e [kʀabə]   lei<u>d</u>er [laɪdʌ]   Ba<u>gg</u>er [bagʌ]   Rei<u>s</u>e [ʀaɪzə]

The symbol [ʌ] represents a vowel-like articulation of the *er*-ending (see also section 4.8).

4.4   State of the Velum

If you run your tongue along the roof of your mouth, you will notice that the hard bony part (the hard palate) ceases about halfway back and it continues as a soft area ending at the tonsils (the faucal opening). This soft area is called the soft palate or velum. The area behind the faucal opening, the pharynx, allows air to pass into the mouth and also into the nasal passages. To stop air going into the nose we can shut off the passages by moving the velum against the back pharynx wall. Since the back of the mouth has fewer nerve endings than the front (e.g. tongue tip, gums, lips), it is difficult to tell exactly what is going on, but in the production of the English word *hidden* the consonantal sequence at the end is [-dn] without any intervening vowel; this sequence is produced with only one articulatory movement, the lowering of the velum, which allows air into the nose and changes [d] into [n]. With the velum lowered air goes into both the nose and the mouth; sounds produced with the velum in this position are called **nasal**. With the velum closed air can only go into the mouth; such sounds are **oral**.

German has pairs of oral and nasal sounds, as in the examples in (3).

(3)   B̲ein [baɪn]   d̲ein [daɪn]   Ba̲g̲ger [bagʌ]
        m̲ein [maɪn]   n̲ein [naɪn]   ba̲n̲ger [baŋʌ]

(Note that the velar nasal [ŋ] does not occur in word-initial position in German, any more than it does in English: [ŋa] and [ŋɪ], for example, are not possible; see, however, a slightly more complex approach to this issue in section 5.8.1.)

The two features of phonation and nasality are quite independent of one another. They can co-occur or the movements involved may begin and end at different times in the speech continuum. Different languages use different combinations of the mechanisms: German, like English, has both voiceless and voiced oral sounds, but only voiced nasal ones, e.g. [p b m] but not [m̥], where the subscript circle indicates voicelessness.

4.5   Oral Articulators

When the air is passing through the mouth, there is quite a wide range of possible modifications that can be made to it. We have a number of articulators in the oral cavity, as indicated in figure 1, some of which are movable, some of which are not. These are referred to as active and passive articulators, respectively. What is important in speech production is the relative position of the articulators to one another, and which ones are being used. Relative position is a matter of manner of articulation; which articulators are being used is a matter of place of articulation. We shall deal with each separately.

4.6   Manner

An active articulator can be in a number of different spatial relations to a passive one. If we take as an initial example the tip of the tongue (apex) and the hard ridge of bone behind the top teeth (alveolar ridge), we can see a number of different possibilities of relationship, which modify the air-stream in different ways. If the sides of the tongue are in full contact with the side teeth and the tip is tight against the alveolar ridge, no air can escape until it is released somehow. The air pressure builds up in the mouth, as long as air is coming up from the lungs. If the vocal cords are vibrating and the velum is closed, the removal of the tongue tip from the alveolar ridge will cause a quick release of the air in the mouth, giving a **plosive** sound. We represent this as [d]; its full description is a **voiced, oral, alveolar plosive**. It is also a **stop**, because the air-stream is stopped in the mouth. Because the air is released, it is a plosive; if the air was not released, it would still be a stop, but not a plosive. Keeping the same articulatory position in the mouth but changing the phonation to voiceless will give us [t], a **voiceless, oral, alveolar stop**; changing the position of the velum but keeping the vocal cords vibrating will give us [n], a **voiced, nasal, alveolar stop**. (Note that in the case of [n], and any other nasal stops, the stoppage is still in the mouth, at the alveolar ridge for [n]; it is not in the nose.)

The position of the articulators for [d] can be modified slightly by removing the tongue tip away from the alveolar ridge very slightly, so that the air is forced through a narrow gap causing local (i.e. at the alveolar ridge), audible friction. The resultant sound is continuous, as distinct from the stop, and is called a **fricative**. The resultant voiced sound is [z], a **voiced, oral, alveolar fricative**; the voiceless equivalent is [s]. We may note that German, like English, does not have any nasal fricatives, e.g. [z̃], except in rapid speech.

Instead of releasing the tongue contact at the alveolar ridge, we can release the side contact. Such sounds are called laterals, because the air escapes from the mouth around the sides of the tongue, since the middle part of the oral cavity is blocked by the alveolar contact. If the sides of the tongue leave only a narrow gap, the air passing through will cause friction. A **voiceless, oral, alveolar lateral fricative**, symbolized [ɬ], occurs in Welsh, represented in spelling by *ll*, but lateral fricatives do not occur in German. With a wider gap for the air to pass through no friction occurs resulting in a **lateral approximant**, symbolized [l]. This type is often referred to simply as a lateral, without the reference to its being an approximant.

If the gap between the tongue tip and the alveolar ridge is similarly made greater than for the fricative, the resultant sound is also described as a (central, i.e. non-lateral) **approximant**. (This sound type is sometimes referred to as **frictionless continuant**.) In English we have a **voiced, oral, post-alveolar approximant**, [ɹ], the sound at the beginning of *red*. (It is post-alveolar because the tip and blade of the tongue are held slightly to the rear of the ridge.) Approximant articulations in German are much more restricted than in English and are produced with different articulators (see below, section 4.12).

The set of sound-types, **stop, fricative** and **approximant**, can be produced with any of the articulators which we are going to discuss in the next section. Laterals are more restricted in that the tongue has to be one of the articulators.

There is one other manner of articulation that is needed for the description of German: the trill. The trill is a sequence of rapid tap movements, that is, the active articulator taps briefly against the passive one and this is done a number of times in succession. In the German spoken in South Germany, Austria and Switzerland we find a **voiced, oral, alveolar trill**, [r]; in Standard German the trill is produced with the back of the tongue and the uvula (see figure 1 and section 4.9), giving a **voiced, oral, uvular trill**, [ʀ].

If no other articulators are used and the tongue is no nearer the roof of the mouth than is required for approximants, then **vocoid** articulations are produced. (These are usually called vowels, but since this term, along with consonant, is better reserved for phonological discussions, we shall not use either of them in the presentation of phonetics.) Since no contact is required for vocoid articulations, we cannot have recourse to the characteristics used so far in this section on manner, or in the following one on place of articulation, where points of contact and/or narrowing of the vocal tract can be specified in terms of the articulators concerned. What we have to deal with here is an area within the mouth in which the tongue can move about without making contact with any other articulator. This is usually referred to as the vowel area and is shown on figure 2.

Although it is roughly speaking ovoid in shape, it is a convention to regularize the area into a trapezoid, as in figure 3. This is referred to as a vowel diagram.

The two dimensions represented by the diagram are front and back horizontally, and high and low vertically. The bulk of the body of the tongue can be moved about along these two axes to change the shape of the space in the mouth through which the air passes (the resonance chamber). This produces different vocoid qualities.

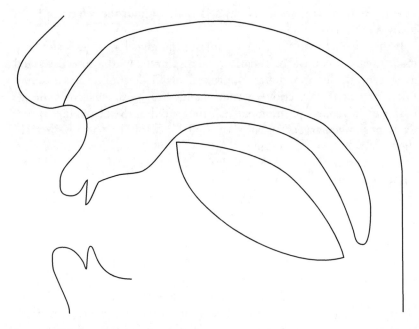

Figure 2 The vowel area

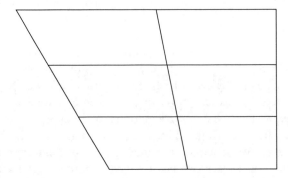

Figure 3 Vowel diagram

4.7 Lip Position

The lips are quite elastic and can be spread and pursed in varying degrees; they also have a neutral position during rest, which can also be used during speech. Sounds produced with pursed lips are called **rounded**, those with spread lips **spread** or **unrounded**. Lip position is a feature of both **contoid** articulations (i.e. stops, fricatives, laterals and trills, the sounds with contact between the articulators) as well as vocoid ones. In German, [ʃ], the initial consonant in *Schein* and [ʒ], the initial consonant in *Journal*, are accompanied by lip-rounding, as are their English counterparts. It is also the main difference between the words *Biene*, with spread lips, and *Bühne*, with rounded ones. Although it is common practice to treat lip position as a feature of vocoid articulations, it is important to remember that it is very often a feature of whole syllables, as in the last two examples.

4.8 Vocoid Articulations

To start with we describe vocoids that are both voiced and oral, though, as we shall see, they do not have to be so. The extreme points of the diagram (rather like north, south, east and west as points of the compass) give us fixed positions from which we can measure other, intermediate positions. They can be accompanied by spread or rounded lips, except for the front, low position, which makes lip-rounding very difficult, if not impossible, because of the openness of the mouth. In figure 4 we give the symbols used for these positions, rounded on the left of the oblique, spread on the right.

The following are examples of those sounds which occur in Standard German. Length is indicated by a following colon; sounds without such a mark are relatively short.

(4) Bühne [byːnə]
     Biene [biːnə]
     Buch   [buːx]
     Bach   [bax]
     Bahn   [baːn], [bɑːn]

[ɯ] does not occur in German; [ɒ] does not occur either, but it does in Standard British English *hot*. The two pronunciations of *Bahn* vary from speaker to speaker.

In order to give further fixed points of reference, the high-low dimension is divided into three equal distances; the resultant points plus the extreme ones together make up what are called the Cardinal Vowels.

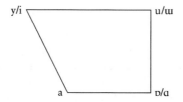

Figure 4   The extreme vocoid positions

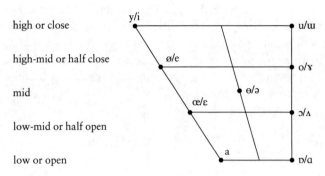

Figure 5   The Cardinal Vowels and position of rest

Figure 5 shows all these positions, with the position of rest marked in the centre, with rounded and spread pairs of symbols.

Further examples of the vocoids found in German will be given in section 4.12. The position of rest, accompanied by neutral lip position, only occurs in unstressed syllables in German and English alike, e.g. *Gebet* [gəbéːt], *about* [əbáʊt], where the acute accent indicates the stressed syllable. (Note that this is not the IPA convention for marking stress.) The different tongue-heights are referred to by either of the alternative names given in figure 5. Examples of full phonetic descriptions of these cardinal vocoid positions are given in (5).

(5) [y] – voiced oral high front rounded vocoid
     [ʌ] – voiced oral half-open back spread vocoid
     [ɛ] – voiced oral half-open front spread vocoid
     [o] – voiced oral half-close back rounded vocoid.

In passing, we should note that there is an overlap between the terms **high vocoid** and **approximant,** when the latter is made in the area of the hard palate (front) or velum (back). Strictly speaking, [j] = [i] and [w] = [u]. The convention of two symbols (and two phonetic descriptions) stems from the fact that vocoids of very short duration are found in the syllable margins, especially in syllable-initial position, and are classified phonologically as consonants; hence they are written [j] and [w], as in English, and are described as approximants. However, from a phonetic point of view, there is no reason why we cannot write English *yes* as [ies] and *wet* as [uet].

The examples we have discussed so far have all been voiced and oral. It is perfectly possible to produce vocoid articulations without any voicing. This occurs in German (and English) in syllable-initial position in words like *Hand* [ḁant], *hübsch* [ɣ̥ʏpʃ], *Hock* [ɔ̥ɔk], where the small circle underneath the main symbol represents voicelessness, that is, open

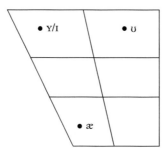

Figure 6   Some non-peripheral vocoids

vocal cords. Phonologically, such voiceless vocoids are interpreted as being the 'same sound', a consonant usually written [h], but this is a matter for the next chapter.

If we lower the velum during a vocoid articulation, then we produce nasalized vowels. These are common in French, for instance, and have come into German with borrowings from that language in words like *Teint* [tɛ̃] 'complexion', and *Restaurant* [ʀɛstorɑ̃], though these are by no means the only possible pronunciations of these words. (Loan words typically have various pronunciations, for example English *garage* [gæɹɑʒ] or [gæɹɪdʒ]; see further chapter 5.) Voiceless, nasal vocoids do not occur in German.

Having established a set of cardinal positions upon which to base judgements of particular instances of vocoid production, linguists need at times to indicate articulations not represented by these extreme points on the periphery of the vowel area. To enable them to locate vocoid qualities more precisely in their symbols, a number of diacritics can be added to the cardinal symbol so that closer, lower, rounder, fronter, more spread and backer varieties can be pinpointed. Since it is not the purpose of this book to go into such detail, we will not discuss them further, but they are incorporated into the IPA chart reproduced at the beginning of the book. However, where particular languages consistently have articulations in one or more of these intermediate positions, a special symbol has been provided for it. This applies to English [æ], the vowel in *hand*, and German [ɪ, ʏ, ʊ] in *Wind*, *hübsch* and *Lust*, respectively, which are given in figure 6.

In other cases one of the cardinal symbols is used without a diacritic to indicate such positions, as we shall see in section 4.12.

What we have said so far refers to vocoid articulations in which the tongue stays in the same position. However, since the tongue is not in contact with any other articulator, it can be moved about during the production of a vocoid. The steady-state vocoids are called **monophthongs**; the moving vocoids cover quite a range of possibilities. A simple movement from one position to another is referred to as a **diphthong**: it

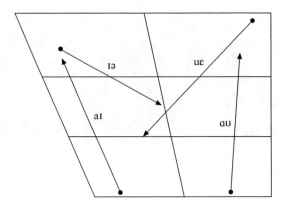

Figure 7   Some diphthongs

is normal practice to indicate the starting and finishing points, i.e. [ai] means a movement from [a] to [i]. In figure 7 we give a number of such movements.

Diphthongs can be classified according to the general direction of the movement; thus, [aɪ] is front, closing, [ɑʊ] is back, closing, [ɪa] is front, opening, and [ɪə] is centring. It is possible to change lip position during the course of the diphthong, as in [ɑʊ] and [ɔɪ]. The movement can, of course, continue by changing direction; in theory such changes of direction are limited only by breathing ability. However, in practice languages seem to limit the number of movements to two within one syllable; longer sequences of movement would be interpreted as more than one syllable. (See further chapter 5 for the notion of syllable.)

4.9   Place of Articulation

In section 4.6 we saw a few examples of place of articulation, in particular the contact of the tongue tip and the alveolar ridge. We must now consider other possibilities, and see how these apply to German.

It is convenient to go from the front of the mouth backwards. For each place of articulation we give the symbols for the voiceless and voiced stops, the voiceless and voiced fricatives, and the voiced nasal stop. Other possible combinations of features, such as voiceless nasal fricatives, are represented by means of diacritics, e.g. [s̃] (see IPA chart for details). Many of these other possibilities are not relevant to German and need not concern us here.

Firstly, both lips can be used, the bottom lip being moved upwards towards the top one, the latter moving very little. Sounds produced in this way are called **bilabial**:

p b   ɸ β   m

The bottom lip can also be brought into contact with the bottom edge of the top teeth, usually with the teeth just tucked inside the lip, to produce **labiodental** sounds:

*p̪ b̪   f v   ʋ

(*There are no official symbols for the labiodental stops in the IPA alphabet, so we have used the diacritic for dentality. Such sounds can only be made by speakers who have no gaps in their teeth, through which the air can escape.)

We then come to a whole range of sounds which involve the tongue as active articulator. As indicated in figure 1, the tongue can be sectioned up into the tip (apex), the blade (lamina), the front and the back. These are only convenient labels for the bits which are regularly used in speech production, but, of course, there are no physical demarcations of these areas (unlike the end of the bone in the roof of the mouth, which marks the boundary between the hard palate and the velum). Furthermore, the exact part of the tongue used in any particular type of articulation may vary between speakers and in different contexts in one and the same speaker. It is important to remember that in the case of all the sounds discussed and symbolized below, the sides of the tongue behind the main place of articulation are in close contact with the side teeth to make sure that the air does not escape that way (cf. section 4.6, above).

The tip of the tongue can be placed against the back of the top teeth to produce **dental** sounds, or between the top and bottom teeth to produce **interdental** ones. Similar sounds can be produced by using the blade instead of the tip. To distinguish these two types of dental articulation we can use the terms **apicodental** and **laminodental**, respectively:

t̪ d̪   θ ð   n̪

If the tip or blade is retracted slightly to rest on the alveolar ridge, instead of on the teeth, we produce **apico-** or **laminoalveolar** sounds:

t d   s z   n

If the tip is retracted even further, or even curled back, so that the underside comes into contact with the roof of the mouth at the beginning of the hard palate, the sounds are **retroflex**:

t ɖ   ʂ ʐ   ɳ

A larger part of the tongue can be used in articulation, e.g. the tip and the blade at the same time. If the tip is placed on the alveolar ridge and the blade on the front part of the hard palate, the resultant sounds are **palatoalveolar**. Again the IPA alphabet does not provide separate symbols for the oral and nasal stops, so we use a superscript [ʲ]:

tʲ dʲ   ʃ ʒ   nʲ

If the middle section of the tongue is used in association with the hard palate, the sounds are called simply **palatal**:

c ɟ   ç ʝ   ɲ

The back of the tongue can be brought into contact with the velum, producing **velar** sounds:

k g   x ɣ   ŋ

The back of the tongue can be moved slightly further back so that it comes into contact with the uvula, giving **uvular** sounds.

q ɢ   χ ʁ   ɴ

There are other possible combinations of articulator contact, but we are restricting our presentation here to those that are needed in the description of German, plus one or two others. However, there are two further manners of articulation, which were mentioned in section 4.6, and which are relevant to German: the lateral and the trill. The lateral articulation in German has apicoalveolar contact and is symbolized [l]; the trill on the other hand is produced in one of two places, either with the tip of the tongue against the alveolar ridge: [r], or with the back of the tongue against the uvula: [ʀ].

4.10   Resonance

One further matter must be addressed which affects all sounds and which is most clearly appreciated in the production of vocoids. This is the feature of resonance. In the production of vocoids the position of the tongue relative to the rest of the mouth determines the shape of the gap through which the air passes, the resonance chamber. But, even if the tongue is in contact with some part of the roof of the mouth, the gap behind the point of contact can be altered by means of the movement of the free part of the tongue (and other articulators, too, such as the pharynx). In English the lateral approximant can have a number of different resonances. The two usually described are those found at the beginning of *limp* and the end of *full* in a standard pronunciation (RP); they both occur in a word like *little*, [lɪtɫ], in a narrow transcription. The wavy line through the symbol represents back resonance, which is produced by raising the back of the tongue towards the velum somewhat without any contact, that is, roughly the position taken up for the vowel [o] in figure 5. This reduction to two types of resonance, **front** and **back**, is an oversimplification, but this English example serves as a suitable illustration of resonance.

In fact, any contoid articulation can have a variety of resonance characteristics; any position can be taken up by the free part of the tongue, and also the muscles of the faucal opening and the pharynx can be tightened and relaxed in varying degrees. All of this has an effect on the shape of the resonance chamber and, hence, the quality of the sound so produced. For our purposes we need to note that in German [l] and [n] typically have a very front type of resonance in the case of many speakers; the body of the tongue is in the position of [i]. This is particularly noticeable with post-vocalic [l], so that many English learners of German have difficulty distinguishing between pairs such as *Gehalt* [gəhalt] and *geheilt* [gəhaɪlt], when spoken by a native speaker in context. On the other hand, [ʀ] has a typically central or back resonance. This often affects a preceding front vowel, in that the tongue is positioned more centrally than in cases where no [ʀ] is articulated. In other words, some speakers have different tongue positions for the vowels in *Wind* [vɪnt] and *wird* [vɨʀt]. Furthermore, for many speakers, words which have an *r* in the spelling at the end of a syllable with or without a following consonant are pronounced with syllable-length back resonance without any lingual contact of the sort involved in [ʀ], e.g. *Haar* [haː], *Bart* [bˠaːtˠ], where [ˠ] is used to indicate back resonance. (For more detail regarding the pronunciation of orthographic *r* in German, see chapter 5; a detailed investigation of coda /r/ in German can be found in Simpson 1998, and Lodge, forthcoming.)

4.11 Voice Onset Time

Our final discussion of characteristics of speech production is centred on the time interval between the start of an utterance and the onset of voice. The vocal cords can start to vibrate at various times after the utterance has begun. If we take bilabial closure and release followed by a vocoid by way of exemplification, the following are possible:

(i)   [pḁ] = no vibration at all;
(ii) [pʰa] = vibration starts after the lips are opened;

(iii) [pa] = vibration starts as the lips are opened;
(iv) [̥ba] = vibration starts after the lips are closed, but before they are opened;
(v) [ba] = vibration starts as the lips are closed.

The timing represented by (ii) is usually referred to as aspiration (indicated by the superscript [ʰ] in the transcription); the little circle is used to indicate the voicelessness in (i) and (iv). In utterance-initial position in a stressed syllable German uses (ii) and (iv), e.g. *Pass* [pʰas] and *Bass* [̥bas]. After another contoid articulation, namely [ʃ], (iii) occurs, e.g. [ʃpaːs]. This is just like English [pʰæn], [̥bæn] and [spæn]. If the articulation in question is preceded by vibrating vocal cords, (v) occurs, e.g. *der Bass* [deʌ bas].

4.12   The Transcription of German and English

The amount of phonetic detail that we can represent in our transcriptions can vary considerably and depends to some extent on the use to which we put them. If we want to indicate a lot of detail, such as the different types of voice onset time discussed in the previous section, then we can represent these differences by using the diacritic symbols as in the representations of the English words *pan, ban* and *span*. On the other hand, we may think that in dealing with a language like German, where these different possibilities occur in different specifiable contexts, we can leave out the diacritics and rely on the simpler letter representations, as in [pas] versus [bas]. The detailed kind of transcription is referred to as **narrow**; the less detailed kind as **broad**. For the purposes of this book the broad kind of transcription is perfectly adequate.

As a simple guide to the kind of transcription used in this book, we now present sample transcriptions for both German and English, giving various combinations of consonants and vowels. Remember that phonetic transcriptions are designed to be consistent and unambiguous; one symbol represents one sound only. Because the vowel sounds are quite different in German and English, there are greater differences in their transcription than in that of the consonants.

German

Platz [plats]   Spaß [ʃpaːs]   Klapper [klapʌ]   knapp [knap]   Dieb [diːp]
Bruder [bʀuːdʌ]   Krabbe [kʀabə]   Schwalbe [ʃvalbə]
trotz [tʀɔts]   Stange [ʃtaŋə]   Wetter [vɛtʌ]   glatt [glat]   Tod [toːt]
drei [dʀaɪ]   leider [laɪdʌ]   golden [gɔldn] or [gɔldən]

klein [klaɪn]   Skandal [skandaːl]   Zucker [tsʊkʌ]
  Glück [glʏk]   Krieg [kʀiːk]
grau [gʀɑʊ]   Züge [tsyːgə]   Folge [fɔlgə]
falsch [falʃ]   Affe [afə]   straff [ʃtʀaf]   brav [bʀaːf]
Wein [vaɪn]   schwül [ʃvyːl]   brave [bʀaːvə]
Sklave [sklaːvə]   Kasse [kasə]   was [vas]   las [laːs]
Sohn [zoːn]   Hase [haːzə]   lasen [laːzn]
Schuh [ʃuː]   Stein [ʃtaɪn]   Flasche [flaʃə]   Tisch [tɪʃ]   deutsch [dɔɪtʃ]
Genie [ʒeniː]   arrangieren [aʀɑ̃ʒiːʀən]   Passage [pasaːʒə]
China [çiːna]   ich [ɪç]   Löcher [lœçʌ]   Dolch [dɔlç]
Dach [dax]   Buch [buːx]   Loch [lɔx]
jung [jʊŋ]   Boje [boːjə]
Möwe [møvːə]   schmal [ʃmaːl]   Hammer [hamʌ]   Lamm [lam]
nett [nɛt]   Schnee [ʃneː]   inner [ɪnʌ]   dünn [dʏn]
Länge [lɛŋə]   denke [dɛŋkə]   sank [zaŋk]   sang [zaŋ]
legen [leːgŋ] or [leːgən]   Höhle [høːlə]   hielt [hiːlt]   wohl [voːl]
rau [ʀɑʊ]   hören [høːʀən]   hört [høːʌt]   Herr [hɛR] or [hɛʌ]
  Vater [faːtʌ]
Hund [hʊnt]   Geheul [gəhɔɪl]

English

(Note that the transcriptions below represent standard British English
(RP); it may not equate with your own variety of English):

pain [peɪn]   Spain [speɪn]   happy [hæpɪ]   tip [tɪp]
bush [bʊʃ]   brush [bɹʌʃ]   ruby [ɹuubɪ]   job [dʒɒb]
tent [tent]   sting [stɪŋ]   later [leɪtə]   short [ʃɔt]
dine [daɪn]   drown [dɹɑʊn]   hardly [hɑdlɪ]   sand [sænd]
king [kɪŋ]   squeeze [skwɪiz]   lucky [lʌkɪ]   knock [nɒk]
go [gəʊ]   gloat [gləʊt]   digger [dɪgə]   wriggle [ɹɪgɫ]   peg [peg]
church [tʃɜtʃ]   watching [wɒtʃɪŋ]
judge [dʒʌdʒ]   hedging [hedʒɪŋ]
few [fjʊu]   wafer [weɪfə]   knife [naɪf]
vow [vɑʊ]   hover [hɒvə]   swerve [swɜv]
think [θɪŋk]   ether [ɪiθə]   bath [bɑθ]
this [ðɪs]   other [ʌðə]   bathe [beɪð]
soil [sɔɪɫ]   parson [pɑsn]   pass [pɑs]
zoo [zʊu]   Jersey [dʒɜzɪ]   haze [heɪz]
shoe [ʃʊu]   usher [ʌʃə]   wash [wɒʃ]
Jeanne [ʒæn]   pleasure [pleʒə]   rouge [ɹuuʒ]
mummy [mʌmɪ]   James [dʒeɪmz]   clam [klæm]
nanny [nænɪ]   clown [klɑʊn]
singer [sɪŋə]   finger [fɪŋgə]   think [θɪŋk]   thing [θɪŋ]

look [lʊk]   silly [sɪlɪ]   fall [fɔɫ]   little [lɪtɫ]
red [ɹed]   error [eɹə]   every [evɹɪ]
yet [jet]
white [waɪt]
here [hɪə]   ahead [əhed]

4.13   Further Reading

The following are suitable introductions to general phonetics: Ladefoged
(1993); Clark and Yallop (1995); Ball and Rahilly (1999). A description
of German is available in Kohler (1977).

EXERCISES

1   From the German examples above, collect together all the words that
have the same stressed vowel, e.g. *Affe* and *straff*. Add any more you
can think of.

2   Compare the German and English stressed vowels; what are the main
differences?

3   Which of the following are voiced: [p ɡ j s ʒ o f]?

4   Which of the following are nasal: [b ŋ m w ã ʌ t]?

5   Which of the following are alveolar: [k χ n s ɛ v ʃ d]?

6   Describe in full each of the following: [t q ŋ z ɔ e ũ ɸ].

CHAPTER FIVE

Phonology

5.1 Preliminaries

What we have presented in chapters 1–3 has told us nothing about the spoken language *per se*. Most of the aspects of German morphology and syntax apply to both the spoken and the written language. But we must now recognize that speech and writing are not the same thing at all; this is why we introduced articulatory phonetics in the previous chapter as a way of describing speech. The relationship between the two media of communication is by no means straightforward and a few brief comments on this difference might be useful at this point. Speech is always considered primary by linguists; the main reason for this is that a young child will speak naturally in the course of its development without any instruction provided there are no pathological problems. On the other hand, children do not learn to read and write without instruction. These are taught skills. The nature of the media themselves also shows up crucial differences: intonation patterns (the rise and fall of the pitch of the voice) cannot be represented directly in the written form. A rising intonation is often represented by a final question mark, but many other nuances of meaning indicated by the pitch and quality of the voice have to be represented in an entirely different way in writing. As an example of an ambiguous written sentence which would be differentiated in the spoken language, consider (1):

(1)   Die Maus bemerkt sofort die Katze, nicht den Goldfisch.

Since *die Maus* and *die Katze* can both be either nominative or accusative, it is not clear from the written version which is in contrast with *den Goldfisch*. In speech emphatic stress would be placed on *Maus*, if that were the accusative object, or on *Katze*, if that word were.

In the previous chapter we were concerned with describing the articulatory characteristics of a range of sounds, many of which are used by native German speakers, though the descriptions are intended to be universal, not language-specific, that is, a voiced oral bilabial stop is just that regardless of the language being spoken. In phonology, however, we are concerned with how native speakers recognize meaning in the sounds of continuous spoken German. Some phonetic differences are meaningful to a German, others are not. Using the word 'know' in the special sense of Chomskyan linguistics (see the Introduction), we can say that native speakers of German know that the difference of voice onset time in *Tank* [tʰaŋk] and *Dank* [daŋk] corresponds to a difference of meaning between the two words, whereas the difference of voicing in *Grad* [gʀaːt] and *Grade* [gʀaːdə] does not convey a difference of meaning, because they are 'the same word', the singular form and the plural one, respectively. (Please note that we have not given meanings for the German words in this chapter, as they are largely irrelevant to the discussion.) More precisely, we want to say they are the same lexical item: they are two different words but they belong to the same item in the lexicon (vocabulary) of German, in just the same way as *bin*, *bist*, *war* and *gewesen* are all different words, but belong to the same verb, which by convention is represented by the infinitive form *sein*. (See further chapter 6.) Thus, to return to our examples of voicing differences, the first one contributes to the distinction of meaning in *Tank* and *Dank* in a way that the second instance does not. In the latter case the grammatical number of the lexical item has changed, but not its meaning.

In German, then, we can see that the organization of the sounds is such that sometimes [t] and [d] are distinctive, at other times not. What the linguist has to do is make statements (establish rules) about what the different circumstances ('times' in the previous sentence) are. By looking at a few more examples, we can see that in initial and intervocalic positions [t] and [d] contrast: *Tier*, *dir*; *Leiter*, *leider*; in syllable-final position they do not. We never find any standard German words that end in [d], though such words do occur in dialect forms. If we look at the variants of one lexical item, what we find is that [t] contrasts meaningfully with an alternating pair [t] and [d], for example *Rat* [ʀaːt], genitive *Rates* [ʀaːtəs], versus *Rad* [ʀaːt], genitive [ʀaːdəs].

On the basis of the meaningful contrasts we can set up two distinctive phonological elements, usually referred to as **phonemes** and symbolized between slant lines: /t/ and /d/, as opposed to the square brackets of the phonetic, physical realizations. Linguists who based their phonology on phonetic considerations only without any reference to other levels of structure (for instance, Jones 1950, Gleason 1955, Hockett 1958) would say that the [t] of *Rat* must be the same element as the [t] in *Rad* because of their phonetic identity. This requirement of the analysis has been referred to as biuniqueness (see Chomsky 1964, Hyman 1975, Lass 1984). But, if we want to account for the native-speaker knowledge of the language, a mental capacity (competence), then it would be difficult to claim that in their mental lexicon German speakers store words like *Rad* in two forms, one having a /t/, the other a /d/ as stem-final consonant. This is not to deny the phonetic reality of their articulation, rather it is a statement to the effect that we must take account of the fact that Germans know which lexical items have alternating forms and which do not. The more important fact of the matter is that [ʀaːt] (*Rad*) and the [ʀaːd-] of *Rades* are the same lexical item, just as with *Grad* and *Grade* above, and, therefore, the change from [t] to [d] does not constitute a difference of meaning. These two phonetic forms must be treated as alternative realizations of the same element in the phonology of German. One way of doing this is to state that the alternating sounds are contextually determined variants of the voiced phoneme /d/. If we do this, we will also need a rule to the effect that syllable-final voiced stops are devoiced, that is, are realized as voiceless. This can be tentatively formalized as: /d/ → [t], which must be read as 'the phoneme /d/ is realized as (represented by the arrow) [t]'. To this rule we must add the information that it is to be applied only when /d/ is in syllable-final position. A more appropriate formulation of the rule affecting /d/ is given as (27) below. We can now differentiate *Rat* and *Rad* in the lexicon, which represents the mental store house of the native speaker of German for her/his lexical items (see chapter 6). They are stored as /raːt/ and /raːd/, respectively. (The use of /r/ to represent the phoneme that is realized as [ʀ] in initial position is partly one of typographical convenience, but also reflects the abstract nature of the phoneme /r/, which has other realizations to be discussed below. The representation of the long vowels will be modified in section 5.7.)

This example shows us that there is, indeed, a difference between phonetics and phonology. When we come to define the phonemes of German, we shall say that /d/ is a voiced alveolar stop. Because this is a phonological definition, voiced does not mean simply 'with vibrating vocal cords', but it means 'capable of alternating with voiceless equivalents syllable-finally'. Our devoicing rule converts the phonological, abstract representation into a phonetic realization. Rules in this sense are to be seen as a mapping of phonetic output onto phonological forms in the lexicon. We can also see from this what we mean by saying that phonology is an abstraction: **voiced** has a specific meaning in German phonology because of syllable-final devoicing; in English, on the other hand, it does not have that meaning, since syllable-final devoicing does not occur in this way. Phonetically speaking, of course, it has the same meaning whatever language we are discussing.

We shall discuss the different classes of phoneme in some detail in sections 5.3–5.7. For the time being, we will simply present the set of consonant phonemes for German in (2).

(2) p t k
     b d g
     pf ts
     m n ŋ
     f s ç ʃ
     v z j ʒ
     l r h

(We must note here that in this chapter we are only dealing with a standard pronunciation.) However, phonemes, whether consonants or vowels, do not combine indiscriminately; they are subject to combinatorial constraints, which are often referred to as **phonotactics** (= 'the syntax of phonemes') and are part of the native speaker's knowledge. Not only this, but the phonemes are combined into a higher structural unit, the **syllable**, which we will discuss first.

5.2   Syllable Structure

We shall show in the following sections that the notion of the syllable is needed for our phonological statements in German. The right-hand boundary of a syllable will tell us, for instance, that no voiced obstruent can occur there, or that /r/ will be realized as [ʌ] after a long vowel. As we said above, the phonemes of a language are organized into higher units of structure, somewhat in the way words are organized into higher units, the phrase and the sentence. *Das große Buch* is not just a sequence of three words; it constitutes a noun phrase, which functions as a unit in sentences (see chapter 2). Similarly /pas/ is not just a sequence of three phonemes but a syllable as well, which can combine with other syllables in different words, as in *verpassen, Passage, Vierpass*.

The syllable is difficult to define from a purely phonetic point of view (see, for example, Ladefoged's discussion, 1982: 219–24). Many linguists have tried to combine both phonetic and phonological considerations in their definition. An important feature that has been invoked to determine a universal syllable structure is sonority. Individual languages deviate from this universal structure in various ways, which then require language-specific treatment. Such universal characterizations of the syllable are based on relations of sonority within the syllable and observations of the most commonly occurring sequences in various languages.

Sonority can be roughly equated with the distance between the articulators in the production of any sound. Thus, high vowels have less sonority than low vowels, stops have less than fricatives. However, it is not just distance apart, but the other articulators involved in production play a part in determining the amount of sonority a sound has. For instance, nasal stops have more sonority than oral ones and even oral fricatives, because of the addition of the nasal cavity, and voiced sounds have more sonority than their voiceless counterparts. The extremes of this scale of sonority are [ʔ] with the least (none) and [a] with the most. (3) is based on Ladefoged (1982: 222), showing samples of relative sonority.

(3)   Most sonorous → → → → → → → → → → → → → → → least sonorous
          ɑ ɛ ɪ u i l n m z v s ʃ d t k

In determining the order in which sounds will appear in a syllable, sonority is distributed as follows: the greatest sonority is found in the nucleus (the vowel in stressed syllables) with diminishing amounts the nearer to the margins (onset and coda) a sound is. If we apply this to sequences of sounds in German, we can see how syllable structure is reflected in this scale. If we have [halm], this constitutes one syllable: the greatest sonority is in [a] with less in [h]; there is decreasing sonority in [-lm]. This gives us the relationships in (4).

(4)
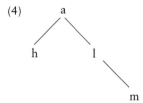

On the other hand, if we take [haml], the sonority relations at the end of the word are different, as in (5). In this case, since there are two peaks, there are two syllables.

(5)
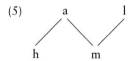

Although this works well in many instances, there are some exceptional structures which are difficult to explain in terms of sonority. If we apply the scale to a sequence like [ʃtam], we end up with (6).

(6)
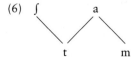

and yet no German would say that that word had two syllables. In fact, many languages, and in particular the Germanic ones (English, Dutch, Swedish, Danish, Norwegian, German, for example) have either /sC-/ or /ʃC-/ syllable onsets despite the fact that they run counter to the sonority scale. If we want to maintain the sonority scale as a useful guide to syllable structure, we simply have to accept that these exceptional onset clusters are a feature of these languages. Exceptions to generalities are certainly commonplace in languages (think of irregular verbs, for instance).

Syllables are divided up into sub-units and syllable places in which various patterns of behaviour can be perceived. The syllable is first of all divided up into an **onset**, which in German may be empty, and a **rhyme**. The rhyme is divided into a **nucleus**, which is where the vowels occur, and a **coda**. Onsets and codas can have one or more consonantal places. (7) gives the basic structure of all syllables; σ stands for **syllable**.

(7)

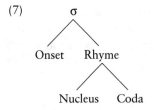

Each of the subdivisions of the syllable can be simple or complex. We have already seen that more than one consonant can occur in the onset or in the coda. In (8) we give the structure for *stank*:

(8)

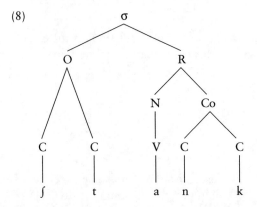

The nucleus can be complex, too: a long vowel or a diphthong. By no means all combinations are possible, and such constraints on combinations are part of the native speaker's knowledge. A German speaker knows that (8) is a legitimate syllable structure in the language and that */ftaɪrkm/ is not.

We must note that there is a difference between an accidental gap in the possibilities, and an actual constraint, for which we can determine a principle. /ʃpaɪn/ is not a German word, but it conforms to the phonotactic regularities of the language (compare *Speise*, *Pein*, *Stein*); in other words, it could be a German word, but it does not happen to be one. On the other hand, */fpaɪŋ/ is not even possible: any fricative other than /ʃ/ or /s/ in initial position of an onset cluster is impermissible and /ŋ/ does not follow diphthongs.

All syllables have to have a nucleus, but the onset and coda are optional, so may be empty. The nucleus is a vowel, if it is stressed, but may be a consonant, such as /l/ or /n/, if it is unstressed. When two or more syllables occur in sequence in a word, it is possible for them to overlap, that is to say, the coda of one syllable is the onset to the next. We shall give some of the reasons for this at the end of this section; for now we need to note that (9), using C for consonant and V for vowel, is a possible syllable structure in German, exemplified by *retten*. The consonant that belongs to both syllables is referred to as **ambisyllabic**.

(9)

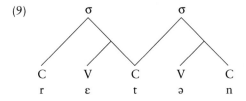

We do not propose to set out in detail all the possible combinations, but we shall pick one or two aspects to discuss more fully. If we start with monosyllables, then the maximum onset is three consonants and the maximum coda is four, as in *Sprung*, *Strand* and *ernst*, *Herbst*, respectively. However, the consonants that can be members of such clusters are very limited. In a three-consonant onset only /ʃpl-/, /ʃpr-/ and /ʃtr-/ are possible, with the addition of a few loan onsets such as /skl-/ *Sklerose* and /skr-/ *Skrupel* (which may be pronounced with [ʃk-] by some speakers). (Note that exceedingly rare loan clusters such as /sfr-/ in *Sphragistik* are not to be included in a set of rules, since most native speakers – even well educated ones – do not know the words they occur in; *Sphragistik* = *Siegelkunde*, that is, the study of seals on documents. Kohler (1977) includes a number of such rarities in his lists.)

A constraint on two consonant clusters is that sounds of the same class do not normally co-occur, for example, */pk-/, */-pk/, */-fç/, */-sʃ/, */nm-/, */-mn/ are not possible. (The dash after the cluster indicates onset, the dash before it, coda.) There are a few exceptions to this restriction: in codas /-pt/ and /-kt/ are allowed, but these are the only combinations of two stops that are, and a number of non-native onsets have been borrowed in the learned vocabulary from Greek, for example *Pterodaktylus* with /pt-/, *Sphäre* with /sf-/. It should be pointed out that, whereas /pt-/ and similar loans will have to be incorporated as proper onsets as in (10), the sequences which involve the automatic insertion of the unstressed vowel [ə] (schwa, see section 5.7), such as *Geburt*, must be assigned to separate syllables, as in (11).

(10)

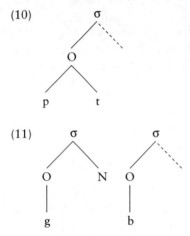

(11)

The first nucleus in (11) is empty, the place where [ə] occurs.

The vowels of monosyllables are also subject to some phonotactic restrictions, but these tend to be in the rhyme rather than between onset and nucleus. We have already noted that /ŋ/ does not combine with other consonants, nor does it follow long vowels. However, one syllable type is missing completely from the monosyllables in German: (C)V, where (C) stands for any number of consonants or none and V indicates a short vowel. Thus there can be no German words like */ʃpɔ/, */gra/, */lɛ/, */tʏ/. If we take a long-vowel nucleus and add more consonants in the coda, the situation is rather different. In this case VVCC and VVCCC, where VV indicates a long vowel or diphthong, are possible but the final consonants can only be alveolar obstruents /t/, /d/ or /s/, as in *hielt*, *Freund*, *Obst*. We must note that forms like *Obst* have two sonority peaks:

(12)   o: s

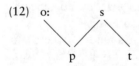

This applies to some combinations with a short nuclear vowel, too, for example *hübsch*, *Lachs*, and forms like *Akt* with two voiceless stops cannot be said to follow the rule of decreasing sonority, since both /k/ and /t/ have about the same amount of sonority (see (3) above). One way to avoid treating such forms (which are perfectly normal from a German point of view) as irregular, is to say that /ʃ/, /s/ and /t/ are extrasyllabic in such cases, that is to say, the rules of syllabification (and stress-assignment, see Giegerich 1985) ignore them. This means that words that contain consonants which do not fit in with the sonority scale have phonological rhymes such as those in (13).

(13)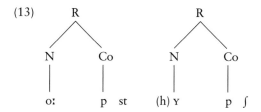

Such extrasyllabic consonants have no syllable place to start with, but will be adjoined to the most appropriate syllable of their word, when the derivation is complete. If the words are simple monosyllables, as in the examples in (13), they will be attached to the end of the syllable. If, on the other hand, there are additions to the basic morpheme, that is, suffixes are added, as in *hübsche*, *aktiv*, they then take up the onset position of the ending, as in (14).

(14)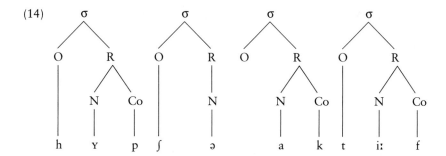

In the representations of syllable structure in (14), we have included an empty onset where the syllable is vowel-initial in *aktiv*. If we handle all such German syllables in this way, we have a neat explanation both of the possibility of [ʔ] as an onset to any vowel (see further section 5.7), and of the syllabification of extrasyllabic consonants in suffixed words: the latter simply fill the empty onset and rule out [ʔ]. *[ʔaktʔiːf] is not a possible pronunciation of *aktiv*, despite the fact that the stress is on the final syllable. So, all German syllables have an onset and a nucleus, but not necessarily a coda.

In disyllabic words such as those in (32) below, for example, *Krabbe*, *Affe*, *Sonne*, we have to decide whether we want the same rules of syllabification for monosyllables applied twice, or whether we need an additional set. This is because such disyllables have a short vowel in the

stressed syllable. If we apply the rules we have for monosyllables, there
are two possible answers, exemplified by *Sonne* in (15).

(15)   a.

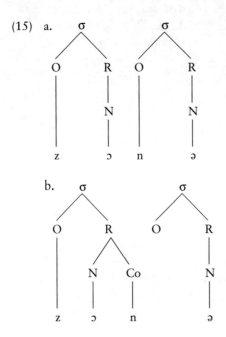

b.

(15a) means that we have to accept a different kind of syllable structure
in disyllables, because (C)V is ruled out in monosyllables (see above). (15b)
is not appropriate, because the final syllable is vowel-initial, which means
that a glottal stop onset is possible, and that is not the case with words like
Krabbe *[kʀabʔə] and *Affe* *[ʔafʔə]. If we want to keep our rules of
syllabification the same for all word types, then we shall have to reject both
alternatives in (15). We shall then have to say that the medial consonant of
such words belongs to both syllables, that is, it is ambisyllabic. In this
way the first syllable ends in a consonant, just like *Mann* and *dick*, and
the final syllable begins with a consonant and blocks the occurrence of
[ʔ]. We then have the structure in (16), where the ambisyllabic place is
marked Co/O. (The final nucleus will be lexically empty, as in (11).)

(16)

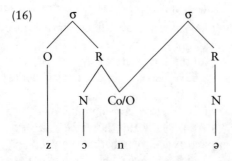

Vowel-initial suffixes, such as the genitive ending *-es*, will produce ambisyllabic consonants of single consonant codas, even after long vowels. This is exemplified in (17) with *Rad – Rades*.

(17)

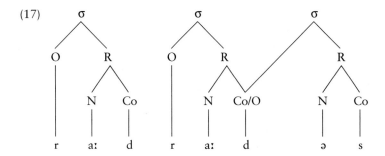

5.3   The Obstruents

Obstruent is a term used to cover both stops and fricatives, which can often be grouped together in phonological statements, if they behave in a parallel manner, as in German with the alternations of voiced and voiceless realizations. The discussion in section 5.1 demonstrates that the phonetic descriptions of a language will be our starting point for making phonological statements, but that they will not on their own determine the full analysis. The function of a given sound or class of sounds is reflected in its behaviour, that is, the patterns of occurrence in the lexical items of the language. To discuss the patterning of [t] and [d], we had to refer to relations between different versions of the same lexical item, for example, singular and plural forms, and we have to make use of the term **syllable** as a structure which is involved in describing where the obstruent devoicing takes place.

Obstruents as a group behave in a parallel fashion to one another. Firstly, we can say that /p t k f s/ are distinct from each other and from /b d g v z/ in syllable-initial position, although /s/ only occurs in this position in a few loan words. Consider the examples in (18).

(18)   Pass   Bass
        Tank   Dank
        Kunst   Gunst
        fein   Wein
        Sex   sechs

In syllable-final position none of the voiced ones occur:

(19)   knapp   [knap]
        hat   [hat]

dick   [dɪk]
straff   [ʃtRaf]
groß   [gRoːs]

However, it is not as simple as this. As we have already noted, there are a number of words where the voiceless and voiced pairs alternate depending on their position in the syllable, for example:

(20)   grob   [gRoːp]   grobe   [gRoːbə]
       Lied   [liːt]   Lieder   [liːdʌ]
       zog   [tsoːk]   zogen   [tsoːgən]
       blies   [bliːs]   bliese   [bliːzə]
       relativ   [Rɛlatiːf]   relative [Rɛlatiːvə]

[f] and [v] only occur in such alternations in loan words such as *brav*, and in the adjectives ending in *-iv*. In those cases where a voiced one of the pair occurs, the syllable structure is such that it is no longer final, but before a vowel. Whether we say the consonant is ambisyllabic or in syllable-initial position makes no difference to these particular forms, nor to our rule dealing with devoicing. What is important is that it is not syllable-final. In these cases the alternation of the voicing characteristic occurs within the same lexical item, that is, it does not carry a change in meaning, as in *Pass*, *Bass*, etc. in (18). The statement that we made above in relation to *Rat* and *Rad* regarding the devoicing of the final /d/ applies to all stops and fricatives in German: any syllable-final voiced member of the set is realized as voiceless. The phonological forms of the items in (20) are thus: /groːb/, /liːd/, /tsoːg/, /bliːz/. (The representation of the long vowels is to be modified in section 5.7.)

There are two other alternations that involve stop and fricative articulations: [ç]~[g], and [ç]~[x]. The former is found in *König – Könige*, *wenig – wenige*. The determining factor in these cases is the unstressed [ɪ] preceding the alternating consonantal forms. The devoicing rule occurs as above, but with a fricative form in syllable-final position. A more precise formulation of the rules will be given below; for the moment we simply need to note that we need two rules: devoicing and fricativization. In the standard variety we may note that in compound words such as *Königreich*, *königlich* and *Königtum* the realization is not always the same: if the following consonant is an obstruent, we find [ç], as in [køːnɪçtuːm]. If it is one of the other consonants, we find speaker variability between [k] and [g], as in [køːnɪklɪç]~[køːnɪglɪç]. In the former case it would seem that the syllable boundary occurs between an underlying /g/ and the following consonant, as in *Königtum*: /køːnɪg$tuːm/, where $ represents the syllable boundary. /g/ is thus syllable-final and must be realized as [ç]. On the other hand, the sequence is treated as a possible onset cluster by some German speakers by realizing such words with [g] (see Giegerich 1986: 114 on non-standard voicing in such cases and even in words with a [-dl-] sequence). Because the final syllable of *König* must have a coda, because [ɪ] and the other short vowels cannot end a syllable (see section 5.2), the /g/ must be ambisyllabic in these forms. This gives us the syllable structure in (21), where the long vowel is treated as two vowel places, as suggested earlier.

(21)

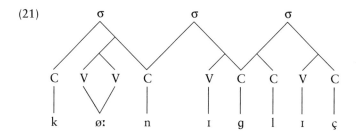

(Other varieties have different realizations in such words, as we shall show in section 9.3.1.)

Next we must turn to [ç] and [x]. These alternate in one and the same lexical item, especially where Umlaut is involved, as in

(22) Buch [buːx]   Bücher [byːçʌ]
      Loch [lɔx]   Löcher [lœçʌ]
      Dach [dax]   Dächer [dɛçʌ]

The front vowels ([yː], [œ] and [ɛ]) are followed by [ç], the non-front (central and back) by [x]. If we look at further examples which do not involve alternations, the same general pattern emerges, as in

(23) hoch [hoːx]   siech [ziːç]
      doch [dɔx]   sich   [zɪç]
      nach [naːx]   Pech   [pɛç]

In addition [ç] occurs after other consonants in the same syllable, regardless of the preceding vowel, as in

(24) Milch   [mɪlç]
      Dolch   [dɔlç]
      Mönch   [mœnç]
      Storch [ʃtɔʀç]

Finally, we find it in word-initial position before front vowels, as an alternative pronunciation to [k] in Greek loan words, such as *Chemie* and *Chirurg* (compare these words with *Chor*, *Charakter*, which always

have [k]). This initial position is also significant in the case of the
diminutive suffix *-chen*, as in *Häuschen*. There are potential meaningful contrasts such as *Kuhchen* [kuːçən] 'little cow' and *Kuchen* [kuːxən]
'cake', *Tauchen* [tɑʊçən] 'little rope' and *Tauchen* [tɑʊxən] 'to dive'. If
we considered only the phonetic form in each case, we would come to
the conclusion that [ç] and [x] were in opposition here; they follow the
same vowel, namely a back one. However, the internal structure of the
words is different, since *-chen* is a separate morpheme (see chapter 3).
We can, therefore, say that [ç] occurs in morpheme-initial position, whatever the preceding sound: *Chemie*, *Kuh + chen*, *Tau + chen*. The morph-
emic structure of the words with [x] is different: *Kuchen* and *tauch + en*.
We must therefore conclude that [ç] and [x] are variants of the same
phoneme, which we will symbolize /ç/.

   We have shown how the concept of meaningful contrasts helps us to
determine the different phonemes of a language. The alternations, on the
other hand, are predictable from their environment: if a voiced stop or
fricative is in syllable-initial position or ambisyllabic, it is realized as
voiced; if it is in syllable-final position, it is voiceless. These alternations
have been related to the same morpheme, for instance *grob – grobe*, *Rad
– Rades*, etc., but we also find forms that are predictable in other circumstances, whatever the word or morpheme. For example, a voiceless stop
in German, if it is at the beginning of a stressed syllable, will delay the
onset of voice in the following vowel, that is, it is aspirated, as in *Pein*
[pʰaɪn], *kein* [kʰaɪn]. On the other hand, they are not aspirated between
vowels or following another consonant in an initial cluster: *Gitter* [ɡɪtʌ],
Stein [ʃtaɪn]. These occurrences, like those within the same morpheme,
are predictable; they are variants of the same phoneme. All such predictable variants are said to be in **complementary distribution**, that is, they
are distributed in such a way that they do not enter into meaningful
contrasts. In German [pʰ] and [p] do not distinguish meanings; they are
allophones of the same phoneme; the latter by convention we put in
slant lines: /p/. Allophone is the technical term for the actual realization
of a phoneme. The relationship between phoneme and allophone is one
of abstract classification (phoneme) and phonetic reality of the abstract
entity in the flow of speech. Phonemes are representations of the store
of native-speaker knowledge about the sound system of the language;
allophones are representations of the actual utterance. By convention we
put such realizations between square (phonetic) brackets. To that extent
we speak uttering allophones, not phonemes. We must emphasize again
that a phonetic entity may be in different allophonic relationships in
different circumstances, that is, a phonetic form may be an allophone of
two (or more) phonemes. Thus, [ç] is an allophone of /ɡ/ in *König*, but
of /ç/ in *sich*, because of the different patterns of distribution that we
have just discussed.

We have so far used a symbol to represent phonemes – /t/, /d/, /ç/, but we have not yet determined how to define them. Each symbol represents a complex of features which define the phoneme's distinctiveness from all other phonemes of the language. The phonetic features that are predictable do not appear in the definition. We give examples of the obstruent phonemes in (25).

(25) /p/ voiceless labial stop
      /b/ voiced labial stop
      /f/ voiceless labial fricative
      /t/ voiceless alveolar stop
      /d/ voiced alveolar stop
      /s/ voiceless alveolar fricative
      /ç/ voiceless dorsal fricative

Notice that we have used the features **labial** and **dorsal**, rather than the more usual phonetic terms **bilabial**, **labiodental**, **palatal** and **velar**. This is because the more precise designation of [labial] can be predicted on the basis of the manner of articulation: stops are bilabial, fricatives are labiodental. In the case of [dorsal] the terms **palatal** and **velar** are dispensed with and replaced by [front], [dorsal] and [back], [dorsal], respectively. It is also possible to have [central], [dorsal] sounds, if we recognize at least three points of contact between the tongue and the roof of the mouth, as in the series: *Kind – kann – Kunst*; *Gift – gab – Gunst*. In the case of German /k/, /g/ and /ç/, /j/ will all be classified as [dorsal]. Even in a more traditional analysis with [velar] the variant realizations are not distinctive, so we do not need to incorporate frontness and backness into any of the specifications, except for /j/. The vowels will supply the appropriate lingual contact feature to /k/, /g/ and /ç/, whereas /j/ will need to be specified as [front] as well, since its place of contact does not alter.

We can now return to the form of the rules needed to deal with the allophonic variation of /g/: [k] ~ [g] ~ [ç] and that of /ç/: [ç] ~ [x]. We define /g/ as the voiced dorsal stop. Devoicing of final stops and fricatives is given as (27), but we need another rule to change the feature [stop] to [fricative] in the environment of a preceding unstressed /ɪ/. We can write this as follows (omitting the formal representation of unstressed):

(26) [stop] → [fricative] / ɪ _____
                  [voiced]
                  [dorsal]

The slant line means: 'in the environment' (which is indicated by what follows it), and the dash indicates the place where the change occurs,

provided the features [voiced] and [dorsal] are present, as indicated
below the dash. If these features were not specified in the rule, the other
two voiced stops and the voiceless ones would be affected too, which
would be wrong. (26) will apply first, then devoicing, which will be of
the form:

(27)   [voiced]   →   [voiceless] / _____ $
                                    [obstruent]

where $ = the syllable boundary, and [obstruent] is there as a cover term
for [stop] and [fricative] to stop the rule from applying to other types of
consonant, which do not devoice, such as /l/ and /n/.

  If we go from the phonemic form of a word or morpheme to its
realization in speech by means of the rules, this is called a derivation (see
chapter 1). For the *-ig* ending under discussion the derivation of the
consonant will be as follows:

(28)   /-ɪg/
                [voiced]
                [dorsal]
                [stop]

Rule (26)   →   [voiced]
                [dorsal]
                [fricative]

Rule (27)   →   [voiceless]
                [dorsal]
                [fricative]

The front resonance comes from the preceding vowel, giving the required
[ç]. This resonance from the vowel applies equally to /ç/ preceding vowels,
but in morpheme-initial position and after consonants a separate rule is
needed:

(29)   Ø   →   [front] / $\left\{ \begin{matrix} C \\ + \end{matrix} \right\}$ _____
                                   [voiceless]
                                   [dorsal]
                                   [fricative]

where Ø = zero and the braces {} indicate a choice: either C (a consonant)
or + (a morpheme boundary), but not both. This rule adds a feature to
the specification of /ç/.

We must note a couple of restrictions on occurrence: the voiced fricatives do not follow short vowels in words with the syllable structure of those in (32) below, and no alternating voiced/voiceless pairs occur after short vowels, so that phonemic forms such as */bad/ or */vɪz/ are ruled out.

5.4 Affricates

Since we have now dealt with the stops and some of the fricatives, this would be a good place to consider two instances of complex phonemes: /pf/ and /ts/. These are usually referred to as **affricates**; that is a term used for a sequence of stop and homorganic fricative (i.e. one made using the same articulatory organs) which behaves as though it were a single consonant rather than two. It is thus a phonological concept, not a phonetic description: the same sequence of sounds may be an affricate in one language but not in another, e.g. [tʃ] in English *church* is an affricate phoneme, but [tʃ] in German *deutsch* is a sequence of two phonemes. In many instances it does not matter a great deal whether /pf/ and /ts/ are single units or two units in succession. This seems to be the case with medial and final positions. In final position, for instance, various combinations can occur: [-pʃ] *hübsch*, [-ps] *Gips*, [-lf] *elf*, [-ɱf] *fünf*, [ʀf] *Dorf*, [-tʃ] *Deutsch*, [-ks] *sechs*, [-ms] *Gesims*, [-ns] *Hans*, [-ls] *Hals*, [-ʀs] *Kurs*. (These do not include any combinations caused by inflexional endings, e.g. the genitive -*s*, because such words are morphologically complex.) The commonest is consonant + [s], then consonant + [f]; none of them can occur in that order in initial position, with the exception of the rare combination [tʃ], as in *Tscheche*. [pf] and [ts], on the other hand, do occur in the same order in any position. Furthermore, they can combine with other consonants in initial position, e.g. *Pflaume*, *Pfriem*, *zwei*. In section 5.2 we noted that the only three-consonant onsets permitted in German are /ʃpl-/, /ʃpr-/ and /ʃtr-/ along with a few loan ones like /skl-/ and /skr-/; basically, the pattern is /ʃ/ + voiceless stop + /l/ or /r/. In comparison with the typical clusters as in *Splitter*, *Sprung* and *Strauch*, sequences such as [pfl-] and [tsv-] would make very odd three-consonant clusters. This is perhaps the strongest argument for treating /pf/ and /ts/ as single affricate phonemes, at least in initial position. In the other positions the situation is less clear. Because historically these sequences come from double consonants (see chapter 8) they occur mostly after short vowels: *Apfel*, *ätzen*, *Topf*, *Witz*, whereas single consonants can also occur after long vowels: *bitten*, *bieten*. (There are some exceptions to this general rule, for example *Schnauze*, *Schneuze*, but these can, in any case, be treated as instances of the affricate.) There are also occasions where it is clear that we are dealing with a sequence of two phonemes, for instance across a morpheme boundary, as in [ʀaːts], genitive of *Rat*. (For rather different discussions of /pf/ and /ts/, see Kohler 1977: 171–2, and Fox 1990: 37–8.)

5.5 Nasals

We have not yet considered the nasal consonants of German. There is a three-way distinction in final position: *Lamm*, *rann*, *Rang*; the last of these is restricted in occurrence, so that it does not appear in initial position, though the other two do: *mein*, *nein*. However, although this seems simple, a number of linguists have suggested a more abstract analysis (see Dressler 1981, and the discussion in Kohler 1977, and Lass 1984). Because, like /pf/ and /ts/, the velar nasal behaves like two consonants in that it does not follow long vowels and, in this case, cannot appear in morpheme-initial position, the proposal is to analyse it as a sequence of two phonemes: /ng/. Thus *Rang* is represented phonologically as /rang/, *Finger* as /fingr/ (for the analysis of /r/, see section 5.6), and *Angst* as /angst/. Before /k/ and /g/ it is analysed as a variant of /n/, taking its velar articulation from the following stop, thus *Dank* is /dank/, *Anker* is /ankr/, and *Tango* is /tango:/. The difference between forms like *Finger* and *Enge* with [ŋ] and *Tango* and *evangelisch* with [ŋg] is one of syllable structure. In the former [ŋ] is ambisyllabic, in the latter the syllable boundary falls between [ŋ] and [g]. If we accept the /ng/ analysis in all cases, we have to have two rules, which are ordered with respect to one another: assimilation of /n/ to a velar realization, then the deletion of /g/ after [ŋ], provided no syllable boundary intervenes. These we can give as (30) and (31).

(30) /n/ → ŋ / __ $\begin{Bmatrix} /k/ \\ /g/ \end{Bmatrix}$

(31) /g/ → Ø / ŋ __

where Ø = zero.

  This solution throws up theoretical issues, two in particular. Firstly, do we want grammars to contain abstract phonemic forms, which are not set up to account for any alternative realizations? (For a full discussion of the issues involved in abstract analyses, including the German velar nasal, see Lass 1984: ch. 9.) Secondly, do we want the concept of deletion, which is the process of turning something into nothing, and which can be used to save all kinds of abstract analyses? In this particular instance it is possible to avoid such an analysis by establishing [ŋ] followed by /k/ and /g/ as an allophone of /n/, subject to a general rule of assimilation of alveolars, which we shall discuss in section 5.8.1, and having a separate phoneme /ŋ/, when it is not followed by /k/ or /g/. The velar nasal conforms to the pattern of any other single consonant after a short vowel in being ambisyllabic; the only difference is that it cannot occur syllable-initially. Thus, all the words in (32) have the same syllable structure.

(32)   Klapper   Wetter   Becker   Krabbe   Widder   Bagger   Affe   Wasser
       Esche   Rache   Schelle   Sperre   Kummer   Sonne   Anger

(Historically speaking, all these intervocalic consonants were once long.) We shall, therefore, accept that German has a phoneme /ŋ/.

5.6   Other Consonants

We have now considered the stops, fricatives and nasals. Of the consonants given in (2) /ʃ/ and /ʒ/ have not yet been mentioned, although they are fricatives (obstruents). The latter is a loan consonant, occurring in words of foreign origin, e.g. *Journal, arrangieren*, though some German speakers replace it with /ʃ/. However, for those who do use it, it fills an otherwise empty slot in the system as the voiced partner of /ʒ/.

There are three further distinctive consonants: /l r h/. The first two are often referred to as **liquids** (in other languages as well), but this is not a phonetic term (and, consequently, is not included in the chapter on phonetics). Rather it is a cover term for these sounds, which, although they are very varied from a phonetic point of view (in German a lateral, a trill, an approximant and a vocoid make up the range of possible realizations), are said to behave phonologically in the same way. In German they are certainly found in the same places in syllables; they can follow most consonants in initial clusters, for instance /pr-/, /pl-/, /pfr-/, /pfl-/, /tr-/, /kl-/, /bl-/, /dr-/, /ʃr/, /ʃl-/, /fl-/, but not */tl-/, */nr-/, */nl-/ or */rl-/, and they combine equally freely with consonants in final clusters, in this case in front of them, for instance /-rp/, /-lp/, /-rt/, /-lt/,/-rʃ/, /-lç/, /-rn/, /-lm/, /-rl/, but not */-rŋ/ or */-lr/. They can also both occur as syllabic consonants, that is, they constitute a syllable of their own; this is a characteristic they share with the nasals. In words like *Esel, Wetter, Atem* and *Boden* the second syllable may be just the consonant, for example [eːzl], and has no preceding vowel phase; in the case of /r/ it is always a vocoid articulation, for example [vɛtʌ] (see further below). This may be sufficient to put them together in a class of their own, even though the nasals behave the same way as regards syllabicity. However, there is little to be gained by introducing the term **liquid** and we can just as well treat them as separate sound types, that is, one-member classes. After all, it is not uncommon in languages to have phonemes which do not group with any others and German is no exception, because, even if we have a class of liquids, /h/ is still a phoneme on its own. In terms of distinctiveness /l/ can be defined as the lateral in German; /r/ is more complicated, and we need to discuss it in more detail.

To start with we find an alternation of a vocoid articulation, which we have so far transcribed as [ʌ], and a uvular trill, [ʀ], as in *fuhr* [fuːʌ] – *fuhren* [fuːʀən]. The vocoid occurs in syllable-final position, the trill in what we have referred to as ambisyllabic position. The trill also occurs in syllable-initial position, for instance *Rang* [ʀaŋ]. In other circumstances there is considerable variation, not just between speakers, but also in one and the same speaker. In initial clusters, after a voiceless consonant, voicing may not start until well into the trill phase. In final clusters we find the greatest variety. Firstly, we must distinguish between a long vowel followed by /r/ and one or more consonants and a short vowel followed by a similar cluster, for example *erst* and *Wirt*, respectively. The majority of speakers of standard German have a vocoid in the first environment, that is [eːʌst]; some even in the second, that is [vɪʌt]. Those who do not have the vocoid after a short vowel either have the trill, [vɪʀt], a uvular approximant, [vɪʁt], or a voiceless uvular fricative, if the following sound is voiceless, [vɪχt].

Then there is the question of the *-er* ending, which is also realized as [ʌ], as in *Vater* [faːtʌ], *welcher* [vɛlçʌ]. In the phonological representations we can interpret this as /r/, as in /vɛtr/ *Wetter*. Such an analysis makes /r/ parallel to /l/ in its status as a syllable, and reflects the fact that there is always the possibility of inserting [ə] before any syllabic consonant in related forms of the same lexical item, as in *inner* [ɪnʌ] – *innere* [ɪnəʀə]. It also assumes that [ə] is not needed as a vowel phoneme in German, but we shall return to that in section 5.7. Finally, many speakers use back resonance in the rhyme with no separable segment that could be identified as the /r/, especially when the vowel is /a/, as in *Bart* [bɑːtˠ], where the vowel phase is lengthened and the final consonant has back resonance; after the long vowel /aː/, /r/ may not be realized at all, for example *war* [vaː], *Haar* [haː]. (For further examples of /r/ variation, see chapter 9.)

Given the considerable phonetic difference between the realizations of /r/, an uvular trill and a back-of-central, half-open vocoid, it is difficult to see what feature(s) can be used as the defining characteristic(s). In the case of the obstruents we could give place and manner features as distinctive, along with phonation as appropriate. /l/ is distinctively lateral.

If we accept the principle of process rules, then we can define /r/ as the trill phoneme in German and have feature-changing rules for the syllable-final and syllabic allophones. This would be in line with the obstruent devoicing rule (27), where the phonation feature of the voiced obstruents is changed. If, on the other hand, we look more closely at the phonetic characteristics of the allophones of /r/, we find that they do have back resonance in common. We could, therefore, define /r/ simply as the [back] consonant.

The final consonant /h/ is something of a bridge between the consonants and the vowels. It is often referred to as a glottal fricative (see MacCarthy 1975, Fox 1990), but this is a somewhat misleading description, if it is supposed to be based on some phonetic characteristics. Any friction that is caused during the production of /h/ comes from the air passing through the entire cavity and is not restricted to any one point. From a phonetic point of view, in fact, we are dealing with a series of voiceless vocoid articulations (see also Kohler 1977: 160). The onset of any vocoid can be voiceless in German, giving realizations such as [ḁat] *hat*, [e̥eːbən] *heben*, [u̥uːn] *Huhn*, [o̥oːx] *hoch*. The vocoid articulation has to be the same throughout; it is not possible to have a different voiceless vocoid from the voiced one, for example *[ɔ̥ant]. The voiceless vocoids are, therefore, in complementary distribution, just like [ç] and [x] discussed above. They can be interpreted as variants of the same phoneme, which is in contrast with other consonants, for example *Band, Land, Hand*. The traditional symbol for this is /h/ and is quite suitable, provided we remember the phonetic reality underlying it. /h/ is a good example of the difference between vocoid/contoid on the one hand and vowel/consonant on the other; it is a series of vocoid articulations, but it is a consonant phonologically, in that it occupies the syllable-onset position. We may note further that if it were a vowel, it would be capable of having a preceding glottal stop (see section 5.7), but forms such as *[ʔḁant] are impossible. Finally we may note that it does not occur syllable-finally. Since all its realizations are voiceless, it can be defined as the [voiceless] consonant in German. This still keeps it distinct from all the other voiceless phonemes, because they have other defining characteristics, too, for instance /p/ = [voiceless] [bilabial] [stop].

5.7 Vowels

We must now turn to a consideration of the vowel system. There are three sets in stressed syllables in German: short monophthongs, long monophthongs and diphthongs. We exemplify each in (33).

(33)   *short monophthongs*   *long monophthongs*
       [ɪ]   sich   [iː]   siech
       [ɛ]   Bett   [eː]   Beet
       [a]   satt   [aː]   Saat
       [ʏ]   füllen   [yː]   fühlen
       [œ]   Hölle   [øː]   Höhle
       [ʊ]   muss   [uː]   Mus
       [ɔ]   Botte   [oː]   Bote

                         diphthongs
                         [aɪ]   nein
                         [aʊ]   Zaun
                         [ɔɪ]   neun

Vowels are always the nucleus of stressed syllables; unstressed ones may have syllabic consonants, for example *Gabe* [gáːbə], *Gabel* [gáːbl]. We mark the main stress of a word with an acute accent over the appropriate vowel. (This is a deviation from the conventions of the IPA, but it avoids making decisions about syllable boundaries, which would be required by operating in accordance with the conventions.)

One particular aspect of the German vowel system must also be mentioned, especially as it is of considerable significance in the morphology, too, which we discussed in chapter 3: that is, Umlaut. In (22) we gave alternant forms of the same stem morpheme, one without Umlaut and one with: *Dach – Dächer, Loch – Löcher, Buch – Bücher*. On the other hand, in (33) the Umlaut vowels are given separately, with the implication that they constitute separate phonemes. This is because there are two types of Umlaut vowels: those that alternate, as in (22), and those that do not, as in *füllen, fühlen, Hölle, König*. (Strictly speaking, if Umlaut is a label for a relationship between two vowels, the latter type should not be called Umlaut.) The latter can be seen as contrasting phonemes, but the alternating vowels can hardly be seen as separate phonemes, given what we said in section 5.3 in relation to the voiced/voiceless alternations in the obstruents. First of all we should ask what the nature of the relationship is in phonetic terms. If we look at the examples in (34), we can see a regular pattern of back, non-Umlauted vowel and front, Umlaut one.

(34)   Mann   [man]   Männer   [mɛnʌ]
       Wahl   [vaːl]   wählen   [veːlən]
       Gott   [gɔt]   Götter   [gœtʌ]
       Sohn   [zoːn]   Söhne   [zøːnə]
       musste   [mʊstə]   müsste   [mʏstə]
       Fuß   [fuːs]   Füße   [fyːsə]

The diphthong that enters into an Umlaut relationship, e.g. *Haus* – *Häuser*, is slightly irregular in that the [ɔ] of [ɔɪ] is a back vowel rather than a front one, as a result of historical changes which need not bother us here. This back–front relationship of the Umlaut vowels has been constant throughout the history of High German (for a brief discussion, see Lodge 1989, and chapter 8; for a more detailed treatment, see Keller 1978) and it is noteworthy that, although Umlaut is no longer regular from a morphological point of view (see further chapter 3), it is phonetically predictable.

If we define the vowel phonemes fully, then /a/, /aː/, /ɔ/, /oː/, /ʊ/ and /uː/ will all be specified as [back], which will be subject to a feature-changing rule ([back] → [front]) in cases of Umlaut. (The phoneme symbols we have just used will be revised later, once we have discussed unstressed vowels in loan words.) If we wish to avoid a feature-changing rule, we can have partially but distinctively specified vowels. In (35) we give the non-Umlauted vowels in terms of frontness, tongue-height and/ or lip-position. Since the long (VV) and short (V) pairs have the same specifications, we only give the long ones, with different features on different lines.

(35) /iː/   /eː/   /aː/   /oː/   /uː/
    [front] [front]
          [low] [low] [low]
                   [round] [round]

The vowels that never enter into Umlaut pairs as the non-Umlauted member, /iː/, /ɪ/, /eː/ and /ɛ/, are already specified as [front]. In those circumstances where Umlaut applies the other vowels will acquire the specification [front], as in (36).

(36) [eː]   [øː]   [yː]
    [front] [front] [front]
    [low]   [low]
           [round] [round]

Note that Umlaut [eː] and phonological /eː/ now have the same specifications. Any remaining features of the vowels will be filled in by default rules to give [back], [high] and [spread] in the appropriate places. The front rounded vowels which are not members of Umlaut pairs, as in *füllen* and *König*, will have the phonological forms in (36) with [front] already specified in the lexical entry.

In discussing Umlaut we have not mentioned [ɛː], as heard in *Käse*, *käme*, *wählen* in the speech of some Germans. It is the Umlaut partner of /ɑ/ and is also found in some non-alternating forms, as in *Käse*. It is often considered artificial, a spelling pronunciation of long *ä(h)* (see MacCarthy 1975: 33; Kohler 1977: 175; Keller 1978: 554–5). Certainly many speakers use [eː] instead, and some may fluctuate. This fluctuation may be sociolinguistic in nature or it may be determined by the phonological environment. For instance, some speakers have [ɛː] in *Käse, käme* and *wählen*, but when the vowel is followed by [ə], [ʌ] or nothing, [eː] is used, as in *Fähe, Häher* and *zäh*, respectively. It would seem that this is a marginal phoneme in standard German, even though it occurs in some dialects.

If we group long vowels and diphthongs together and refer to them both as long vowels, we can distinguish the following types of syllable nucleus in German:

(37) a. short or long vowels in stressed syllables,
      b. secondary-stressed long vowels,
      c. unstressed short vowels,
      d. [ə], unstressed only.

(37a) means that any of the vowels in (33) may occur in stressed syllables, accompanied by the other types of nucleus or not, as the case may be. Type (37b) only occurs after the main stress of a word, as in *Heimat* [háɪmaːt], *Bischöfe* [bíʃøːfə], *Arbeit* [áːʀbaɪt], whereas (37c) occurs either before or after the main stress, as in *Elefant* [elefánt], *Philosophie* [filozofíː], *Kollegium* [kɔléːgɪʊm], *Tympanon* [týmpanɔn]. Note that the last set of examples are all loan words, though in some native words we also find such vowels, for example *Freundschaft* [fʀɔ́ɪntʃaft], *Mischung* [míʃʊŋ], *König* [kǿːnɪç], although [ɪ a ʊ] are the only ones; the others do not occur in native suffixes. Under (37c) vowels with the same quality as the stressed long vowels, for instance [i e o] in the above examples, are nevertheless short. This raises the question as to how to analyse such short vowels in unstressed syllables. On the basis of vowel quality it would be possible to say that they were shortened variants of the long stressed ones (see Fox's discussion, 1990: 32–3). However, there are no minimal contrasts in German which rely on these unstressed short vowels: their distribution can be seen as complementary and there are a few alternations within the same morpheme which deserve mention. Keller (1978: 555) suggests that [ɪ ɛ ʏ œ ʊ ɔ] only occur in closed syllables, that is, those that end in a consonant, and [i e y ø u o] only in open ones, i.e. those that are vowel-final, with [a] occurring in either type. However, if we compare *Kolonne* [kolónə] with *Kollege* [kɔléːgə] (see Fox 1990: 32), it must be acknowledged that the first vowels have only a single [l] following them, even though they have different qualities. In the second case we need the concept of ambisyllabicity again: the [l] of *Kollege* belongs to both syllables (note that the spelling reflects this in many cases with a double letter). We can then say that [ko-] of *Kolonne* is an open syllable, and that the first syllable of *Kollege* is [kɔl]. We then have the necessary statement of complementary distribution. In unstressed syllables we therefore have a single set of monophthongs, the quality of which varies according to syllable type with the exception of [a]. If we find it necessary to associate these with one or other of the sets of stressed monophthongs, the decision may rest on alternations within the same morpheme. Once again these are found in loan words, as in *Proféssor – Professóren*. Here we have [ɔ] alternating with [oː]. Similarly in *Fótus-fötál* we have [øː] alternating with [ø], and in *Cäsar–cäsárisch* [eː] alternating with [e]. There seem to be no examples of alternations of short vowel–short vowel. We might, therefore, wish to conclude that the short unstressed vowels were all variants of the long stressed ones with quality differences according to syllable type. This would give us the following phonological representations, using different symbols for the long and short stressed vowels without the length marks: /filozofí/, /elefánt/, /kolégə/, /kolɔ́nə/, /proفésor/. It is unnecessary to indicate length in the phonological forms, because the symbol shows which vowel is long in stressed syllables, /zɪç/ versus /ziç/, /bɔtə/ versus /botə/. The only problem is the [a] – [aː] distinction. To keep the representation consistent we need a different symbol for the long stressed vowel; /ɑ/ is suitable for this purpose (see MacCarthy 1975, and Fox 1990), for example /zat/ versus /zɑt/. (The examples are from (33).)

The alternations in the vowels discussed above are typical of the loan-word vocabulary of German, though there are also some native alterna-tions of the same sort, e.g. *vór – vorüber, über – überzéugen*. There are also some exceptions to the distributional characteristics in the unstressed vowels such as *Búchstabe – buchstabíeren*, where the first syllable is closed in both cases, but the alternation is [uː] – [u], rather than the expected [uː] – [ʊ]. It may be that suffixes which take the main stress, such as *-ier(en), -(er)ei, -ant*, are all exceptional in that they seem to allow nuclei of type (37b) to occur before them, contrary to what was stated above, as in *Schmeicheléi*. The scope of this book does not allow us to go into great detail and many such interesting areas will have to be glossed over superficially. However, one point we can make with regard to these particular suffixes is that languages always have exceptional forms and classes and rarely present us with neat and tidy pictures of their structure.

A good example of linguistic 'untidiness' is the way in which loan words are pronounced. Words like *Teint*, *Chance* and *Pension*, which come from French, are often pronounced with nasalized vowels, e.g. [tɛ̃], [ʃãsə], [pãsjɔ̃], respectively, but it is difficult to say that German there-fore has nasalized vowel phonemes. Rather, we say that German speak-ers borrow these vowels along with the words concerned. We can see that such vowels are marginal in the phonological system of German, because there are alternative Germanized or partly Germanized versions as well, that is, they are made to conform to the phonological structure of German words, as in [taŋ], [ʃáŋksə], [paŋksjóːn], [pãsjóːn] or [pɛnzjóːn]. Such variation may be of sociolinguistic importance, that is, a particular form may be indicative of the particular social background of the speaker, or the social relationship between participants in a conversation. Clearly, such loan words are not fully incorporated into the language system; the fact that there is quite considerable variation is a measure of this.

We have still not discussed type (37d). This vowel, usually referred to for convenience as **schwa**, is only found in unstressed syllables. Unlike the short vowels, it does not need a following consonant. Thus, *Tasche* [taʃə] is an acceptable phonological structure in German, *[mɪʃʊ] is not. The only short vowel that can occur in similar circumstances is /a/, and then only in loan words. (Interestingly, [ɪ] can occur in diminutives and truncated forms, e.g. *Betli, Azubi, Schuhi*, but not in any other roots and suffixes.) The question we have to ask is whether it is a phoneme in its own right, or whether it is a variant of one of the other phonemes. It is rarely in meaningful contrast with the other vowels: instances such as *totem* [toːtəm] versus *Totem* [toːtɛm] (Kohler 1977: 176), or *Anna* [ana] versus *Anne* [anə] are somewhat contrived. In the first pair the first word has a morpheme boundary in it, *tot + em*, whereas *Totem* does not, and names ending in -*a* or -*e* are marginal and some are certainly loans. MacCarthy (1975: 33) suggests /ɛ/ as the most appropriate phoneme to which schwa could belong, pointing out that many South German speakers have an unstressed vowel closer to [ɛ] than to [ə], as in *gute* [guːtë]. However, it is not necessary to accept either of the two options, separate phoneme or allophone of another phoneme. In (11) in section 5.2 we proposed an empty nucleus in lexical entry forms realized as schwa. In those cases where schwa is word-final, for example, *Gabe, arbeite, gute*, the same applies. We need to say that there is an empty nucleus at the end of such words, which is automatically realized as schwa, except in those cases where another vowel follows in connected speech, for example, *hab' ich, geb' ich*. Note that the effect of the empty syllable is apparent in that in both these cases the /b/ is realized as [b], not [p], as it would be in syllable-final position: compare, for instance, *geb' ich* [geːbɪç] with *gab ich*, where there could also be an initial glottal stop in *ich*, [gaːp(ʔ)ɪç]. If we treat schwa as an empty syllable nucleus, it is the unspecified vowel in German, that is, it has no phonological features defining it, and can be seen as the default vowel in German unstressed syllables, the one that occurs, if none of the others do.

When vowels are in syllable-initial position, there is often a glottal stop onset to them, as in *Abend* [ʔaːbənt], *arbeiten* [ʔaʀbaɪtn], *ewig* [ʔeːvɪç], *offen* [ʔɔfən], *Verein* [fʌʔaɪn]. Although it is common before a stressed vowel, even unstressed vowels may have it at the beginning of a breath group, as in *ʔEr geht ʔauf der Straße.* This glottal stop is not a contrastive phonological unit, because it is predictable, namely it occurs in front of any vowel at the beginning of a syllable. Consequently, it will not appear in the phonological form of words; phonologically *offen* is /ɔfn/, whether it is pronounced with a glottal stop or not.

5.8 Connected Speech

So far we have looked at a number of theoretical matters and analysed various words and word-types in isolation, that is, we took the word as an isolatable entity. This may be a legitimate thing for a linguist to do, since there are many important generalizations that can be made on the basis of the word, as we have seen. However, when language is actually used by speakers, they rarely use single words as utterances, though they are, of course, possible; consider the following interchange between speaker A and speaker B:

(38) *A*: Fertig!
       B: Gut!

More usually a number of words is used and in most cases these will be strung together without any breaks between them. We do not use the words of our language as if we were reading them out of a dictionary. For instance, the sentence *Was soll ich ihm geben?* will not be uttered as in (39), except in the particular circumstance of exasperation on the part of the speaker at not having been heard or understood by the addressee, even after several repeats.

(39) [vás zɔ́l ʔíç ʔíːm géːbən]

A natural, colloquial version of the sentence would be:

(40) [vas ˌzɔ́l ç ĩm géːbm̩]

(where the small circle before [z] indicates partial devoicing) with just two stresses and with the other syllables either unstressed or reduced. German, like English, stresses a relatively small number of syllables in any utterance compared to the total number occurring (or potentially occurring) in it. (39) has six syllables, of which two receive stress in (40).

Stress is only one of the features of natural, connected speech, and a full investigation of it goes well beyond the scope of this book. (For a book-length treatment of stress and intonation in German, see Fox 1984.) Some of the other features are more easily handled in an introductory book, so we shall restrict our discussion to them. These are sometimes referred to as rapid speech processes (see Dressler et al. 1972; Zwicky 1972; Lass 1984: ch. 12), though they may occur even in reading a text out loud. Note, too, that we have used the term 'process' again, and this assumes some kind of change of form. Again, this could be avoided by choosing a set of declarative statements to describe what occurs. One thing needs particular emphasis: the features of natural speech that we shall be describing are not haphazard degenerations of the 'proper' form of the words involved, but are regular, though optional, and can be described in terms of rules, just like the allophonic rules we discussed in the previous sections. The fact that they can be defined by rule means that they do not apply in any way an individual speaker thinks fit, but are properly constrained by the form of the grammatical knowledge of German. For instance, *angeben* can be pronounced [aŋgeːbm̩], but *umgeben* cannot be *[ʊŋgeːbm̩], only [ʊmgeːbm̩]. This is because /n/ is allowed to be realized with various places of articulation in German, but /m/ is not.

We shall discuss the general characteristics of assimilation, lenition, shortening and deletion, and exemplify them with examples similar to those in Kohler (1977: 207–30).

5.8.1 *Assimilation*

Assimilation is the term used for the phenomenon we have just described in relation to *angeben* above, namely, the sharing of features by two adjacent sounds, one of which would not have those features in other circumstances. In the case in point the /n/ of *an-* is realized as a dorsal nasal in front of a dorsal stop: /n/ and /g/ share the same feature of dorsality. The sounds do not even have to be adjacent: in the early stages of Umlaut in High German an /i/ or /j/ in a following unstressed syllable caused a back vowel in the stem to become front, for example *gast* ('guest'), plural *gesti* ('guests') (see chapter 8). The frontness spreads to the preceding syllable. This assimilation at a distance is often called harmony, but the principles governing this and contiguous assimilation are the same. However, the types of assimilation we shall be discussing in this chapter will all be of the contiguous type.

Any phonetic feature may be shared by the adjacent sounds: place, manner, phonation, nasality, and so on. Perhaps the commonest feature that is assimilated in German is place, so we shall deal with that first. As in English, it is the alveolar stops and nasal /t d n/ that assimilate to a following obstruent:

(41) hat besucht   [hap bəzuːxt]
      hat gemacht   [hak gəmaxt]
      in Mainz   [ɪm maɪnts]
      den guten Mann   [deŋ guːtəm man]

The other stops and nasals do not show this variation of place. In terms of the realization rules we discussed in section 5.3, this can be seen as an extension of the allophonic principle, though as optional variants rather than obligatory ones. Thus, in the examples in (41), [p] and [k] are allophones of /t/ in the word *hat*, and [m] and [ŋ] allophones of /n/ in the last two examples. Either we choose a feature-changing rule as in (42), where [α place] means that the two place features must match (α is an algebraic variable), or we do not specify place at the phonological level for /t d n/ at all.

(42) [alveolar]   →   [α place] / ____   C
                            [stop] [obstruent]
                                  [α place]

where word and syllable boundaries are irrelevant. If /t d n/ are unspecified for place, as in (43), the place feature will be supplied by the following obstruent or the default rule (44) will apply to give an alveolar realization.

(43) /t/   /d/   /n/
      [voiceless] [stop]   [nasal]
      [stop]

(44) Place   →   [alveolar]

Where an obstruent follows /t d n/, they will inherit the place of articulation from the obstruent by **spreading**: the feature spreads from right to left to fill in the gap of the unspecified place feature. In the examples in (45) the nasal assimilates to a preceding obstruent, when the former is syllabic. The spreading in this case goes from left to right.

(45) Gruppen   [gʀʊpm]
      haben   [haːbm]
      dürfen   [dʏʀfm̩]
      lachen   [laxŋ]
      backen   [bakŋ]
      zogen   [tsoːgŋ]

The other kind of place assimilation is restricted to /s/ and /z/ before /ʃ/, /ʒ/ or /j/. In this case the tongue-contact is palato-alveolar, but the lips

are not rounded for the realizations of /s/ and /z/, as they are for /ʃ/ and
/ʒ/. We have used the symbol [ç] to show the difference:

(46)   das Schiff   [daç ʃɪf]
        des Journalisten   [dɛç ʒuʀnalɪstn]
        las schon   [laːç ʃoːn]
        des Jungen   [dɛç juŋən]

Assimilation can go in either direction: in (41) a preceding alveolar
changes its place to that of a following obstruent, in (45) the assimilating
nasal follows the obstruent which determines its place feature. In the
first case we have regressive assimilation, in the second progressive
assimilation. In the following cases in (47) an oral stop takes on nasality
from an adjacent nasal.

(47)   zum Beispiel   [tsʊm maɪʃpiːl]
        in den   [ɪn nen]
        ein guter   [aɪŋ ŋuːtʌ]
        eben   [eːmm̩]

In the case of *eben* note that place assimilation is progressive and nasality
assimilation is regressive. Note also that in *ein guter* we have syllable-
initial [ŋ]. This does not violate the phonotactic constraint on syllable-
initial /ŋ/ referred to in section 5.5. Phonotactic constraints are
phonological, i.e. they obtain with regard to phonemes; [ŋ] in [ŋuːtʌ] is
an allophone of /g/.

Progressive assimilation of voicelessness is found at syllable boundaries, for example:

(48)   dasselbe   [daszɛlbə] or [dassɛlbə]
        ratsam   [ʀaːtzaːm] or [ʀaːtsaːm]
        eßbar   [ɛsbaːʌ] or [ɛsb̥aːʌ]
        weggehen   [veːkgeːən] or [veːkg̊eːən]

Note that the voiceless initial stops are represented by the symbol for a
voiced one with the voiceless subscript circle. This is because they are
not produced with as much energy as the voiceless /p t k/, which would
also be aspirated in this position; *weggehen* cannot be realized with
aspiration after either of the voiceless stops. (For further examples, see
Kohler 1977: 217–18.)

5.8.2   *Lenition*

Lenition ('softening') is a rather complex phenomenon and the term tends
to be used as something of a catch-all for various historical developments

and synchronic alternations (see Bauer 1988b; Anderson and Ewen 1987; Lass 1984). It relates to sonority in terms of voicing and opening of the articulators. Thus, if a stop is regularly realized as a fricative in certain conditions, then it is interpreted as being subject to lenition, and phonologically it is still a stop. In German, for instance, we find alternants such as [zaːgən] and [zaːɣən] for *sagen* in many speakers. However, it could equally well be interpreted as a kind of assimilation: between two vowels, the most sonorant sounds, the stop is made more sonorous in that it is realized as a fricative, an 'opener' sound. In German it is only /b/ and /g/ which are affected by leniton in intervocalic position, and the resultant realization may be a fricative or an approximant, as in:

(49) habe   [haːbə]   [haːβə]   [haːwə]
     lege   [leːgə]   [leːjə]   [leːjə]
     Kruge   [kʀuːgə]   [kʀuːɣə]

(/g/ does not seem to be realized as an approximant after a back vowel.) Some of these examples are also dialect forms, in some cases with no stop realizations, which we will discuss in chapter 9 (section 9.3.1).

Intervocalic voicing of voiceless obstruents, even across word-boundaries, occurs when both syllables are in unstressed position. In some instances it occurs following the loss of final [ə]. The following examples are from Kohler (1977: 219):

(50) muß ich   [mʊz ɪç]
     hat er   [had eʌ]
     schaff' ich [ʃav ɪç]
     mach' ich [maɣ ɪç]

5.8.3 *Shortening*

In section 5.7 we showed that in loan words short versions of the long vowels occurred in syllables before the primary stress, (37c) above. Shortening also occurs as a feature of continuous speech. Given a particular stress pattern in an utterance, the weak forms must occur, if the words are not stressed. A parallel from English is appropriate: if the definite article is not stressed, then it is [ðə] before a consonant and [ðɪ] before a vowel; only rarely is it pronounced [ðiː]. In German *den* in *in den Garten* will be [den] in most circumstances; only in cases of special emphasis, when it takes the main stress, will it be [deːn]. Note the short, unstressed vowels in example (51).

(51) Der Mann sah den Hund in ihrem Garten.

     [deʌ mán záː den hʊ́nt ɪn iʀəm gáʀtn]

Shortening of long consonants is not common in German, partly because double consonants only occur across word or syllable boundaries,
as in *in Neustadt, unnatürlich*. When two identical consonants come
together in an unstressed sequence, shortening, or degemination, as it is
usually called with respect to consonants, may take place. Even if the
consonants differ in articulatory strength but share all their other features, they can be simplified to one, as in:

(52)   dasselbe   [dasɛlbə]
       weggegangen   [veːĝəgaŋən]

5.8.4 Deletion

This is the name for cases of alternation with zero, no phonetic realization. (The theoretical implications of deletion have been referred to briefly
above in section 5.5 in connection with [ŋ] and we shall not consider
them further. Note that degemination can be seen as deletion rather than
shortening.) The commonest sounds to alternate with zero in German
are [t] and [ə]. [t], which is the realization of /t/ or /d/ in syllable-final
position, can be deleted when it is the middle one of three consonants,
provided that it is morpheme-final, as in:

(53)   westlich   [vɛslɪç]
       hältst   [hɛlst]
       entkommen   [ɛŋkɔmən]
       endlich   [ɛnlɪç]

(English has a similar rule of consonant-cluster simplification, but it
differs in detail and is more complex; see Lodge 1984: 9–10 and 136–7).
    Schwa alternates with zero before nasals, /l/ and /r/ in nouns, adject-
ives and related forms, as in:

(54)   Atem   atmen
       eitel   eitle
       trocken   Trockner
       Eifer   eifrig

These alternations are obligatory (and are even indicated in the spelling).
We discussed schwa in section 5.7 and suggested that it should be treated
as an empty syllable nucleus. In those cases where there is no phonetic
realization the empty syllable remains empty and nothing happens. In
the other cases there is either a syllabic consonant (/l/ and /n/), schwa
and a consonant (/l/, /n/ and /m/) or [ʌ] (/r/). There are also instances of
optional schwa deletion when verb-final [ə] occurs in front of unstressed

ich, or even after a single stem-final consonant when *ich* precedes the verb, as in:

(55)   hab' ich
       mach' ich
       trockn' ich
       ich hab'
       ich mach'
       *ich trockn'

(The last of these is not possible because it would leave an impermissible phonetic sequence as a coda. For a longer discussion of schwa in standard German, see Giegerich 1987.)

Alternations with zero can be handled basically in one of two ways: **deletion**, removing something from the phonological structure, or **epenthesis**, the addition of something to the structure at a place marked in the representation, such as an empty syllable nucleus, or at a place where it is necessary to break up an otherwise impossible sequence.

It should be pointed out that there are some problems with the interpretation of certain realizations as instances of deletion. For example, Kohler (1977: 216) gives *zumindest zwei* with [-s s-] and *einst stritten* with [-s ʃt-] as instances of deletion. However, it is by no means clear that on every occasion the sequence of articulated contoids is any shorter than one would expect from the 'undeleted' version. In other words these sequences should, at least in some cases, be transcribed [-ss ss-] and [-çç ʃt-], respectively. In other words, these are instances of manner assimilation, not deletion.

As an example of how these processes relate a realization to the underlying forms of the lexicon, we will take *in der* in unstressed position, as in the sentence: *Er ist in der Stadt.* In (56) the phonological forms are at the top and each process is given on the left of the colon.

(56)   in der   /ɪn der/
       stressed realization: [ɪn deːʌ]
       weak form (i):   [ɪn deʌ]
       weak form (ii):   [ɪn dʌ]
       progressive nasalization: [ɪn nʌ]
       degemination: [ɪn ʌ]

Each of the forms on the right in square brackets is a possible realization. The ordering of the rules is not fixed as given in (56); provided that the conditions for the operation of any rule are met, for instance the stress pattern is right, it can apply. That means that progressive nasalization could be applied after weak form (i), giving [ɪn neʌ] as yet another possible realization. On the other hand, degemination can only apply after progressive nasalization, because only then are the conditions properly met.

5.9 Further Reading

For a discussion of sonority, see Ladefoged (1982); Kiparsky (1979), and Selkirk (1984), present different models of the syllable based on sonority; for an application of sonority to German syllable structure, see Giegerich (1986).

For fuller discussion of consonant clusters, see Kohler (1977) and Fox (1990); for a technical discussion of German syllable structure, see Giegerich (1985), (1986) and (1987), and Wiese (1996).

For a useful discussion of the difference between phoneme and allophone, see Davenport and Hannahs (1998: 95–113).

For alternatives to a derivational approach to phonology, see Lass (1984), Archangeli (1988) and Carr (1993). A more detailed treatment of underspecification and markedness is given by Steriade (1995), and for a comparison of derivation and declarative phonology, see Coleman (1995) and Kaye (1995). Wiese (1996) is a comprehensive treatment of the German phonological system using underspecification and a limited amount of derivation.

An introduction to Optimality Theory, an attempt to avoid all rule-based derivation, is given by Roca and Johnson (1999) and Kager (1999).

On the phonetic details and phonological interpretation of coda /r/ in German, see Simpson (1998) and Lodge (forthcoming).

For a comment on this rather complex area, see Lodge (1992: 44–5) and (1997: 165); Local (1992) discusses the matter in more detail.

EXERCISES

1 Describe in detail the constraints on onsets and codas of German mono-syllables. Use the defining phonetic features of the phonemes to make statements about the possible combinations.

2 Using a dictionary, pick out 25–30 loan words, transcribe them in phonetic script, give the language from which they were borrowed, and give the characteristics which mark them as loans, e.g. *Bibliothek* [bɪblɪoté:k], Ancient Greek, the final syllable takes the main stress, and there are full vowels in pretonic position.

3 Choose a written text and transcribe it into IPA script indicating those places where in speech assimilation would normally occur.

CHAPTER SIX

Lexis

6.1 The Lexicon and the Nature of Lexical Entries

In the preceding chapters we have been looking at the various types of knowledge a native speaker will have relating to the German language: knowledge of how to form words and how to put sentences together using words, and of the way the sounds of a language are organized. In addition, he or she will also have knowledge of what the words of a language actually are, and how they are characterized in terms of meaning, grammatical category, and their behaviour in sentences. Phonological and morphological rules will go some way towards defining the possible words of a language, but there must also be an inventory of the words which are present in a language at a particular time. This inventory is commonly called the **lexicon**.

But the lexicon is more than just a list of the words of German at any given time. For one thing, it will contain, we are assuming, not just words but also other types of **lexical items**. Some of these will be bound morphemes. Consider the following examples:

(1) Zeit ung   Zeit schrift   be zieh en   Ess zimmer
     newspaper   *magazine*   *to cover*   *dining room*

In the discussion of morphology in chapter 3 it became clear that not only parts of words such as *-schrift* in *Zeitschrift* or *-zieh* in *beziehen*, which can stand alone as words in their own right, and are referred to as free morphemes, will be listed in the lexicon of the language, but also affixes such as *-ung*, *be-* and *-en*. It is important to be aware of the fact that some authors limit the use of the term 'lexical item' to words, and even to particular types of word (see, for example, Katamba 1994). This reflects the individual author's view of what is contained in the lexicon.

In keeping with the view put forward here, we are assuming that lexical items include words, morphemes and even phrases (see section 6.5 below). Sometimes in the course of this chapter we shall speak of 'words' rather than of 'lexical items'. This is done for simplicity and because for much of what we have to say about lexical items and their meanings, words represent the typical case. It should be borne in mind, however, that most of what is said about words in fact applies to all types of lexical items in the system described here.

Every lexical item has a lexical entry, which is a representation of the knowledge we have about lexical items. In chapter 3, section 3.2.2, we saw examples of lexical entries for affixes. There we listed 4 types of information: category, phonological representation, what the affix attaches to, and a semantic characterization. We must now look rather more closely at lexical entries and the information they contain. Firstly, we must distinguish between affixes, as described in chapter 3, section 3.2.2, which must by definition carry information about what they attach to, and all other lexical items, which will not of course contain this information but must carry details of how they fit into a structure in which they are to be used. Like affixes, they will also carry information about meaning, but this will be a different sort of information from that we assumed for affixes, where the meaning of an affix can be defined in terms of how it relates to the root to which it attaches. An important distinction to be made between types of information in a lexical entry is that between general and idiosyncratic lexical information. General information will relate to a whole class of words (see section 6.3), sounds (see chapter 4), or thematic roles (see section 6.2). In order for such information to be available, it will therefore be sufficient to indicate that an item belongs to category N or V, say, without specifying the characteristics of that category within the lexical entry. On the other hand, idiosyncratic information about particular aspects, for example phonological or thematic aspects of an item in question, will need to be fully specified. The types of information contained in a lexical entry (other than an affix) will be roughly as follows:

(2)   category
      phonological representation
      meaning
      thematic representation

For the verb *stell-* the entry might look something like this:

(3)   stell-
      a.   V
      b.   /ʃtɛl/

c.   'stell'
d.   agent <theme, location>

Note that we have given *stell-* as a stem, with no inflectional endings. The information given in the lexical entry (3) tells us a number of things about the lexical item *stell-*: (3a) tells us that it is a verb, (3b) gives the basis for its pronunciation and (3c) what it means, specified merely as a representation of the meaning here. (3d) gives the information on how the verb fits into syntactic structures.

The phonological representation of lexical items, the information in (3b) above, is dealt with in chapter 4. In this chapter we shall look at each of the other aspects in turn, beginning with (3d).

6.2   Thematic Structure

The information in (3d) above says that the verb *stell-* has a subject which is an agent (the person putting something somewhere) and two objects, one of which is a theme (the 'something'), and one a location (the 'somewhere'). Agent, theme and location are what are known as **thematic roles** (or **theta roles**) and they relate to the **argument structure** of the lexical item in question. The notion of argument structure derives from the fact that some lexical items, particularly Vs and Ps, represent relations between other entities, usually entities whose meaning is expressed in NPs. Each relation can have a certain number of such entities to which it relates; these are its arguments and constitute its argument structure. An intransitive V, for example, takes one argument, expressed in its subject, and a transitive V takes two, expressed in its subject and its object, or three if it must also take an indirect object or prepositional complement. Each argument corresponds to a thematic role, which is the role the argument bears with respect to the relation. *Stell-* has an agent, the person doing the putting, a theme, that which is put, and a location expressed by a PP such as *ins Regal* ('in the shelf') or *auf den Tisch* ('on the table'). The latter two are in brackets in (3d) to indicate that they are objects. This is merely a convention; there are lots of possible ways of putting down on paper something which represents a structure in the mind. We have here followed common practice (see, for example, Williams 1981). The theory of thematic roles is often known as **theta theory**.

The information given in (3d) is usually referred to as the **thematic structure**. The thematic structure of lexical items provides a link between the semantics of an individual word and the syntax and semantics of the sentence in which a word appears. It might appear that the semantics of a sentence is just the sum of the meanings of all its words, but it is in fact much more than this, as the meaning of a sentence includes syntactic aspects such as the relations expressed in thematic structure. In addition, the meaning of a sentence also includes pragmatic aspects to do with the function and appropriateness of the sentence in a particular context and additional aspects of propositional or truth-conditional meaning concerned with whether a sentence is true or false in relation to the world.

In earlier versions of generative grammar it was often assumed that the information given above in (3d) was actually of two types. The first was a **subcategorization frame**, which would look something like the following:

(4)   [—— (NP)(PP)]

indicating that the V takes two objects, in an NP and a PP. A subject is always assumed but because it is not inside the VP it is not given in a subcategorization frame. The other type of information was a set of **selectional restrictions**, which might look like this:

(5)   [+human] —— [-abstract] [-abstract]

These indicated what semantic properties the subject and objects of *stell-* could have.

However, it is now generally considered to be clear that the information in (4) can at least to some extent be derived from the information given in (5) because which categories are appropriate (4) will actually depend on their semantic properties (5). Furthermore, the choice of categories (4) will almost wholly depend upon information such as that in (3d) above. For this reason, semantic information such as that in (3d) appears to be sufficient to tell us what we need to know. The fact that, for example, the object is an NP need not be specified because there is a **canonical structural representation** for each thematic role, that is, it has a typical manifestation in a particular syntactic category. An agent, for example, must always be an NP, it cannot be PP or a VP. Selectional restrictions such as those in (5) can be derived from the **lexical conceptual structure**, part of the meaning of a lexical item, sometimes described as those aspects of meaning which are linguistically relevant. So (3c) and (3d) will together give us all the semantic and syntactic information we need to be able to use *stellen* in a sentence.

It is generally assumed that the information given in the lexical entry, especially that about the structure into which a lexical item fits, as given in (3d), is essential for all levels of grammar. Chomsky (1981) posited the **projection principle** which expresses exactly this, namely that representations at every level of the syntax respect the properties of lexical items. And it will be recalled from 3.6 that we are assuming information from morphemes is contained in the words formed out of them. So this information, activated when a word is used, does not get lost but continues to influence how the word can be used in any situation.

6.3 Categories of Lexical Items

In (2) above we said that one of the pieces of information given for a lexical entry is the category of the lexical item; this is (3a) in the sample entry in (3). As discussed in chapter 3, and following the practice adopted by writers such as Lieber (1981) and Ouhalla (1994), we assume that not only words but also morphemes belong to particular classes. Thus the word *Tisch* belongs to the category noun (N); so does *Frau*; so does *-ung* as in *Zeitung*, *-er* as in *Maler* and *-in* as in *Malerin*.

As discussed in chapter 3, this view allows us to preserve the notion of 'head' as that element, whether bound or free, which determines number, gender, case and category of the whole word. As the above examples show, both *-frau* in *Putzfrau* and *-in* in *Malerin* or *Linguistin* determine that the word in question is a feminine noun.

However, it is not always easy to determine the category of a particular lexical item. While traditional terms in German such as *Nennwort* ('naming word') for nouns and *Eigenschaftswort* ('quality word') for adjectives suggest that a particular category is defined semantically, this is not in fact the case; a word like *Schönheit* ('beauty'), for example, denotes a quality but is a noun. Even structural definitions such as 'an adverb qualifies a verb' do not really help as an adverb may qualify other parts of the sentence; the adverb *sehr*, for example, qualifies adjectives, as in *sehr schön* ('very beautiful'). Traditional categories are also inconsistent in other ways: *sein* is traditionally called a possessive adjective, or even, in some grammar books, a pronoun, but it is in fact a determiner as the following examples show:

(6) a.   Ein blaues Buch wurde verkauft
           A blue book was sold

     b.   *Ein seines Buch wurde verkauft
           A his book was sold

     c.   Sein blaues Buch wurde verkauft
           His blue book was sold

     d.   Es wurde verkauft
           It was sold

     e.   *Sein wurde verkauft

These examples suggest that *sein* in (6c) and *ein* in (6a) have the same distribution, whereas *sein* cannot appear in the same position as the adjective in (6a) and (6c); a sentence in which this happens, (6b), is ungrammatical. Furthermore, a pronoun *es* can appear (6d) in place of the whole NP *ein blaues Buch* (6a), but the word *sein* cannot; (6e) is also ungrammatical. Crystal (1987: 92–3) discusses some of these problems briefly with reference to English and Fox (1990: 148–55) describes them more fully with particular reference to German.

In general, we would want to assume the following categories for German:

(7) N: Tisch   Frau   -er   -ung
     V: ess-   angeh-   -en   betret-
     A: grün   viert-   -lich   -isch
     Pron: er   dies   solch-   welch-
     P: bis   pro   bei   eingerechnet
     Det: der   ein   dies-   sein-
     Adv: schnell   hier   hin   allerdings
     Particle: ja   mal   sowieso   zwar
     Conj: aber   bevor   wenn   ohne dass

Note that, as the inflectional ending *-en* determines the category (V) of all words formed by its attachment, then *ess-* and *angeh-* could in principle be unspecified as to category. They are never heads and do not, therefore, determine category. We shall not discuss this question here, simply assuming for the reasons given in chapter 3, section 3.5, that roots such as *ess-* are in fact verbal. The assumption that prefixes such as *-er* and *-ung* are nouns, just as are words such as *Tisch* and *Frau*, suggests that the basis for assignment to categories must be syntactic rather than semantic. Nouns are not so much words which represent 'things' as entities with the categorial features of nouns. Their distribution in syntactic structure will of course not always be the same: the distinction between bound and free morphemes expresses the fact that bound morphemes cannot stand alone in syntactic structures, but must be attached to the appropriate root or affix.

The categories N, V, A and Adv are considered to be **open classes** whereas the others are **closed classes**. Open classes can in general be augmented by the formation of new words using the principles of word-formation as outlined in chapter 3. Thus the class of words of category N can be added to by the following types of word:

(8) Zeitungsfrau   On-Taste   Hochbootung
     newspaper lady *on-button* *booting up*

The class of words of the category A can be added to by new adjectives formed from new or existing nouns using one of the A endings or forming a compound A:

(9) schwiegermütterlich   trollig   sommersprossenartig
     like a mother-in-law   *idiotic*   *freckle-like*

Closed classes cannot be added to, largely for semantic reasons: it is unlikely that new relationships of the type expressed in a preposition or conjunction will come into being. This is much more likely in the case of nouns and verbs, where discoveries, inventions and advances in science and technology give rise to concepts for which new words are needed. However, it would not be entirely true to say that closed classes are closed because they are conceptually exhaustive, as a comparison of different languages will indicate. Russian, for example, has a preposition *iz-pod* meaning roughly 'out from under', whereas German does not. Other languages, such as Turkish, lack the range of pronouns found in German and English. Nevertheless, prepositions in German and pronouns in Turkish are closed classes and cannot be extended in those languages.

Each lexical category will be associated with a particular set of meanings. This is important, as Fanselow (1988a: 45) points out, for restrictions on word-formation, but it also plays an essential role in language acquisition, whether first or second, and in our ordering of semantic knowledge of lexical items: categorial information will provide at least part of the meaning of any particular item. This categorial aspect of the meaning of lexical items is related closely to sentence meaning. For example, verbs, by their very nature, are relations, and thus, as we have seen above, have an argument structure which is projected from the lexicon. This means that they may take a number of arguments, usually one, two, or three. For example, the verb *essen* ('eat') may have one argument, as in *Hans isst* ('Hans eats') or two as in *Hans isst Brot* ('Hans eats bread'). *Geben* must have three as in *Hans gibt Maria das Buch* ('Hans gives Maria the book'), and so on. Each of these arguments is assumed to correspond to a thematic role. These are the roles which a particular lexical item can assign to other elements of the sentence, and which help determine the overall semantic interpretation of a sentence.

6.4   The Meaning of Lexical Items

To return again to (3) above, another line in the lexical entry of a particular item was its meaning, (3c). We simply gave a representation of this in (3), without addressing the question of meaning and how meaning is represented.

The whole question of what meaning is and how it is represented is a very complex one. It is clear that lexical items, that is, words and phrases, **refer** to something. In other words, there is something which is external to the language which is represented by a word or phrase. In formal semantics this is generally referred to as the **extension** of an expression. In general we shall be speaking here of the meaning of words, but it must be remembered that what we have to say applies in principle to any lexical item, whether simple or complex. Because that which a word at first glance appears to refer to may not exist, it makes sense to say that a word in fact refers not to an entity in the outside world, but to a **concept**. A concept, then, is an idea or mental construct. The following are all examples of possible concepts:

(10)   Tisch   Einhorn   Hexe   Meeresjungfer
       table   *unicorn*   *witch*   *mermaid*

Of these only the first could be said to have existence. Nevertheless, the other three exist as concepts, even if the concepts have no corresponding objects in the real world.

If the assumption is made, as it is here, that affixes have fully specified lexical entries (see Olsen 1986b: 75), then these must also refer to concepts, rather than corresponding to objects in the world.

Similarly, Jackendoff (1983: 109) argues that 'word meanings must be treated as internalized mental representations' and not as simply the set of all the objects in the world to which the concept associated with a particular word refers.

Another question which has arisen in this context is whether the meaning of a word is dependent upon the individual speaker's concept, or whether it is independent of its possession by particular speakers, a view taken, for example, by Katz (1980).

These issues, which are universal issues of the philosophy of language, are far too complex for us to go into here. We shall merely assume, with Jackendoff (1983: 120ff), that the meaning of a lexical item must contain at least three types of information, namely:

(11)   a.   necessary conditions, for example, 'thing' or 'colour' or 'emotion', which always form part of the meaning of the word;
       b.   graded conditions which specify a central value for an attribute or object such as 'red' or 'cup'; Jackendoff calls these **centrality conditions**; and
       c.   typical conditions which may have exceptions. Following Putnam (1975) and Fanselow (1981) we shall call the latter stereotypes.

For the word *Regal*, this information would be as follows:

(12) a. 'thing', 'artefact'
      b. a specification of the central value of size and shape which would
          allow any object to be considered with regard to whether or not it is
          an instantiation of the word '*Regal*'.
      c. 'for putting things in/on'

(12a) and (12b) make up what is often, in formal semantics, called the
intension of an expression. We said in chapter 3 that in particular the
third category of information, stereotypes associated with a word, is of
great importance for the formation and interpretation of compounds. It
is also important for the stylistic figure of metaphor, which is an implementation of a conceptual process of comparison, and is frequently based
on stereotypical information about lexical items, rather than on information which the lexical item includes of necessity. In the following
phrase:

(13) das Blatt ist wie ein Tiger
      the leaf is like a tiger

it is presumably the stereotypical stripedness of tigers, not their necessary characteristic of being animals, which is used for the basis of comparison. See chapter 7 for a further discussion of metaphor.

In addition to the information given above in (11), the meaning of a
lexical item can be assumed to contain a level of lexical conceptual
structure, as mentioned in section 6.2 above, which is a representation of
linguistically relevant aspects of meaning such as selectional restrictions
imposed by a particular word on the words that can occur with it. Thus
the V *essen* ('to eat') will contain the information that its agent must be
human, whereas *fressen* ('to eat') will contain the information that its
agent must be non-human, as the following four sentences indicate:

(14) a. Hans hat den Kuchen gegessen
          Hans has eaten the cake

      b. *Hans hat den Kuchen gefressen

      c. Der Hund hat den Kuchen gefressen
          The dog has eaten the cake

      d. *Der Hund hat den Kuchen gegessen

Sentence (14b) is in fact possible if used facetiously and this very fact
indicates that it is deviant. Its deviance, and its humorous (and possibly
insulting) effects stem from the fact that Hans, by being made the subject

of a verb which only allows a non-human subject, by implication is not human. This information about selectional properties of words is also important for extended meanings such as metaphors. Note that metaphorical uses of the German for 'to eat' use *fressen* rather than *essen*:

(15) a. Das Auto frisst die Meilen
          The car eats up the miles

      b. Kinder und Haushalt fressen mich total auf
          The children and the housework take up all my energy

      c. Ich mag diesen modernen Haarschnitt nicht; da sehen die Enden so
          abgefressen aus
          I don't like this modern haircut; the ends look chewed off

Some studies (e.g. Pustejovsky 1993a) would also consider thematic structures to be part of the meaning of a lexical item. Notice that in (3) above we have listed this as a separate part of the lexical entry, in (3d). This, again, is a matter of universal semantics which goes beyond the scope of our discussion here and is not especially important for understanding what the information in the lexicon of a German speaker consists of.

6.5 The Nature of Lexical Items

In the previous section we pointed out that lexical items are not necessarily words, although we have in general been using words for illustration throughout the chapter, as typical examples of lexical items. We have already said that morphemes must be listed in the lexicon. However, it seems likely that not just words and morphemes are lexical items. As a rough rule of thumb, relating to what we assume to be the psychological reality of the concept of lexicon, that is, its place in the actual processes of the brain involved in language, we should expect all those things to be listed in the lexicon which are not formed anew on each occasion that a linguistic utterance is produced. Clearly this will not apply to sentences as a rule. A sentence such as

(16) Hans hat Brot aus dem Brotkorb genommen
      Hans has taken bread from the bread-basket

is constructed as needed, not called up out of a list, in the way that items such as *Brot, genommen, ge- . . . -en* as a past participle morpheme, and even the compound noun *Brotkorb* are. But some sentences and phrases *are* presumably called forth from an inventory. Take for example idiomatic phrases and sentences such as:

(17) a. Es ist gehüpft wie gesprungen
      b. Es regnet in Strömen
      c. unter einer Decke stecken
      d. Hinz und Kunz

These are not created by a speaker in the moment of use on the basis of the rules of German, but are reproduced as complete wholes. A native speaker of German knows such expressions. A learner of German can learn them, and they can typically be found in dictionaries of the language. Further evidence for their status as lexicalized entities is provided by the fact that they cannot be translated literally. The translation of (17a) into English is not (18a) but (18b) below:

(18) a. It is all the same whether you jump or leap
      b. It's six of one and half-a-dozen of the other

Similarly, suitable translations of (17b), (17c) and (17d) would be English idiomatic expressions such as 'it's raining hard' (or even 'it's raining cats and dogs'), 'to be hand in glove', 'every Tom, Dick and Harry' respectively. We would want to say that (17a)–(17d) are lexicalized in German but that (16) *Hans hat Brot aus dem Brotkorb genommen* is not.

What we are therefore assuming is that all elements of language whose form or meaning cannot be deduced from existing lexical items must themselves be lexical items. Sometimes a complex lexical item may seem quite transparent – that is, both form and meaning seem deducible from other lexical items – but upon closer inspection this is seen not to be the case. The word *Brotkorb* from the sentence in (16) above is an example. *Brot* and *Korb* are lexical elements which can be put together to make the compound *Brotkorb*. However, a *Brotkorb* is not simply any basket in some way related to bread. A washing basket containing bread is not a *Brotkorb*. A basket of eggs kept next to the bread is not a *Brotkorb*. These specific elements – that the basket must be of a particular size, and it must be used habitually to contain bread on a table – are not deducible from *Brot* and *Korb* alone but must be stored in a separate lexical entry for *Brotkorb*. This is what leads us to the assumption that *Brotkorb* is lexicalized. In chapter 3 we showed that loan words such as *Linguist* or *Pazifist* may also not necessarily be transparent on the level of meaning.

The view that only items not entirely reducible to others are really lexical items with a separate entry is not held by all linguists. Some consider phrases and collocations such as

(19) a.   das Fenster zumachen
           to close the window

      b.   Urlaub machen
           to go on holiday

to be lexical items, because although, they argue, the form and meaning
of these phrases is **compositional,** that is, they contain no extra elements
not contained in the individual words and morphemes themselves, the
actual form cannot be known without recourse to an inventory (see
Sproat 1985). So phrases such as those in (19) above, often referred to as
Funktionsverbgefüge in German (see, for example, Helbig and Buscha
1987) might quite reasonably be supposed to be lexical items.

   It is worth noting that, although a lexical item always has a clearly
characterizable form and meaning, one of the particular characteristics
of stylistic manipulation of language is to change the relationships usually existing between a lexical item and the elements of its entry. Thus,
for example, *Brotkorb* may indeed be used to mean a basket of eggs kept
next to the bread, especially if used to distinguish this particular basket
of eggs from another one. Or verbs such as *singen, sagen* may be used
with only a theme instead of an agent, as in:

(20) *ein Gedicht sagt auf
       a poem recites

with the meaning 'a poem is recited'; compare expressions in English
such as 'this book reads well'. Chapter 7 contains a discussion of how
German can be stylistically manipulated in these and other ways.

   In general there is agreement about the fact that the lexicon contains a
list of lexical items, though not, as we have seen, about the exact contents of this list. Usually generative grammar theory before about 1970
did not view the lexicon as the place where word-formation processes
happened. Some linguists in the 1970s (such as Jackendoff 1975) distinguished the processes of derivation and inflection with regard to their
location, assuming that the former was a lexical process whereas the
latter was located in the syntax. Many later writers (such as Lieber
1981) saw the lexicon as the place where all morphological operations
took place. Other authors, notably Di Sciullo and Williams (1987), maintain that morphological processes, which in their view are similar to
syntactic processes, do not actually take place in the lexicon. In general,
those approaches which assume that some or all morphological processes take place within the lexicon of a language are referred to as
'lexicalist', and 'non-lexicalist' is the term given to those that assume
that the lexicon is merely a static list of items and their descriptions.

There is some confusion about the term, though, and it is sometimes used inconsistently.

We will assume, then, that the lexicon contains idiomatic phrases as well as morphemes and words. But we still need to consider whether complex forms – derived words such as *Anbeter* and inflected forms such as *steht* – all have entries in the lexicon. We have already noted that compounds tend to have meanings that are not entirely compositional and would therefore need to be listed. But it could be argued that derived and inflected words do have compositional meaning. There are different answers to the question of whether they have lexical entries or not. Kiparsky (1982b), for example, maintains that only simple forms are listed; Allen (1978) has two separate lexicons – a conditional one for regular complex forms and a permanent one for idiosyncratic complex forms and simple forms. Jackendoff (1975) maintains that all words of a language are listed whether or not they are complex or idiosyncratic. Di Sciullo and Williams (1987) offer the view, which we shall follow here, that the lexicon contains all idiosyncratic elements of the language: 'semigrammatical objects' which cannot be derived by other means. Consider Di Sciullo and Williams's 'hierarchy of listedness' (1987: 14):

(21)   morpheme > word > compound > phrase > sentence

All morphemes are listed, because they cannot be derived, most words are listed because they have 'a meaning or some other feature' that does not follow from their composition, and so on. This applies to all the elements of the hierarchy, with those at the right-hand side, that is, sentences, least likely to be listed because their meaning is least likely to be non-compositional, that is, to contain elements not directly derivable from their constituent parts. In Di Sciullo and Williams's view, whether or not a particular form is listed will vary from speaker to speaker. Nevertheless, there is usually assumed to be a common core of elements which are in every German (or other language) speaker's lexicon. This idea is behind the designation of words as **lexicalized** or **non-lexicalized**. Lexicalized words or phrases are assumed to be part of all (or all average) German speakers' lexicons; morphemes are therefore almost all lexicalized, with the exception of examples such as *-icht*, discussed in chapter 3, which are unknown to some speakers. The notion of lexicalization in relation to morphology is discussed in chapter 3. Here the only further point to be made is that lexicalization can have the effect of making the grammatical and semantic origins of words obscure to a native speaker. Words such as *gegebenenfalls* ('if appropriate') or *dank* ('thanks to') are much less likely to be analysed as 'given the case that X applies' or 'caused by X, who/which is to be thanked for this' by native speakers, for whom they are just unanalysed lexical entries than for non-native speakers, for whom the words will not perhaps be fully lexicalized and who will reconstruct them from their original underlying semantic and syntactic structures.

6.6   Relations among Lexical Items

In section 6.4 we said that part of the meaning of a lexical item is defined in terms of necessary conditions which determine whether the concept to which it refers is in fact an example of that particular item. Theories which posit such information as part of meaning are often called **decompositional** theories of word meaning; a word such as *Frau*, according to this type of theory, is said to have various components such as *erwachsen*, *weiblich* and *menschlich*. Other approaches are **non-decompositional**, that is, they favour the expression of meaning in terms of unanalysed concepts and networks of inferences amongst concepts. We shall not discuss these differences further here as they relate to universal semantic issues. But, however such meanings are seen to be encoded in individual lexical items, it is clear that this must occur in such a way as to make relations between individual lexical items clear. Such relations are an essential aspect of a native speaker's knowledge of the language.

The idea that the meanings of lexical items are related to one another in particular ways is usually seen in the context of structuralism (a view of language prevalent in the early to middle years of the twentieth century, which particularly emphasized the arbitrariness of the way words related to meanings and the importance of the different ways in which meanings could relate to one another) and the semantic theories which follow a general structuralist direction, such as Geckeler (1971). However, as Lyons (1977: 250) points out, the theory of these relations, and the view that words are part of a complex system related by meaning, goes back to the ideas of von Humboldt in the nineteenth century and even further to Herder in the eighteenth. Most of its best-known proponents such as Porzig (1934), Trier (1934) and Weisgerber (1954) have written about the German language. The theory is usually referred to as the theory of **semantic fields** (or **lexical fields**; we shall use the two terms interchangeably here) and is concerned with such fields as subdivisions of the lexicon of a particular language. Lyons (1977: 251) also discusses the distinction between theories which take the 'objects, properties and relations external to language' as their starting point and those which use as their basis the lexemes of a particular language. Clearly these must be different points of view, for the lexemes of one language do not encode meanings in exactly the same way as those of another. Concepts, to which lexical items make reference, divide up perceived reality differently in different languages, as any translator is aware. A typical example given to illustrate this is the area of colour terminology. German says *blau* for some colours the English would tend to call purple and *rot* for others; though there is an intermediate area referred to by the words *purpur* ('purple') and *lila* ('lilac'), it is interesting to note that both these words are foreign loan words, difficult to inflect and therefore not especially liked by many German speakers. Although some inflection is possible, as the following example shows

(22) Ich habe ein lilanes Kleid gekauft
      I have bought a lilac dress

it is defective: masculine accusative *einen lilanen Tisch* sounds odd, as does the feminine in any case. (Note that *n* has to be added between *lila*-and the appropriate ending to make it pronounceable.) Sometimes *lilafarben* or *purpurfarben* are substituted as these can be fully inflected. Even their meanings are not entirely clear: especially *purpur* will be seen by different German speakers to refer stereotypically to a colour resembling scarlet, purple or various shades in between. Usage may vary historically and with context. *Lila*, too, is sometimes used for what we tend in English to call 'purple' and sometimes for the lighter shade we call 'lilac'. But it is surely not because the appropriate words are loan words that Germans tend to divide what we would call purple between red and blue. It is rather the other way round: historically speaking, gaps in the system were only gradually perceived and words were imported to fill them. It is significant that the loan words tend to be used for synthetic colours. For example, many flowers that we would consider purple are classified as *blau* by Germans, even though, in fact, purple flowers are far more common than blue ones. This suggests that the German word *blau* describes an area further along the spectrum towards red than does the English word *blue*. A purple dress, on the other hand, would most probably be described as *lila*, and, at times when this is a fashionable colour, the area covered by the term will become clearly distinct from that covered by *blau*. Sometimes the reverse situation applies: German has more terms than English and divides a conceptual field up into more sections. This would certainly be true today of the distinctions expressed by German *Junge* ('boy'), *Jugendliche* ('youth') and *Mann* ('man'). *Junge* is used for boys up to about 15, thereafter *Jugendliche* until about 20, and *Mann* for anyone older. But English now rarely uses 'youth'. News reports, books on sociology or medicine generally use the term 'boy' up to about 16 or 17, and thereafter 'man'. Sometimes the gender-neutral 'teenager' or 'young person' is used for young men between about 14 and 19. The age of majority is the same in both countries, but Germans clearly have a perception of 'youths' as a particular category of person, which has no direct feminine counterpart (though its plural form can be used for a mixed group), just as the English term does not. This example shows that lexical items relate to the concepts they encode in a particular way in a particular language.

6.7   Sense Relations

The structure of semantic or lexical fields is determined by relations of meaning between different words or sets of words in the lexicon of a language. These relations are known as **sense relations**. Words can, for example, have similar, contrasting or opposing meanings and most of the relations of sense assumed to exist between the items in the lexicon are based on the type or degree of closeness or opposition.

Antonymy is a relation of direct opposition; **antonyms** are lexical items which are opposed in meaning. Lyons (1977: 271) makes the point that it is not clear whether humans have an inherent tendency to dichotomize, which leads to the perception of opposites in language, or whether the number of opposites in language causes us to 'polarize judgements and experiences'. Both Fox (1990: 276f) and Lyons (1977: 279) distinguish between gradable words, which are strictly antonyms, and ungradable words, which are **complementaries**, and whose relation to one another is one of **complementarity**. **Gradable** words are those which indicate possession of a particular quality in a particular degree. Such words include *hoch, niedrig, heiß, kalt, gut, schlecht* (respectively 'high', 'low', 'hot', 'cold', 'good', 'bad'). It is perfectly reasonable to say

(23)   Der Stuhl ist höher als der Tisch
       The chair is higher than the table

Hoch and *niedrig* are antonyms, and indeed all gradable lexemes potentially have antonyms.

But if we look at ungradable opposites such as *verheiratet* ('married') and *ledig* ('single'), we see that they cannot be used in such constructions:

(24)   *Hans ist lediger als Peter
       Hans is more single than Peter

is very odd and could at best be used facetiously. For this reason their opposition is said to be one of complementarity – either one or the other applies, but not something in between. (See Lyons 1977: 271ff for a discussion.)

Another relation of opposition which is often distinguished from antonymy and complementarity (see Lyons 1977: 281ff) is **converseness**.

This is the relationship that exists between words such as *Ehemann* and *Ehefrau* and *Lehrer* and *Schüler*. Each one implies the presence of the other. Lyons (1977: 273) would also include active and passive forms of verbs here: *sehen* and *gesehen werden* are in a relation of converseness, as are comparative forms of graded antonyms: *höher* and *niedriger*. Lyons also distinguishes what he calls **directional opposition** which involves 'an implication of motion in one of two opposed directions with respect to a given place'. Thus *gehen* and *kommen* are directional opposites as are *herauf* und *herunter*. Again, we see here that languages do not encode such relations in the same way. German uses *kommen* often where English would not use *come*:

(25) a. Als ich gestern um 8 Uhr ins Büro kam, . . .
     b. Ich bin nicht dahingekommen

These would be translated into English as

(26) a. As I got to my office at 8 yesterday . . .
     b. I didn't manage to get there

Another directional opposition in English which is not realized in the same way in German is the distinction between *bring* and *take*. Consider the following example:

(27) Ich habe ihn zum Arzt gebracht

which in English would be:

(28) I took him to the doctor

In fact verbs like *kommen* and *gehen* on the one hand, and *bringen* and *nehmen* on the other, are not directional opposites in the strict sense in German, as they are in English. *Kommen*, for example, could be said to relate to the speaker's imagined perspective within the event being described, rather than to the speaker's actual position at the time of speaking. Thus:

(29) Ich kam um 8 Uhr ins Büro

is said from the perspective of being in the office after one had arrived, rather than of being in the office at the time of speaking, which would be the case with English *came*. *Bringen* is even less directional, as it suggests something more akin to taking along with you, whether to the location of the speaker or away from it, and *nehmen* is not necessarily its opposite.

It is possible to distinguish many other sorts of opposition, but we shall not go into these here. Not all lexical items are related by contrast, however. The relation of **synonymy** is that which exists between two lexical items which mean the same, for example the following pairs:

(30)   Gesicht, Antlitz   (*face*)
       Mineralwasser, Sprudelwasser   (*mineral water*)
       Spital, Krankenhaus   (*hospital*)
       Uterus, Gebärmutter   (*uterus*)
       abkratzen, sterben   (*die*)
       die Flinte ins Korn werfen, das Handtuch werfen   (*give up*)
       das Handtuch werfen, aufgeben   (*give up*)

Such words and phrases are called **synonyms**. Although all native speakers of a language have a general sense of which lexical items could roughly be regarded as synonyms, it is by no means an easy term to define. It could be maintained that only words such as *Gebärmutter* and *Uterus*, where one is a foreign word and the other a native German word, are truly synonymous (see chapter 3, section 3.5). However, this is not necessarily the case even here, for in fact one is a word used by a doctor (*Uterus*) whereas the other is used by a layperson. This suggests that some essential core of meaning – usually referred to as the **denotation** – is the same for both words, while the difference is one of stylistic level, function or appropriateness. In fact this could be maintained for all pairs of words which could roughly be called synonymous. In the example just given, by virtue of one word being technical and the other not, the words are not identical in this particular respect. *Gesicht* and *Antlitz*, though both refer to the same part of the body, namely the face, are different in level: *Antlitz* is formal and literary whereas *Gesicht* is the word in everyday use. In both the cases just discussed, we could say that a difference of register (technical as opposed to non-technical, literary or non-literary) is involved. Register is dealt with in detail in chapter 9. *Mineralwasser* and *Sprudelwasser* are not necessarily synonymous, though they are, or were until recently, often used synonymously. *Mineralwasser* is naturally occurring water which contains minerals, whereas *Sprudelwasser* could also be tonic water, which does not contain minerals, and could include *Heilwassser*, a mineral water for which there are certain regulations and for which the intended effect has to be definable. Furthermore, *Mineralwasser* does not have to contain carbon dioxide, and if it does not, it could not be called *Sprudelwasser*, which is sparkling. Until fairly recently, *Mineralwasser* was generally sparkling, if bought in a restaurant, and so *Sprudelwasser* could have been seen as what is called a **hyperonym** of *Mineralwasser*. This means that it is a word representing a concept superordinate to that represented by *Mineralwasser* (we shall discuss this below). Now that mineral water, both still and sparkling, has become enormously popular among Germans, it is unlikely that *Sprudelwasser* would be used as either a hyperonym or a synonym of *Mineralwasser*. *Spital* and *Krankenhaus* both refer to the same place but *Spital* is the dialectal variant of the standard *Krankenhaus*, used in Austria and parts of Bavaria (see chapter 9 for further examples).

Alternative lexical items like those given in (30) all vary in **connotation**, that is, those aspects of meaning lying outside the denotation of the lexical item, which are generally associated with it. Though there are different sources for these various connotations (they may arise from variation in degree of technicality or from regional variation, for example), the effect is similar: synonyms are rarely exactly interchangeable in the same context.

One way in which synonymy is prevented in a particular language is by what Aronoff (1976: 45) has referred to as **blocking**. This is the prevention of more than one derivation from a stem (see chapter 3) with a particular meaning. Thus, for example, the noun from *weiß* is *Weiße*; this lexical item by its presence prevents the formation of a noun **Weißheit*, although this formation would be quite regular. And indeed, there is uncertainty among speakers of German as to what the corresponding German word for 'whiteness' should be. It is interesting to observe that the noun seems more natural in English (as in Melville's famous chapter 'The Whiteness of the Whale' in *Moby-Dick*), and that this applies to several colour terms: *Röte* ('redness') is common, as is *Bläue* ('blueness'), but *?Gelbe* ('yellowness') is, unlike its English counterpart, considered unacceptable by most speakers of German. Similarly, the existence of **grünartig* is prevented by *grünlich*, and of **fremdlich* by *fremdartig*. Clearly blocking does not always occur and, as Di Sciullo and Williams (1987: 10ff) point out, Aronoff's description is not entirely clear. They suggest, in fact, that blocking could be a generally applicable mechanism. This would mean that synonyms are usually blocked, but when they do exist, they tend to take on different aspects of meaning – different connotations, for example, as in the words in (30) above. In fact, when two derived forms of the same base word exist, there are always some different aspects in the concepts they denote. Thus *darwinisch* ('Darwinian') means 'of Darwin', as in *darwinische Theorien*, whereas *darwinistisch* ('Darwinistic' or 'Darwinesque') means 'in the manner of Darwin'; *darwinistische Theorien* are theories after the manner of Darwin. Di Sciullo and Williams (1987) suggest that blocking occurs not only in the lexicon but also generally in morphology and also in syntax: rules, for example, can be blocked, just as individual words and phrases can.

In the example above, we said that *Sprudelwasser* could be used as a superordinate concept whose meaning included that of *Mineralwasser*, though it is sometimes used as a synonym. Clearer examples are:

(31) Blume: Narzisse   Tulpe   Veilchen

Here *Blume* is the hyperonym of the three other words; it expresses a concept whose meaning includes the meaning of the others. Hyperonym is not a very frequently used term; Lyons (1977: 291) notes that Mulder and Hervey (1972) use it; he himself prefers **superordinate**. Some authors (for example Wales 1989) use **hypernym**; we shall use the term hyperonym here. The converse of hyperonymy is **hyponymy**. The words *Narzisse*, *Tulpe* and *Veilchen* are all **hyponyms** of *Blume*. In other words, their meanings are included in the meaning of *Blume*. Another way of putting it is that they are all types of *Blume*. Furthermore, they are **co-hyponyms** of one another. Lyons (1977: 292) describes synonymy as symmetrical hyponymy, because if each word in a pair is a hyponym of the other, the result is synonymy. This only works if a concept is assumed to include itself, for hyponymy is basically a relation of inclusion: *Blume* includes the other three. There may be several levels of hyponymy: *Blume* could be said to be a hyperonym of *Gartenblume* and *Wildblume*, whereby *Tulpe* and *Narzisse*, at least within the context of plants which grow in Germany, are hyponyms of *Gartenblume*, and *Veilchen* is a hyponym of *Wildblume*. Here, too, we see that the German language makes such hierarchical distinctions differently from the way in which this is done in English. Germans regard *Narzisse* as a garden flower which may grow wild in other countries, whereas in England, *daffodil* is not so clearly a garden flower. *Narzisse* may be said to be a hyperonym of *Osterglocke* ('daffodil'). *Narzissen* which are not daffodils are simply called *Narzissen* in German; there is no distinct term for them and this is a gap in the system. We shall return to this question below.

Another type of sense-relation is the **part–whole relation**, sometimes referred to as **synecdoche**, and although this is a term frequently reserved for literary criticism and stylistics, there is no reason why this should be so, and we shall use it for the lexical sense-relation here. Synecdoche is considered by many authors (Jakobson 1956; see also Boase-Beier 1987a), when used as a stylistic device, to be a subclass of metonymy (see chapter 7). As a sense-relation, synecdoche expresses the relation between *Knopf* and *Hemd* or *Berlin* and *Deutschland* but as a stylistic device it is generally used for the substitution of the part for the whole as in *Berlin unterstützt London* ('Berlin will support London'). Metonymy also involves substitution and therefore the term should only be used of a stylistic device; as a sense-relation it would be meaningless as it would refer to any relation between two lexical items, independently of the nature of the lexical items. The nature of that relation, though it may in fact be one of a limited number of possible relations such as cause/effect, similarity and so on, is not specified. Synecdoche, however, is a different matter, for it expresses a part–whole relation in the lexical items concerned. It encompasses such relations as that between *Tür* and *Griff*, *Mensch* and *Hand*, *Mantel* and *Knopf*. It forms the basis for many NN compounds: *Türgriff*, *Menschenhand* and *Mantelknopf* are all lexicalized compounds. Lyons (1977: 312ff) discusses the interesting question of **transitivity** in this relation: it would be transitive if the fact that B is a part of A and C of B were to imply that C is a part of A. In other words, if the *Haus* has a *Tür*, and the *Tür* has a *Griff*, does then the *Haus* have a *Griff*? The lack of a compound **Hausgriff* suggests that synecdoche is not seen as transitive, at least as far as word-formation is concerned.

Within the system of sense-relations in any language there are many gaps. One of these was mentioned above: there is no separate word in German for *Narzissen* which are not *Osterglocken*. One way of describing a **lexical gap** is as a place where sense-relations seem to call for a term but one does not exist. These gaps can often be most clearly perceived in relation to another language. In the example above, German has a gap for flowers which are not *Osterglocken* but are other types of *Narzisse*, flowers which in English would be called 'narcissi'. This does not mean there is no word for the actual flowers; they would be referred to as *Narzisse* (as, indeed, any word can be referred to by its hyperonym, though not by its hyponym). But there is no word corresponding to English *narcissus*, which appears to be a co-hyponym of *daffodil* in English. In English, at least in everyday language, there is no hyperonym (though the Latin species name is *narcissus*). These facts are illustrated below:

(32)

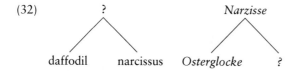

Here we can see that both languages exhibit lexical gaps, but in different places in the system. The mistake of assuming that terms exist for the corresponding points in the representation of lexical information in another language is a common pitfall of translation.

A further example of a lexical gap is illustrated in (33):

(33)

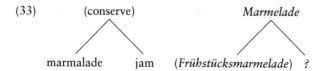

The term *conserve* in English could reasonably be supposed to be a
hyperonym for *jam* and *marmalade*, and probably is in the lexicons
of some English speakers, though it is not very common and for this
reason appears in brackets. German uses the hyperonym *Marmelade*
as an equivalent to *jam*, for there is no separate term for this, and
uses *Frühstücksmarmelade* for a conserve made of citrus fruits and
containing peel. These are usually imported from England and are
therefore not in common use; most Germans simply refer to them as
(*Orangen/Zitronen*)-*Marmelade*. This sort of mismatch causes end-
less confusion to Germans speaking English, who have a conceptual
difficulty with the two English hyponyms. (To many Germans the difference is not at all evident.) This shows the close correspondence
between lexical fields and the conceptual areas (or **conceptual fields**)
they represent.

6.8   Further Reading

For further information on argument structures and thematic structures
of lexical items, see Stowell (1981), Ouhalla (1994: 126ff) or Rappaport
et al. (1993). For a discussion of the meaning of sentences and how
words fit into them, see Crystal (1987: 107).

   On the nature of meaning, see Lyons (1977: 174ff), Crystal (1987:
100ff) or Kempson (1977).

   Pustejovsky (1993b) is a collection of articles dealing with many issues
to do with the lexicon and meaning. Another such collection is Gussmann
(1987).

   On early distinctions in generative grammar between what was
seen as a lexical process of derivation and a syntactic process of inflection, it is interesting to read Jackendoff (1975) and Aronoff (1976).
For slightly later, 'lexicalist' views (assuming all morphological processes took place in the lexicon), see Lieber (1981) or Selkirk (1982).
Malicka-Kleparska (1987) is useful as it gives a brief overview of
some of these developments, and especially of Allen (1978) and Aronoff
(1976).

   Hoppenbrouwers et al. (1985) contains various articles on the meanings of words (see, for example, the article by Carston on non-
decompositional meaning) and on a number of different lexical fields.

   It is difficult to find anything comprehensive on sense-relations in
German, but most of what Lyons (1977) – referred to several times in
section 6.7 – has to say can be applied equally well to German. It is
definitely worthwhile reading Lyons's chapters 8 and 9 and trying to
substitute German examples (other than the ones given here) for the
English ones.

EXERCISES

1 Underline the determiners in the following sentences:

Diese alten Bücher sind wertvoll.

Ich habe meinen Vater besucht.

Mit einem Auto kommt man in dieser Stadt nicht zurecht.

Ihre Probleme sind anders als deine.

Read section 6.3 again if in doubt.

2 Read section 6.5 on lexical items. Which of the following words and phrases would you expect to be lexical items?

Buch
-ung
tschüs
einen Antrag stellen
-ar
Hinz und Kunz
ein alter Mann
ein schwarzes Loch
Schwarzarbeit
ein schwarzer Vogel

3 Give 5 examples of converseness (see section 6.7); here is a first one:

Käufer – Verkäufer

4 Fill in the gaps in the diagrams below with possible words:

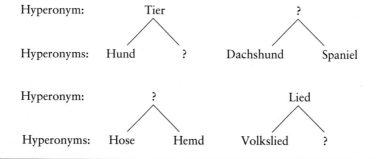

| Hyperonym: | Tier | | ? | |
| Hyperonyms: | Hund | ? | Dachshund | Spaniel |

| Hyperonym: | ? | | Lied | |
| Hyperonyms: | Hose | Hemd | Volkslied | ? |

CHAPTER SEVEN

Stylistics

7.1 Stylistics and the Style of Texts

Views on the scope and nature of the discipline known as **stylistics** vary greatly. In English-speaking countries it is frequently taken to be the linguistic study of literary texts (see, for example, Wales 1989: 437). But this view is by no means universal; in Germany stylistics is not usually confined to the study of literary texts but deals with all types of text. Examples of this approach can be found in Sowinski (1972) and Fleischer and Michel (1975). In viewing all types of text as the appropriate subject of stylistics, the question of how to distinguish between literary and non-literary texts can to some extent be avoided, although some studies (such as Riesel 1970) do see literary texts as a separate text-type. In general, the question of what makes a text literary is the subject of a great deal of controversy; it is addressed by several of the works listed in the final section of this chapter.

In our discussion of style and stylistics, we shall not be particularly concerned with questions about what constitutes a literary text nor with the role of stylistics within literary criticism, another issue open to a number of different views. Instead we shall assume that, although stylistic analysis may well form a starting point for literary criticism, it is not necessarily part of the latter; it is not concerned with value judgements. We are assuming also that it is potentially the study of all types of text and so in this we are closer to the German use of the term *Stilistik*. What we shall be particularly concerned with is the issue of stylistic knowledge as part of the native speaker's knowledge of German, and the relationship between this knowledge and other types of linguistic knowledge.

Having established that stylistics examines the style of texts or, to be more exact, the native speaker's knowledge of how style works, it is necessary to determine what is actually meant by the term **style**. Püschel

(1980) defines style as 'das "Wie" sprachlicher Äußerungen', in other words 'the "how" of linguistic utterances', but there are other views of what is meant by style. It has been seen as a question of choice among a number of semantically equivalent expressions, as an expression of the personality of the writer, and as an ornament which is somehow additional to the everyday form of the language.

7.2   Style and Deviation

Many of the views of style mentioned above are based on the intuition that the style of an expression in some way depends upon the notion of deviation from a norm. This is a particularly common view in the type of stylistics which deals especially with literary texts. See Boase-Beier (1987a: 11f.) for a discussion. The sort of examples put forward to suggest that style involves deviation from a norm include deviant syntax, creative use of metaphor or the use of repetitive patterns. The following two examples show deviant syntax. An English gloss has been given rather than a translation, as a translation would not show the exact nature of the deviation.

(1)   Es kam die Nachricht
      there came the message
      zu gehen an die See,
      to go   to the sea
      nördlich
      northwards

                                         (Meister 1979: 92)

(2)   Jetzt:
      now
      September -
      September
      nachmittags.
      in-the-afternoon

                                         (Meister 1979: 22)

In (1) the infinitive verb form *zu gehen* would normally have come after *an die See* and *nördlich* before: *Es kam die Nachricht, nördlich an die See zu gehen.* In example (2) the deviation lies in the lack of a verb; this is clearly not a sentence of German.

   Other structures are not grammatically deviant in such an obvious sense but nevertheless show evidence of repeated sounds which would, according to Sowinski (1972: 57ff.), be avoided in non-literary discourse:

(3) Hausen die traurigen Fische

$\qquad\qquad\qquad\qquad\qquad$ (Goll; Conrady 1977: 740)

(4) Ein neues Lied will ich euch **singen**
      Nichts konnte mich zur Strecke **bringen**

$\qquad\qquad\qquad\qquad\qquad$ (von Törne 1981: 130)

In (3), the sound [au] is repeated and in (4) *singen* and *bringen* rhyme,
and both are in the same position in the line, which further emphasizes
the repetition of sound.

  Yet other examples of deviation relate to unusual metaphors:

(5) Die graue Nacht ist mit silbernen Nadeln gerafft
      The grey night is gathered with silver needles

$\qquad\qquad\qquad\qquad\qquad$ (Kolmar; Conrady 1977: 813)

The examples above come from literary texts, but many instances of
what is obviously deviant language can be found in non-literary texts,
too. The following come from advertisements:

(6) a. Neu. Ohne Risiko
          Natürlich. Sympathisch
          New. Without risk
          Natural. Kind

      b. Aus Verantwortung für Ihre Haut
          Out of duty to your skin

      c. Nicht mal ein Pflaster auf den Wunden der Natur
          Not even a plaster on the wounds of nature

None of these utterances contains a verb, and they are therefore
grammatically incomplete: they do not constitute sentences. In all these
examples, both literary and non-literary, what makes the utterances
unusual is that the style does not conform to the syntactic and semantic
norms of German.

  The view of style as deviation from a norm, usually referred to as
standard language, gained particular importance in the 1920s and 1930s
in the work of the Prague Linguistic Circle (sometimes known as the
Prague School), an influential group of linguists and stylisticians including Jakobson, Trubetzkoy, Mathesius and Mukařovský. Their view was
that the function of poetic language was to attract attention to itself, a
phenomenon known as **foregrounding**, by virtue of employing deviant
structures, a view which examples (1) to (5) would seem to bear out. But

as Wales (1989: 117) points out, deviation involves establishing a norm and the establishment of such a norm is often not a very satisfactory enterprise, because norms vary: what is normal for a newspaper text may not be for a legal text, and so on. In chapter 9 we will show that in fact there are many different norms appropriate to different situations and types of text.

If style is to be viewed as related to deviation, then it is essential that we can say what is the norm against which deviation is to be measured. One of the difficulties of attempting to define deviant linguistic structures in relation to a norm is that it is virtually impossible, for any given deviant structure, to say what a corresponding non-deviant structure would be. This is because the deviant structure does not stand in a one-to-one relationship with a non-deviant one, but rather represents a choice from a class of possible structures in principle infinite in number. And any one structure may be deviant in a number of ways. In order to speak of deviance in a meaningful way, it is necessary to have recourse to linguistic terms such as 'grammaticality' and 'acceptability'.

If we assume, as outlined in chapter 1, that the grammar of a language generates all and only those structures of a language which are grammatical, then one way of defining a deviant structure is to say that it cannot be generated by the grammar in question. For example, a grammar of German will not generate subjectless sentences, but a poem in German may begin thus:

(7) Geht in die Stadt;
     kauft sich Tee und Brot
     Goes to town;
     buys tea and bread

We can define this sentence as deviant, but not by reference to another non-deviant version, such as:

(8) Er geht in die Stadt;
     kauft sich Tee und Brot
     He goes to town;
     Buys tea and bread

because an equally appropriate corresponding non-deviant sentence would be:

(9) Geht er in die Stadt,
     kauft sich Tee und Brot?
     Does he go to town,
     buying tea and bread?

We could, however, clearly define the deviation by saying that in (7) the Extended Projection Principle is violated. This principle, it will be recalled from chapter 2, requires all clauses to have a subject. Subject-less clauses such as (7) are therefore not generated by the grammar of German, which is assumed to contain the Extended Projection Principle (see also Ouhalla 1994). In the case of (7), then, the deviation can be defined as **ungrammaticalness**.

However, many stylistically deviant structures are not so obviously grammatically unacceptable. Figures such as **zeugma** are syntactically straightforward, but nevertheless appear odd to a native speaker. Here are two examples:

(10) Sie stellte den Antrag, und damit ihrem Kollegen das Bein
      She put the application in and thus tripped her colleague up
      (literally: *she put in an application and thus also her leg in her colleague's
      path*)

(11) Er nahm Abstand, dann den Zug, und fuhr nach Hause
      He distanced himself, took the train, and returned home
      (literally: *he took distance, then the train, and returned home*)

Zeugma (from a Greek word meaning 'yoking') is a figure in which a verb takes two objects which are incompatible because each relates to a different meaning of the verb in question. In (10) the verb *stellen* is used both with *Antrag* ('to put in an application') and *Bein* ('to trip up'), resulting in an unacceptable combination. Example (11) functions in much the same way on the basis of the verb *nehmen*. Semantically these structures are unusual, and are often used facetiously. There are actually in each case two verbs in use, with different selectional restrictions (see chapter 3). In (10) *stellen1* is part of a collocation *einen Antrag stellen* and has little independent meaning within the collocation. The second verb, *stellen2*, is part of the idiom *jemandem das Bein stellen* (to trip someone up). Similarly in (11) *nehmen1* only takes the object *Abstand* as it is part of the fixed collocation *Abstand nehmen* (to distance oneself) and *nehmen2* takes any means of public transport as object. The two objects are conjoined by *und* as though they were both objects of the same verb. Another way of describing what is deviant here is to say that *stellen2* and *nehmen2* are not actually expressed at all, but are neverthe-less somehow supposed to function as the verb for which there is in each case an object. This would bring such examples close to another type of deviation, illustrated in (12).

(12) Er kaufte eine Zeitung und ein Buch

This sentence is not deviant in the following meaning:

(13)   He bought a newspaper and a book

but it *is* deviant if used to mean

(14)   He bought a newspaper and read a book

This is because the verb 'bought' (*kaufte*) can be recovered from the meaning of (12) as the verb whose object is *ein Buch*, because it is identical to the earlier *kaufte* whose object is *eine Zeitung*. However, *las* ('read') cannot be thus recovered from (12) as it is not identical to the verb used earlier with *eine Zeitung*. This is a phenomenon known as **gapping** (see Stillings 1975). Gapping assumes that material is deleted, and is only possible if the deleted material is identical to earlier material which is present, because otherwise interpretation would be impossible. So *kaufte* can be omitted in (12) but *las* cannot. (10) and (11), then, to return to our earlier example, can, as indeed all examples of zeugma can, be seen as violations of gapping principles and this is what makes them deviant. There are other constraints, too: only certain categories can be gapped;

(15)   *Peter kaufte eine Zeitung und Hans kaufte auch
       Peter bought a newspaper and Hans also bought

is not a grammatical sentence of German because NPs cannot be gapped.
   Other types of deviation involve pragmatic considerations. If I enter a cold room and say

(16)   Es ist furchtbar heiß hier im Zimmer
       It is terribly warm in this room

then I am employing **irony**, but there is nothing in the form of the utterance to suggest this, only in its relationship to the context of utterance. Irony involves interpreting utterances as their opposites, or as utterances which contrast in other ways would normally be interpreted.
   All the above examples can be described as deviant by reference to principles of language which are violated. In (7), it was a syntactic principle, the Extended Projection Principle, in (10) and (11) it was the syntactic principle of gapping, and in (16) it was the assignment of a semantic interpretation to fit a particular context. What all the above examples suggest is that stylistic deviance is not merely an unquantifiable or indefinable strangeness in the use of German. It appears that what is involved is a violation of specific principles which form part of a German native speaker's knowledge of the language.

7.3   Stylistic Principles

The problem with the above approach is that it does not go far enough because it suggests that the violation of language principles is not controlled and that although it might be possible to say in each case which principles of German grammar have been violated, it is not possible to predict the shape such violation can take. It suggests that any type of deviation is possible. Yet this is clearly not the case. (7), repeated here as (17), was a possible deviation:

(17)   Geht in die Stadt;
         kauft sich Tee und Brot

but the following sentence is not:

(18)   *In Stadt die geht;
          sich Tee Brot und kauft

Likewise (11), repeated as (19):

(19)   Er nahm Abstand, dann den Zug . . .

is possible, though unusual, but

(20)   *Abstand nahm Zug, dann den er . . .

is not. And where (16) represents a clearly definable figure of irony, assuming that I am saying that it is hot but meaning that it is cold, there would be no recognizable figure used if I entered a cold room and said:

(21)   *Es ist hier
          It is here

All of these examples violate the grammar of German in a way which is not recognizable. While stylistic manipulation of the language may well result in unusual structures, nevertheless they can generally be precisely characterized (for example, as a violation of a particular rule or principle of grammar) and often named (zeugma, irony). This suggests that stylistic deviation is subject to constraints; not just anything is possible.

   If we can recognize and name or at least characterize stylistic deviation, if we can understand stylistically deviant utterances, if we can recognize that structures such as (18), (20) and (21) are not possible, then we must have knowledge of what governs stylistic deviation. It seems that part of a native speaker's knowledge of language in fact constitutes a number of principles governing the possible stylistic manipulation of texts. Notice that this puts stylistic knowledge on a par with syntactic, morphological, phonological or lexical knowledge. We are assuming that the principles which constitute this knowledge interact with principles from other areas of linguistic knowledge just as lexical and syntactic principles or morphological and phonological principles interact. This is a somewhat different view of style from one which sees it primarily as in some way determined by the function to be fulfilled. In contrast to this, the view described here is that style is determined by what its principles allow, just as is the case in other areas of language. The two views, exemplified for English by writers such as Halliday (1971) for functional views and Boase-Beier (1987a) for views based on stylistic knowledge, are indeed not mutually exclusive, as clearly style is largely a matter of choice and choice may fulfil a particular function. If we see deviation as the result of the interaction of stylistic principles with other principles of language, we can explain the intuitions both that some structures are stylistically deviant and that not just any type of deviation is possible. We can also explain why certain types of text exhibit more deviation than others: some stylistic principles are more appropriate to a particular type of text than are other principles or than these are to other text-types. In fact, we have a way of characterizing a native speaker's intuitions about style which goes far beyond what any attempt to relate individual structures to other, non-deviant, ones could do.

We are assuming, then, that one area of linguistic knowledge is **stylistic knowledge**, which can be characterized as a set of principles which interact with other areas of linguistic knowledge. But what are these principles? It is probably not possible to provide an exhaustive list, but we would expect them to include principles which give rise to many figures common to studies of style and to earlier studies of rhetoric, or the art of public speaking and argumentation. To say that principles of style give rise to deviant structures is not to say anything about the texts or text-types in which they occur. These may be literary or non-literary, and if of a type usually described as literary, they may be poetry or prose. This means that, though it is possible that certain principles may be at work in one type of text rather than another, figures cannot be defined on the basis of the type of text they occur in or its intended purposes or effects. But stylistic knowledge alone will not explain the style of a particular utterance or text. This is because style can quite reasonably be seen, as noted in section 7.1, as a question of choice. When we discuss stylistic variants of sentences, such as those in (34), (36) and (37) in chapter 2, we assume that they are, broadly speaking, different ways of saying the same thing. On the other hand, it can be argued that what is said is never 'the same thing' because style at the very least changes emphasis and may carry a particular meaning as in (3) above where the repetition may create a particular image of captivity, or in (6c) where the connotations of *Wunde* (wound) help personify *Natur* (nature). Any study of style must therefore take into account this aspect of choice, and what the reader of a text interprets the assumed choices to have meant.

7.4 Metaphor

Consider the following examples:

(22) Die Nacht war honig,
schwer, schwarz . . .
The night was honey,
heavy, black . . .

(23) ein Glas trinken
to drink a glass

(24) Kaugummigedicht
chewing-gum poem

What these examples have in common is that they appear to say something involving semantic incompatibility: the night cannot be honey, and we do not drink a glass. Something cannot be both chewing-gum and a poem.

Although no comparison is made explicit in any of these examples, it seems that they must represent comparisons. The night is not actually honey, but is described as being like honey, as having some characteristics which honey has. What we drink can be compared to a glass in the sense that it is the amount that the glass holds and that the act of drinking out of a glass involves putting both glass and contents to the lips. The poem in *Kaugummigedicht* is being compared to chewing gum, perhaps in that it appears to have no fixed meaning, just as chewing gum has a variable form.

In (22), the part of the utterance containing the comparison, which is commonly referred to as a **metaphor**, is of the form

(25) A is B   (that is, *die Nacht ist honig*, or 'the night is honey')

but in fact it represents a statement of the form

(26) A is like B   (*die Nacht ist wie honig*: 'the night is like honey')

In (24), assuming the usual interpretation of copulative compounds (see chapter 3), what is being said is of the form:

(27) B that is A   (*Gedicht, das Kaugummi ist*; 'poem which is chewing-gum')

but it is interpreted as:

(28) B that is like A   (*Gedicht, das wie Kaugummi ist*; 'poem that is like chewing-gum')

We can formulate the principle governing the use of structures with these interpretations as follows:

(29)   *The Principle of Metaphor*

    Assign a structure of the form 'A is B' or 'B that is A' a semantic interpretation of the form 'A is like B' or 'B that is like A', respectively.

Our stylistic knowledge of German will include both knowledge of this principle, which is likely to be universal, and of the various ways in which it can be realized in German. This more specific knowledge of how metaphor works in German will include knowing that words can be conjoined as in (24) to form compounds and that copulative compounds are possible (part of the morphological knowledge discussed in chapter 3).

    The principle in (29) describes what may be called standard metaphor, but there are other metaphorical processes such as **metonymy, simile, personification**, all of which are generated as a result of other principles. Metonymy does not include the assignment of a semantic representation containing a comparison, as there is in fact no mismatch in the form of syntactic and semantic representations, but only between the usual semantic representation and the one to be assigned here. In example (23) above, which is an instance of metonymy, the word *Glas* does not have its usual meaning of a vessel which can be used to contain a drink, but must be assigned the meaning of a word such as *Getränk*, that is, (23) must be assumed to mean: *ein Getränk trinken*, 'to drink a drink'. A separate principle must be responsible for this type of utterance:

(30)   *The Principle of Metonymy*

    Assign an element X in a structure a semantic interpretation Y, whereby X and Y are related in terms of similarity, contiguity, a part–whole relation or other association.

This principle, too, can be assumed to be universal, but it can only be used to form actual utterances of German in conjunction with a German speaker's lexical knowledge (see chapter 6) about *Glas*, namely that it is something commonly used to contain drinks. And indeed, such knowledge may differ from culture to culture. 'Möchten Sie noch eine Tasse?' is not impossible in German, but less likely than its counterpart 'Would you like another cup?' in English, where it would be assumed to refer to tea. It seems clear that though (22) above, and possibly (24), are the sort of utterances one would expect in poetic texts, (23) is an everyday expression. Nevertheless, it involves the reader or hearer in a mental process of replacing one concept (*Glas*) with another (*Getränk*). It could in fact be argued that no such mental process is necessary in this case, because *Glas* in the meaning 'drink' has become lexicalized (see chapter 6). This is further borne out by the fact that the plural of *Glas* is usually *Gläser* but if it is used to mean 'drink' it has a different plural: *Glas*. Thus we say

(31)   Er hat nur zwei *Glas* gehabt
       He has only had two glasses

and not

(32)   *Er hat nur zwei Gläser gehabt

if we mean alcoholic drinks. Further evidence that this use of *Glas* is lexicalized comes from the fact that (31) would always be taken to refer to alcoholic drinks, not water or fruit juice. Metonymy, then, like other types of metaphor, is common to all registers (see chapter 9) of language, but everyday language is more likely to use lexicalized metaphors like that in (23), whereas those in (22) and (24) would be more typical of literary or (in the case of (24)), journalistic texts. Metonymy, in expressions like *Kamm* ('ridge' of a mountain, literally 'comb'), *Muschel* ('outer ear', literally 'shell') or *Bein* ('leg' of a table), is so common as to pass virtually unnoticed by most speakers of German. In literary criticism, where particular metaphors are often seen as indicating a particular theme or even ideology, relations of metonymy based on a part–whole connection are traditionally called **synecdoche**.

In **simile**, the relation of similarity is made explicit; this is the case in the following example:

(33)   Nach dem Sturm glänzte das nasse Heu wie Sauerkraut
       After the storm the wet hay glistened like sauerkraut

Here there are no discrepancies between the semantic interpretation and the structural form. The utterance means what it says; but it is the element of comparison, explicit here but implicit in the substitution in (23) and also in (22) and (24), which has led to simile traditionally being subsumed under metaphor. (For a discussion of the relation of these figures to one another see Boase-Beier 1987a: 88–99). In (33) it is again the case that, though the means of interpretation do not differ from one language to another, there is still lexical knowledge involved which is specific to German: the meaning of *Sauerkraut* is part of the lexicon of most German speakers. This is certainly not true of the word *sauerkraut*, the only possible translation, used in English. It is in fact a common feature of all types of metaphor, including simile, that the detailed information needed to process them tends to be language- and culture-specific. Many recent studies of metaphor (such as Lakoff and Johnson 1980) point to the universality of many bases for comparison (such as comparing argument to war) but, while this does apply to metaphor as used in everyday language, it is undoubtedly a frequent characteristic of poetic metaphor that it uses other, much more culture-specific or context-specific elements on which to base comparison.

Personification involves a type of metaphor or metonymy in which an inanimate object is made to appear human. In the terms used here, the personified utterance is actually assigned a non-personified semantic representation. Thus, in

(34)   Das Wetter kann sich heute wirklich nicht entscheiden
       The weather really can't make its mind up today

the actual interpretation is something like 'the weather is very changeable today', whereby the personified elements of making up one's mind are replaced by what is actually possible as a representation of what we understand to be the real world. Such expressions also may have a culturally specific element: (34) would be much more unusual in German than its counterpart in English, where personified statements about weather are far more common.

7.5   Repetition

The following examples represent a phenomenon especially common in texts from literature, in particular poetry, and also from advertisements and journalistic texts:

(35)   Mühlen aus Wind
           mahlen Sandmehl

                               (Ausländer 1977: 256)

           Mills made of wind
           grind the grains of sand

                               (Boase-Beier and Vivis 1995: 57)

(36)   Wenn Sie Wert legen auf den guten Geschmack, kaufen Sie Brot. Brot isst
       man jeden Tag, bei jeder Gelegenheit. Brot ist gesund. Und Brot schmeckt.

Bei Müller gibt es eine fast unendliche Vielfalt von Brot und Brötchen.
Kaufen Sie Brot. Kaufen Sie Müller-Brot.
If good taste is important to you, buy bread. Bread is something you eat
every day, on any occasion. Bread is good for you. Bread tastes good.
Here at Müller's we have an almost unlimited choice of bread and rolls.
Buy bread. Buy Müller's bread.

(37)   Für die Frauen von Haundorf ist das Leben zur Hölle geworden. In die
       Stadt trauen sie sich nicht mehr. Auf den Strassen ist niemand zu sehen. In
       den Häusern sind Türen und Fenster fest verschlossen.
       For the women of Haundorf life has become hell. They no longer dare to
       go into town. On the streets there is no one to be seen. In the houses,
       doors and windows are firmly locked.

In all these cases, sounds, words or structures create patterns of **repetition**. One of the most striking ways of achieving repetition is to use
patterns of identical and varying sounds to give figures such as **rhyme**
(two or more words in which the sequence from the stressed vowel to
the end of the word is identical), **slant rhyme** (initial and final consonant
clusters are identical, but the vowels are different), **half rhyme** (final
consonant clusters are identical but initial consonants and vowels are
different) or **alliteration** (the initial sounds, usually consonant clusters,
are identical). There is also the more general figure of **assonance**, strictly
used to refer to words with identical stressed vowels and different initial
and final consonant clusters, but often used for repeated sound patterns
in general. In (35) there is repetition in the slant rhyme of *Mühlen* and
mahlen, and the half rhyme of *Wind* and *Sand-* and the alliteration of
[m]. This is captured in the English translation as assonance of *mills* and
wind, alliteration of [g] and half rhyme of *wind*, *sand* and *grind*. However, there are many other types of repetition. In (36) the word *Brot* is
repeated and in (37) the four PPs *für die Frauen, in die Stadt, auf den*
Straßen and *in den Häusern*. It seems reasonable to assume that as
native speakers of German, or of any other language for that matter, we
are aware that there is a Principle of Repetition which allows us to
repeat linguistic elements within a text:

(38)   *The Principle of Repetition*

       Repeat linguistic elements which are phonologically, morphologically, syn-
       tactically or semantically similar.

This is without doubt a universal principle of style. But it will always
interact with the various linguistic levels of German, allowing for the
possibility of repetition wherever similar elements exist at any of these
levels.

In (35) it interacts with the morphology and phonology of German to give the particular repetitions in *Mühlen, mahlen* and *-mehl*. The type of repetition in (36), which fulfils the function of pressing the point home as this is an advertisement, is very common in all languages, but it is the actual lexicon and morphology of German which allow the repetition of the word *Brot* in *Brötchen* ('rolls') and in the compound *Müller-Brot*, which can only be rendered by the phrase 'Müller's bread' in English, where compounds consisting of a proper noun and a common noun are far less usual. In (37) the repetition makes use of the freedom of German word order (see chapter 2) to create a series of sentences beginning with PPs. While, as the English equivalent shows, some of this effect can be maintained in English, there is no equivalent for *In die Stadt trauen sie sich nicht mehr* because English only allows certain PPs (and generally not directional ones) in sentence-initial position. Thus the German text in (37) is able to create a stronger sense of the ubiquity of the fear felt by the women of Haundorf because of the facility with which it can move phrases to sentence-initial position for emphasis than are languages without German's rich morphology and therefore without such freedom.

7.6   Iconicity

In many cases in which repetition is used, it is presumably intended to represent some sort of repetitive sound, motion, circumstance or action in the world to which the text makes reference. So the repeated sounds in (35) may mirror the turning of a mill-wheel. This phenomenon is generally referred to as **iconicity**. The concept derives originally from the writings of C. S. Peirce (see Peirce 1931–58) who uses the term **icon** to mean a sign which in form bears physical similarity to the object to which it refers. The term is used in many studies of style such as Epstein (1975) or Ross (1980). The principle at work in the mirroring of content in form can be defined as follows:

(39)   *The Principle of Iconicity*

> Use linguistic structures that mirror that to which they refer at the phonological or syntactic level or in the typographical representation.

This is a universal principle which is at work especially in literary texts, though it may be found to apply in other types of text such as advertisements. As is the case with all universal principles, the way it applies will differ from language to language.

In example (35) above, in which we are assuming that the repeated sounds are used iconically, the repetition is made easier because of the transparency of lexical items in German mentioned in chapter 6. The words *Mühlen*, *mahlen* and *Mehl* are all etymologically connected and thus iconic repetition is achievable in a way it would not be in a language such as English, in which the corresponding words (mill, grind, flour) are etymologically and phonologically distinct. But iconicity does not only manifest itself in repetition. In the following example from Schiller, quoted also by Sowinski (1972: 271), the sounds of the words are presumably intended to echo the sounds the words describe:

(40)   Von dem Dome schwer und bang
       Tönt der Glocke Grabgesang

One could argue here that especially the [ɔ], [oː], [aŋ], and [øː] sounds, and also the regular four stressed syllables in the line, echo the sound of the bell, or at any rate are meant to suggest it. Bulwer Lytton's translation of these lines as:

(41)   From the steeple
       Tolls the bell,
       Deep and heavy,
       The death-knell

                                            (Lytton n.d.: 252)

shows that he has failed to capture the iconic element in English. Though this would not be possible in terms of exact equivalence, as the qualities of English vowel sounds are different from those of German, a competent translator will usually compensate in such cases by using sounds which have similar connotations in the target language. This is possible because phonological iconicity of this type always has a culture-specific, conventionalized element, as the different words used to express the same sound in different languages show: German has *bimbam* where English has *ding-dong*, but in neither language does this suggest a funeral knell. The point here is that neither *bimbam* nor the sequence of sounds in (40) are the actual sounds of bells, but merely call forth these sounds in the mind of the German speaker and hearer. Consequently (41) would not need to attempt the sounds of a funeral knell, but merely something which would suggest this to the English speaker. This phenomenon, of words lexicalized as representations of specific sounds, is common to all languages. Such words, like *krachen* ('to crash'), *plumpsen* ('to fall heavily', 'to flop'), *zischen* ('to hiss'), *platschen* ('to splash'), as well as the corresponding interjections *krach!* ('crash!'), *plumps!* ('flop!'), *zisch!* ('hiss!'), *platsch!* ('splash'), are referred to as **onomatopoeic** words.

The examples above illustrate two different types of iconicity. In example (35), the repeated sounds echo a repetitive movement and in

(40) sounds echo sounds. Examples such as (35) are sometimes referred to as **secondary iconicity** and examples such as (40) as **primary iconicity**. We can define primary iconicity as the direct mirroring of content in the form of the language structures, whereas secondary iconicity is an indirect mirroring, such as sounds representing not sounds but movement, as in (35), a distinction also made by Lyons (1977). We could also say that secondary iconicity is in a sense metaphorical iconicity: content is mirrored not by something resembling it but by something related to what resembles it. What relates the sounds in (35) to the movement they represent is the element of repetition. This could be seen as an interaction of the Principle of Metaphor given in (29) with the Principle of Iconicity given in (39).

Examples (35) and (40) both show the Principle of Iconicity interacting at the phonological level, to affect the sounds chosen to represent a particular cognitive content. However, iconicity can interact with other levels of the language, too, notably the syntax. An instance of primary syntactic iconicity would be Handke's (1969: 134) final line:

(42) Plötzlich, mitten im letzten Satz...
      Suddenly, in the middle of the final sentence...

which is an unfinished sentence and therefore directly echoes the meaning represented. In the following stanzas from the poem 'Worte' by Karl Krolow (Conrady 1977: 918), there is substantial repetition of VPs:

(43) Aber die Namen bleiben
      Im Ohre nur ein Gesumm
      Wie von Zikaden und Bienen,
      Kehren ins Schweigen um.

      Vokale – geringe Insekten,
      Unsichtbar über die Luft,
      Fallen als Asche nieder,
      Bleiben als Quittenduft.

      But the names remain
      As a buzzing in the ear
      The sound of bees and cicadas
      Turning to silence.

      Vowels – redundant insects
      Float in the air unseen
      Fall and settle as ashes
      Remain as the scent of quinces.

In these two stanzas the repeated VPs are:

(44)   die Namen bleiben
       [die Namen] kehren ins Schweigen um

       [Vokale] fallen als Asche nieder
       [Vokale] bleiben als Quittenduft

in three of which the subject, written in square brackets, can only be
retrieved by recourse to the Gapping Principle (see section 7.2 above).
The repetition of the simple unembedded VP structures, in combination
with both repetition at the phonological level in metre and rhyme and
repetition at the semantic level in words for insects (*Zikaden, Bienen,
Insekten*) and words for insubstantial or abstract entities (*Namen,
Gesumm, Schweigen, Vokale, Luft, Asche, Duft*), could be interpreted as
echoing the persistence of words, the topic of the poem. The lexical
items chosen – insects, insubstantial entities and the adjectives *gering*
and *unsichtbar* – echo their lack of substance. The syntactic iconicity
could here be regarded as secondary: repetition represents persistence,
while the lexical repetition both does this and adds the semantic connotations of the words themselves.

Typographical iconicity (called 'graphological' by Fischer 1999) occurs when the meaning of an utterance is reinforced in its typographical
presentation. It is common in advertising, where examples of the type:

(45)   a.   für GROSS und klein
            for big and little

       b.   das richtige **Fett** macht dünn
            the right fats make you thin

are fairly common, but uncommon in poetry, where its effects are not
usually subtle enough. It is perhaps more common in recent German advertising than it is in English, perhaps because the latter tends to prefer
word-play, a type of joke based on lexical ambiguity (see section 7.8).

7.7   Compression

Compression is often felt to be a typical characteristic of certain types of
text, mainly literary or journalistic ones (see Levin 1971). If a linguistic
structure is compressed, some elements have been missed out, but their
presence is assumed in order to make a complete interpretation of the
structure possible. The following sentences all exhibit compression:

(46)   Rudi kaufte eine Zeitung und Julia ein Buch
       Rudi bought a newspaper and Julia a book

(47)   Wertvolles Gemälde gefunden
       Valuable painting found

(48)   'Blumen' ist ein Kaugummigedicht
       'Flowers' is a chewing-gum poem

(46) is another instance of gapping. We interpret the sentence as meaning

(49)   Rudi kaufte eine Zeitung und Julia kaufte ein Buch
       Rudi bought a newspaper and Julia bought a book

As discussed in section 7.2, we can only recover the verb *kaufte* if it is identical to a verb earlier in the sentence. Thus (46) is not in fact grammatically deviant. Grammatical deviation was shown in example (11) above, repeated here:

(50)   Er nahm Abstand, dann den Zug und fuhr nach Hause
       He distanced himself, took the train, and returned home

where the gapping results in the deletion of a verb which cannot be recovered. However, (46), though not grammatically deviant, is compressed in that it requires the reader to supply the missing element *kaufte*.

(47) is an example of the type of compressed expression typical of a newspaper headline, and, in contrast to (46), is ungrammatical. There are a number of elements missing: an article and an auxiliary verb are required in order to render the sentence grammatically acceptable and additional information in the text may reveal the agent of the verb *finden*, and further details about the painting. The meaning assigned to (47) may, for example, be:

(51)   Das Gemälde, das 1978 von der Heinrich-Galerie in Berlin gestohlen wurde,
       ist in Frankfurt von einer Studentin gefunden worden
       The painting which was stolen from the Heinrich Gallery in Berlin has
       been found by a student in Frankfurt

Usually, in cases such as these, the additional information which forms part of the interpretation of the utterance is found in the text which follows the headline. Because the reader knows that headlines are generally disambiguated, he or she will be tempted to read the article (and, of course, to buy the newspaper in order to do so).

In (48) the compound *Kaugummigedicht*, already encountered above in (24), is compressed in that it does not express the relationship between the two elements. From the discussion in section 7.4 we know that this is a metaphorical compound and that therefore the relationship between the two words is one of similarity; thus the compound may be interpreted, along the lines suggested in (28) above, as:

(52) Gedicht, das Kaugummi ähnlich ist
      Poem which is like chewing-gum

In (46)–(49), something must be added to the elements actually present in the structure in order to assign it the correct interpretation. The ability of language to compress structure in this way is not language-specific. We can thus formulate a universal principle:

(53) *Principle of Compression*

      Use linguistic structures which may be assigned an interpretation which contains more elements than the structure itself.

This principle will interact with the grammar of German to give rise to both grammatically acceptable structures of the type in (46) and (48) and ungrammatical ones such as (47), (50) and the example given earlier in (17), repeated here:

(54) Geht in die Stadt;
      kauft sich Tee und Brot
      Goes into town;
      buys tea and bread

The way the principle works in individual languages will be subject to some variation. German, for example, as we saw in chapter 3, favours compounding, and compounds such as *Kaugummigedicht* will therefore be very common. In other languages such as French, such compounds will be far less common, because compounding in general is not used as frequently. Structures such as (50), though reasonably common in English, will tend to be more frequent in German because of the relative frequency of idiomatic collocations of the type *Abstand nehmen*, sometimes called *Funktionsverbgefüge* (see chapter 6).

7.8   Ambiguity

If we look again at an example similar to that in (47), of a type commonly found in newspaper headlines, it will be clear that there may in fact be a variety of interpretations which can be assigned:

(55)   Gemälde gefunden
       Painting found

This may be interpreted exactly as in (51). But there are many other possible interpretations, for example:

(56)   Ein Gemälde von Picasso wurde in einer Scheune gefunden
       A painting by Picasso was found in a barn

(57)   Jedes Jahr werden zwischen fünfzig und einhundert Gemälde, die durch Diebstahl von Galerien in Deutschland verschwunden sind, auf Märkten in Spanien und Frankreich gefunden
       Every year between fifty and one hundred paintings, which have disappeared as a result of theft from galleries in Germany, are found at markets in Spain and France

We cannot tell whether *Gemälde* in (55) is singular or plural, nor whether *gefunden* is part of a verb in the past or present passive. These details depend on the context of the utterance, just as do further details such as agent and location. (For a further brief discussion of a headline, see chapter 9, section 9.1.)

The same is true of the compound which we have already seen several times:

(58)   Kaugummigedicht
       chewing-gum poem

We said in section 7.4 that this was a metaphorical compound, in which there was assumed to be a relation of similarity between the two elements of the compound *Kaugummi* and *Gedicht*. But in fact this need not be the case; the following are also possible interpretations:

(59)   a.   Gedicht über Kaugummi
            Poem about chewing-gum

       b.   Gedicht, das als Reklame für Kaugummi dient
            Poem used as an advertisement for chewing-gum

It is in fact a characteristic of any utterance which is compressed that it can be assigned a number of different meanings. In other words, it is **ambiguous**. Because compression involves assigning elements in a semantic interpretation which are not present in the structure, there is always in principle the possibility of assigning a variety of different elements. Every compressed utterance is therefore ambiguous. We define the Principle of Ambiguity as follows:

(60) *Principle of Ambiguity*

Use structures which may be assigned more than one semantic representation.

Sometimes, as suggested above, though utterances are in principle ambiguous, they are disambiguated in the context in which they occur. If the compound *Kaugummigedicht* occurs in the following text its meaning is clear:

(61) Der Kritiker Peter Metzler nannte Hundekahls Gedicht *Ein Sommer hinter Glas* 'ein typisches Kaugummigedicht', weil es angeblich für jeden Leser etwas anderes bedeute
Critic Peter Metzler called Hundekahl's poem Ein Sommer hinter Glas 'a typical chewing-gum poem', because supposedly it meant something different for every reader

Here the phrase 'für jeden Leser etwas anderes' can be seen as equivalent to *Kaugummi* and thus the relation to be supplied is clearly one of similarity. Such structures can be said to be locally ambiguous, but can be given a non-local or context-dependent interpretation, the elements of which are found elsewhere in the context of the structure.

Compressed utterances are by their very nature ambiguous, as we have seen, but ambiguity does not always rest on compression. Some structures are in themselves ambiguous. Consider the following text:

(62) Die Züge ihres Charakters, mild und reizvoll, ja fast zu brav dargestellt, sind im Hintergrund des Stücks immer präsent

The sentence could be interpreted in either of the following ways:

(63) a. The traits of her mild and pleasant character, almost too decorous in presentation, are always there in the background of the play

b. The traits of her character, presented in a mild and pleasant, indeed in almost too decorous a way, are always there in the background of the play

This ambiguity rests on the fact that most adjectives in German can also be used as adverbs. We cannot therefore tell whether the words *mild* ('mild') and *reizvoll* ('pleasant') in (62) are adjectives describing *Züge* ('traits') or adverbs qualifying *dargestellt* ('presented'). There is, in other words, a systematic ambiguity in the German language between the categories of adjective and adverb. The ambiguity is not resolved in this particular text because the participle *dargestellt* is not given its auxiliary. If it were, then its presence might make it clear whether *mild* and *reizvoll* were adjectives or adverbs. In

(64) a. Die Züge ihres Charakters werden mild und reizvoll, ja fast zu brav
          dargestellt . . .

or

      b. Die Züge ihres Charakters, die mild und reizvoll, ja fast zu brav
          dargestellt werden . . .

there can be no doubt that both *mild* and *reizvoll* as well as *brav* qualify
dargestellt werden and are therefore adverbs, not adjectives qualifying
the woman's personal attributes.

This type of ambiguity will depend upon the particular language. German is ambiguous with regard to adjectives and adverbs whereas English, for example, is not. Knowledge of the stylistic possibilities of
ambiguity in German will include knowledge both of the general principle given in (60) and of those specific aspects of the German language
conducive to ambiguity.

The ambiguity we have thus far discussed is structural, but ambiguity
can also be lexical. Although the phenomenon of lexical ambiguity is
present in all languages, clearly there will be different words which are
ambiguous in different languages, a fact which causes difficulties for
translators when an author has chosen a word which is ambiguous in
the source language but whose target-language equivalent is not. All the
following words are potentially ambiguous in German:

(65) Schloss   Karte   Mutter   See

Schloss, usually considered an example of **homonymy** (several words with
the same form), can either be a word meaning a lock or a word meaning
a castle. As it is in both cases neuter, articles or agreement of adjectives
will not disambiguate the word; this is only possible from semantic clues
in its context. *Karte* is always feminine, and it can mean a map, a menu,
a playing-card or a greetings card. This multiplicity of meaning is referred
to as polysemy; unlike homonymy, which involves different words which
merely look alike, **polysemy** is used when one word has a number of
related but distinct meanings. *Karte* is thus more ambiguous than 'card'
in English, which can mean a playing-card or greetings card but not a
menu, and, again, can only be disambiguated in context. *Mutter*, which
is always feminine, means a mother or a nut, as in nut and bolt. And *See*
is masculine if it means a lake, feminine if it means a sea. It can thus only
be ambiguous in certain utterances, such as:

(66) von See zu See
      from sea to sea/from lake to lake

where there are no articles to make it clear which of the words is meant. What is important to note here is that, as with all the other principles we have considered, though the Principle of Ambiguity is universal, the means by which it is realized in German will not only be specific to the German language in terms of ambiguous structures or categories but also dependent upon which lexical items have more than one meaning.

Lexical ambiguity is the basis for word-play, which results when the two (or more, though it is usually two) meanings of a word are brought into play simultaneously. Word-play is far more common in English, where it is especially used in Christmas cracker jokes ('Where was Solomon's temple? – On his forehead') than in German, though it is difficult to say why. One reason could be that the greater number of markers for gender on nouns and for forms of the verb make lexical ambiguity more difficult to sustain in a syntactic structure in German.

7.9 Cohesion

According to Halliday and Hasan (1976: 4), cohesion is a semantic concept: 'it refers to relations of meaning that exist within the text, and that define it as a text'. Relations of cohesion are text-forming, according to this view, but not structural in the sense in which we speak of the structure of a sentence.

We shall use the term **cohesion** here with a slightly different meaning from that given it by Halliday and Hasan. We shall assume, as they do, that cohesion is a relation which links elements within a text, but we shall assume it can operate at all levels and is not necessarily only a semantic entity. In example (35), repeated here as:

(67) Mühlen aus Wind
      mahlen Sandmehl
      Mills made of wind
      grind the grains of sand

the relationship between *Wind* and *Sand*-, traditionally called half-rhyme or consonance (see section 7.5), in which the initial consonants and the vowels differ but the final consonant cluster (the coda; see chapter 5) is identical, is not a semantic one but is a purely formal repetition. Nevertheless, it adds to what Halliday and Hasan call the **texture** of the poem, that is, its nature as a text which is held together by linked units, in this case of sound. This, in our view, is an instance of cohesion.

Cohesion, then, is defined as contextual linking or the linking of elements within the same text – we could say that one element is in the context of the other – by a variety of means which may be semantic, syntactic, lexical or phonological, or may relate to typographical representation.

Whereas cohesion, being a semantic entity, is, in Halliday and Hasan's terms, a relation which allows elements to be semantically interpreted, in our terms it may also allow an element to be interpreted as part of a pattern. It relates to the principle of repetition mentioned in section 7.5 but goes beyond this, because it may also include such things as pro-nominal reference or answers to questions. A few instances are given in the following text:

(68) Peter schickte Maria neunzehn rote Rosen. Er wußte, daß sie Blumen besonders mochte, aber er hat lange überlegt, ob Rosen oder Tulpen. Neunzehn war für ihn so etwas wie eine magische Zahl: Maria war gerade neunzehn geworden, ihre Hausnummer war neunzehn und am neunzehnten Februar würde sie ihn endlich besuchen.
Peter sent Maria nineteen red roses. He knew that she was very fond of flowers, but he had thought for a long time about whether to send roses or tulips. Nineteen was for him something of a magic number: Maria was just nineteen, she lived at house number nineteen and on the nineteenth of February she would finally visit him.

In this short text, the use of pronouns is one of the means of achieving cohesion. *Er* in the second sentence refers to Peter, *ihre* and *sie* towards the end of the text refer to Maria. The pronouns can only be interpreted by reference to the proper names which precede them. Lexical cohesion is exhibited by *Rosen*, *Blumen* and *Tulpen* in that there is a relationship of hyponymy between *Rosen* and *Blumen* and between *Tulpen* and *Blumen* and of co-hyponymy between *Rosen* and *Tulpen* (see chapter 6). *Neunzehn* is repeated four times and relates semantically to *Zahl* and *-nummer*. There is also alliteration in *rote Rosen* and *Blumen besonders*, and assonance in *magische Zahl . . . war gerade*.

These are all clearly defined relationships of different types, and they occur in texts of all types. It appears, though, that the knowledge of such relationships is unlikely to form part of the native speaker's grammatical knowledge of German because it is knowledge about how to form texts. We thus assume that there is an additional Principle of Cohesion, which may be formulated thus:

(69) *Principle of Cohesion*

Link elements above the level of sentence in order to create a text by using semantic, lexical or phonological links, or links in the typographical repre-sentation of the words.

It may be that we would want to subsume the Principle of Repetition, given in (38), under this one, on the view that repetition is simply a means of creating contextual links between elements. We leave this question open here. As with the other principles given, it will be noticed that this principle must again be universal in nature and application. There is nothing specifically German about using pronouns or repeating lexical items; it is the exact form of the pronouns and other items and structures which is specific to the German language.

7.10   Style and Choice

In the preceding sections we have examined a set of stylistic principles which would appear to be universal in nature. One reason for supposing that they are universal is that there are many studies of such phenomena in other languages and indeed throughout history. Ricoeur (1975) is, for example, a well-known study of metaphor in French, Stanford (1939) an important examination of ambiguity in Ancient Greek, and Nänny (1985) a study of iconicity in English. Furthermore, the principles are extremely general in nature; they contain no information about their particular syntactic or lexical manifestation which might render them language-specific. In this sense they are similar to many of the principles of syntax, morphology or phonology mentioned in earlier chapters. Like these, they form part of a German native speaker's universal linguistic knowledge. But linguistic knowledge also includes an understanding of how they interact with language-specific rules – the rules of compounding or agreement, for example – in order to give rise to the specific structures of German.

At the beginning of this chapter we noted that some views of style regard it as a matter of choice on the part of the author. We must return to this question here, because a view of style as choice may appear incompatible with the notion that style is guided by principles in much the same way as is phonology or morphology. However, it is not really incompatible. There are basically three ways in which the style of texts can be seen as a matter of linguistic choice. The first is:

(i)   Stylistic principles differ from many other principles of the language in that they are optional; their application is a matter of choice on the speaker's or writer's part.

This is not true of a syntactic principle such as the Extended Projection Principle mentioned in section 7.2; this principle is not optional: clauses must have a subject and if a subject is not present in any structure then an empty category (called PRO) fills that position. This does not apply to, say, the Principle of Repetition in the same way. Repetition may be desirable in a poem, as rhyme or alliteration, as syntactic parallelism or semantic reiteration, but it may equally well be absent, indeed it may be avoided in other types of text. Reiners (1990: 28), for example, instructs us

(70)   Nur wenn ein Wort besonders betont ist, dürfen Sie es wiederholen.

He is, of course, speaking here specifically of non-literary texts. Stylistic principles, then, can either be implemented or not, according to the speaker's choice and the type of text in question. In fact, there does appear to be a parallel to this in phonology. In the connected speech phenomena discussed in chapter 4, section 4.7, assimilation may or may not occur for reasons that are not well-understood. However, it is only parallel in that it is optional; there is no reason to suppose that a desire for a particular effect plays any role in the phonological phenomena in question.

But stylistic choice is not just a question of the optional nature of stylistic principles. There is another way in which style can be seen as a matter of choice:

(ii)   The language of a particular text and thus, in a broad sense of the term, the style of a text, is not only the result of stylistic principles but also of choice from the resources provided by the grammar and lexis of the language in question.

A large proportion of the characteristics of any text will not be the result of stylistic principles. If we take a poem by a German poet who is generally considered to use syntactically deviant language, whose deviance lies in its compressed and ambiguous nature, we find sentences such as:

(71)   Es war da
       ein anderes Haus

                                                        (Meister 1979: 20)

       There was
       another house

Example (71) does not show evidence of any of the stylistic principles discussed here. This is in fact exactly what we would expect, given that stylistic principles interact with the grammar of the language, and are optional. The element of choice here is exactly that present in any standard use of German: *Haus* instead of words with similar meanings such as *Gebäude* or *Wohnhaus*, and the construction *Es war da* ... instead of *Da war* ... , both of which are possible and mean the same thing. Thus, because the overall style of a text results from both the implementation of stylistic principles and the implementation of other, non-stylistic principles of grammar, the stylistic choice at a speaker's or writer's disposal is in many cases just a question of choice among the normal resources of the language.

A third element of choice is in the implementation of stylistic principles:

(iii) Stylistic principles allow a choice among the available language structures.

Applying, for example, the Principle of Repetition may affect lexical choice, as in example (36) above, the first three sentences of which are repeated here:

(72) Wenn sie wert legen auf den guten Geschmack, kaufen Sie Brot. Brot isst
      man jeden Tag, bei jeder Gelegenheit. Brot ist gesund
      If good taste is important to you, buy bread. Bread is something you eat
      every day, on any occasion. Bread is good for you

Here the word *Brot* has been repeated, instead of using a pronoun to replace it. But the principle could equally well, as we saw earlier, interact with the phonology or the syntax of German to give repeated sounds or syntactic structures. If this principle interacts with the rules of compounding discussed in chapter 3, it may also give rise to particular types of compound, such as:

(73) a. blei-blau   b. Honig-Haare   c. winter-silber
          lead-blue   *honey hair*   *winter silver*

which contain alliteration (73a and b) and assonance (73c) and are formed according to the rules of compounding in German. Compounds which violate these rules are not acceptable, just as they would not be if there were no stylistic interaction:

(74) a. ?schwimmschwärmen   b. *brotbei   c. *hinterunter

The first, (74a), is a VV compound and is at best marginal (as the ? indicates), the NP compound (74b) and the PP compound (74c) are both unacceptable because compounds with a head of category P are ruled out for the reasons given in chapter 3, section 3.2.3.

Choice is thus an important element in style, but it can no more account for the presence of some structures and the absence of others than syntactic choice can account for the presence of subjects in sentences. Indeed, it is only by assuming that a native German speaker's knowledge of language contains both universal stylistic principles and an understanding of how to implement them in interaction with the grammar of German, that the issue of stylistic choice becomes a meaningful one.

7.11 Further Reading

For views on what makes a text literary, see Eagleton (1983), Boase-Beier (1987a), Fabb and Durant (1990) or Fabb (1997).

On the nature of style, see Fowler (1996), Freeborn (1996) or Thornborrow and Wareing (1998). Sanders (1973: 13ff) gives a useful overview of the various approaches, concentrating on studies of German. Other books which focus on the stylistics of German are Sandig (1986), Reiners (1990), Sanders (1986), Sowinski (1972). A good general work on stylistics is Short (1996).

Garvin (1964) is an important early collection of translated articles from the Prague Linguistic Circle. Later articles written in the same tradition can be found in Odmark (1979).

Vickers (1970) provides a sense of how figures of traditional rhetoric have influenced the way we view style today; see also Freeborn (1996: ch. 6). Brooks and Penn Warren (1950) is a now somewhat dated but nevertheless highly interesting view of the place of rhetoric in the production of texts.

There are numerous books on metaphor. Ortony (1979) or Abraham (1975) are good introductions. Lakoff and Johnson (1980) and Lakoff and Turner (1989) both present a view of metaphor as part of everyday communication, and both these works and Steen (1994) consider metaphor as part of human cognition, that is, the way that we know and perceive reality.

Repetition is discussed by Kiparsky (1973) as central to the notion of style. There is also a discussion in Sowinski (1972) and there are many treatments of particular aspects of repetition such as syntactic and lexical parallelism (Fabb 1997: ch. 6) and rhyme (Freeborn 1996).

Iconicity has been studied extensively, and is mentioned in general works on style, such as those by Freeman (1976) or Posner (1980). The most comprehensive treatment of iconicity to date is to be found in two collections of papers, Nänny and Fischer (1999) and Fischer and Nänny (2000). There are few studies dealing specifically with iconicity in German texts: Fischer (1999) is an exception.

Ambiguity has been widely studied. Probably the most famous study is Empson (1930), which, though obviously dated and also not easy to read, is well worth a look. Su (1994) is an interesting study of lexical ambiguity. Most of the general books on stylistics mentioned above have sections on ambiguity.

Apart from Halliday and Hasan (1976) mentioned in section 7.9, cohesion is also dealt with by Toolan (1998: ch. 2).

EXERCISES

1   Using the poem in example (43), note all the metaphors. Decide which of these are examples of metaphor proper and which are similes or instances of metonymy.

2   In a German newspaper or journal, find an advertisement and note all the different types of repetition it contains, and whether these are repetitions of sound (such as rhyme or alliteration), of structure, or of actual words or morphemes.

3   Make up a headline for the text in example (37), using compression but ensuring that the headline can be understood by reading the text.

4   Produce a translation into English of the two lines in example (40), trying to re-create its stylistic features, and thus improving on Bulwer Lytton's attempt in (41). You might need a dictionary to get the exact sense of the words in (40), but you will find that a good translation often has to deviate from the exact sense.

CHAPTER EIGHT

Historical Background

8.1 Preliminaries

As we noted in chapter 1, it is possible to consider German as the product of historical development. This historical development does not form part of the native-speaker knowledge of a speaker of modern German. Indeed, we have seen instances of former knowledge which has now disappeared; in section 3.4 on morphological productivity and in section 8.4 below we suggest that it is highly unlikely that speakers of modern German would associate *mögen* and *Macht*, especially as the semantic relationship one would expect between a verb and a noun has changed since OHG, and despite the fact that the *t*-ending appears in the straightforward pair *fahren – Fahrt*. In modern German the nominal suffix *-t* is no longer productive and mostly not recognized as such by native speakers. Nevertheless, the historical dimension may inform the linguist as to which is the most likely of competing analyses; in chapter 2, section 2.4 we noted that Indo-European languages had an SOV order in sentences which could be said to have been inherited only partially by modern German. This suggests that classifying German as an SOV language has some justification.

All languages change through time, partly because of internal, purely linguistic pressures and partly because of external, social changes. To some extent linguistic change can be seen as a consequence of generations of children not acquiring exactly the target linguistic system of their parents or carers. Add to this the social pressure of accommodating to one's peers (rather than one's elders), who may be from different social groups or different geographical areas, and change is inevitable. In more recent, literate times there is also the pressure of standardization, in particular in the written form of languages, so that the range of varieties increases from just a number of local dialects to the many overlapping social and regional dialects we find today in a language like German (see chapter 9; Barbour and Stevenson 1990). We shall deal with the internal and external aspects separately.

There are many detailed treatments of the history of German (see section 8.8) and we shall not attempt to reproduce such approaches here. As a framework for the ensuing discussions a basic outline of the position of German is necessary to show its relationship to the other languages of Europe and give a rough timescale of developments. German is an Indo-European language; it is related to the Slavonic languages (Russian, Polish, Czech), the Celtic languages (Welsh, Irish, Scots Gaelic, Breton), the Romance languages (French, Italian, Spanish, Portuguese, Romanian, all descended from Latin) and Greek, besides many of the languages of northern India such as Hindi and Panjabi. Within this large family there is a subgroup known as the Germanic languages, which share common linguistic characteristics. This family, too, is subdivided into further subgroups: North Germanic (the Scandinavian languages), West (English, Dutch, German), East (Gothic; died out). These groups are determined by linguistic characteristics, though this division is not an uncontentious issue. The linguistic unity of West Germanic is questionable; for this reason we give a few examples from the North Germanic languages. They have only two genders, place the definite article as a clitic after the noun, for example, *egget* 'the egg', and have a common stock of characteristic lexical items, exemplified by Norwegian *barn* 'child', *elv* 'river', *fjell* 'mountain', *smør* 'butter', *by* 'town'. (Note that some of these words have been imported into English via the Viking colonization of parts of the British Isles in the ninth century, for example, *bairn* in the North of England and Scotland, *fell* in the Lake District, and the ending *-by* in many place-names. The word *elv* appears in Germany as the River Elbe.) Trask (1996: 176–87) gives an overview of the relationships between languages with a diagram of the Germanic group on p. 186.

It is on the West Germanic group that our attention will be focused, as we examine how modern German developed from it. The division into different historical periods is conventional and based on certain linguistic features disappearing or developing, but such periods are only rough guides and cannot be considered to be determined by clear breaks. Change continues without interruption, so the periods effectively merge into one another and overlap is normal. The rough time periods of development for the language are as follows: 700–1100 Old High German (OHG), a linguistic break with the non-High German varieties; 1100–1400 Middle High German (MHG); 1400 onwards New High German (NHG); we shall retain the term 'modern German' for the language of the twentieth and present centuries. In the rest of the chapter some of the changes which underlie this division will be discussed in some detail.

Although languages change and children do not usually sound exactly like their parents, the changes are not just haphazard, but are subject to general principles. In the following sections a few of these principles will be considered in relation to German at different levels of structure: phonology, morphology, syntax and semantics. The phonology of earlier periods of any language can only be reconstructed. Since there are only written texts up until the very end of the nineteenth century, historical linguists have to use the interpretation of orthographic conventions, direct descriptions from contemporary commentators, rhyme, assonance and alliteration in poetry and informed guesswork, involving a thorough knowledge of phonetics. Quite unrelated and distantly related languages can display very similar patterns of development, often at different periods of time. In addition, these phenomena can be found in language acquisition data. For example, assimilation of place of articulation, discussed in chapter 5, is found in many languages throughout their history: the Latin prefix *in-* assimilated to [im-] before bilabial-initial roots, as in *implicare* ('to involve'), and the Germanic prefix *ant-*, after having changed its vowel quality in an unstressed position, also assimilated to bilabial and labio-dental root-initials, as in *empfehlen, empfangen*. It is also the norm for children to acquire such assimilated forms first. It is often only later that the unassimilated forms are learned, when the spelling system is being acquired. (For comments with regard to this, see Lodge, 1981 on English, and Newton 1970 and Ferguson 1978 on Modern Greek, a language that has obligatory assimilation in certain circumstances.) Given the sort of phenomena we find in both acquisition data and historical development and given what we know about articulation, it is only to be expected that changes such as those just exemplified occur. Certainly, a change from, say, [b] to [l] or [n] to [x] would be very hard to explain and linguists would not expect to find such changes.

8.2 Phonology

We will exemplify phonological development with two important changes from the history of German, one consonantal and the other vocalic, from different periods. The former served to mark off High German and subsequently standard German from other varieties of Germanic. It is usually referred to as the High German sound shift because it differentiates High German from all other Germanic dialects. It took place over the period from AD 400 to 700. The simplest way to demonstrate that such a change took place is to compare modern standard German words with their non-German, related equivalents, for our purposes from English, and we shall show that there is a regular set of relationships. It is

Table 1 Phonological development

English sound	English	German	English	German	English	German
[p]	pound	Pfund	hop	hüpfen	hope	hoffen
[t]	ten	zehn	heat	Hitze	water	Wasser
[k]	can	*kann	bake	*backen	book	Buch

the voiceless stops of English that we take as a starting point. For the time being the examples are in ordinary orthography in table 1.

What are voiceless stops in English have as their German equivalents affricates or fricatives at the same place of articulation. Note that the asterisked items do not fit the pattern, since we would expect to find [kx] not [k]. We shall return to this below. In the case of the predicted forms it depends on the phonological environment whether there is an affricate or a fricative: in syllable-initial position or when the consonant was originally (in Proto-Germanic) geminate (double) we find the affricate, otherwise it is a fricative. The gemination word-internally has sometimes given rise to related pairs of words, for instance, PGmc *atjan > essen* 'to eat' and PGmc *attjan > ätzen* 'to etch' (that is, 'to eat into' as of acid; the asterisk in such cases is used to indicate reconstructed forms).

This sound change did not spread through the Germanic dialects at an even rate. For some reason the three stops were affected variably. The reflection of this in modern German dialects is that, for instance, some areas have *ich, machen, Dorf*, but *dat, Appel, Pund* (parts of West-Central Germany to the west of Frankfurt), others have *ich, machen, Dorf, Fund, das*, but *Appel, Kind* (East-Central Germany), while yet others have the expected system with [kx] in *Kind* (written *Chind* in dialect orthography; Switzerland, for example). The consonantal changes represented in table 8.1 are found in a large area encompassing Würzburg, Nuremberg and Munich.

The way in which this sound shift has spread in the dialects of Germany has led to a three-way division: Low German with no sound shift; Middle or Central German with some of the shifts, but no [pf] or [kx]; and Upper German with all the shifts except there is no [kx] in the northern area of Upper German, as just mentioned. The standard language coincides with this last area as far as these consonants are concerned. Since standardization has to do with social and political factors rather than linguistic ones, the choice of dialect(s) that form the basis of the standard language is a product of historical events and development, not linguistic consistency. Despite the fact that considerable prestige is accorded the standard variety of any language, there are no *linguistic* reasons to support this. Initial [k] is no better than initial [kx]. It is the

place of the Upper Franconian dialects with initial [k] in the development of a unified written language that determined its elevation to the
standard norm in such words as *kann* and *Kuchen*. We discuss the
process of standardization in section 8.8 below. The basic point we
are making here is that the differential development of the voiceless
stops of the West Germanic dialects helps to determine modern dialect
differences.

Let us now consider the general mechanism of the change in phonetic
terms. The phenomenon we see here as part of the High German sound
shift is usually referred to as **lenition**, which we discussed in chapter 5,
section 5.8.2. Although this is not a technical phonetic term, it can be
described in articulatory terms as an increase in the opening between the
articulators concerned (see Lass 1984: 177–83). A zero opening is a
stop; if the closure phase is released slowly, the result is an affricate (stop
+ fricative); if the closure is not made complete at the point of articulation, the result is a fricative. At the alveolar ridge, for instance, this gives
a development as follows: [t] > [ts] > [s]. This kind of development is
found in many languages, historically as well as synchronically (for more
examples, see Lass 1984). A striking parallel with the High German
sound shift is to be found in the present-day Liverpool accent: where
standard English (and most other accents) has initial [p], [t], [k], Liverpool has [pɸ], [ts], [kx], and in other positions in the word [ɸ], [s], [x]
or [ç] (velar or palatal depending on the preceding vowel), respectively.
So *pan* is [pɸan], *ten* [tsɛn], *water* [wɔsə], *brick* [bɹɪç], and so on. (The
difference between Liverpool [pɸ] and German [pf] is only slight. Many
languages associate bilabial stops and labiodental fricatives; the phonological place feature used to cover both places of articulation is [labial];
see above, chapter 5, section 5.3.)

The vocalic changes affect the MHG vowels *ie, uo* and *üe*, usually
assumed to be the diphthongs [iə], [uə] and [yə], respectively, and the
high monophthongs *î, û* and *iu*. (The circumflex is a modern convention
to indicate length in the orthography; *iu* represents [yː].) If we compare
the MHG and modern German versions of the same words, we find the
developments in (1).

(1) MHG bieten [biətən]   NHG bieten [biːtən]
     MHG fuoz [fuəʂ]   NHG Fuß [fuːs]
     MHG müede [myədə]   NHG müde [myːdə]
     MHG wîz [wiːʂ]   NHG weiß [vaɪs]
     MHG hûs [huːs]   NHG Haus [haʊs]
     MHG hiute [hyːtə]   NHG heute [hɔɪtə]

Note that the alveolar fricative from Germanic [t] and the original
Germanic [s] were not identical until the end of the medieval period.

Although the exact phonetic realization is not known, the two were never rhymed in classical MHG poetry. The modern convention is to write a hooked *z* for Germanic [t], which we have not followed for typographical reasons. In the phonetic transcription we have used [ʂ] to indicate that it was different from the [s] of *hûs*, for example.

The three MHG diphthongs have monophthongized and the three long high monophthongs have diphthongized. What we must note here is that the monophthongs must have become diphthongs before the diphthongs monophthongized; if it had been the other way round, then *all* the instances of [iː], [uː] and [yː] would have become [aɪ], [aʊ] and [ɔɪ], respectively, so that *bieten* and *wîz* would have developed along the same lines. In addition, MHG had three other diphthongs *ei*, *ou* and *öu*, usually interpreted as [ei], [ou] and [øy], respectively, which fell together with the modern reflexes of *î*, *û* and *iu*. Thus, we have the examples in (2).

(2)   MHG beizen [beiʂən]   NHG beißen [baɪsən]
      MHG ouge [ougə]   NHG Auge [aʊgə]
      MHG fröude [frøydə]   NHG Freude [fʀɔɪdə]

The vowel changes that set off modern standard German from MHG can be summed up in (3).

(3)   MHG ie   → NHG [iː]
      MHG uo   → NHG [uː]
      MHG üe   → NHG [yː]
      MHG ei ⎫
             ⎬ → NHG [aɪ]
      MHG î ⎭
      MHG ou ⎫
             ⎬ → NHG [aʊ]
      MHG û ⎭
      MHG öu ⎫
             ⎬ → NHG [ɔɪ]
      MHG iu ⎭

Again, it is important to note that these changes did not affect all German dialects in the same way. Thus modern Alemannic speakers have diphthongs still in *bieten*, *gut* and *müde*, whereas Upper Franconian speakers in the north of the Upper German area have monophthongs in these words (see further chapter 9).

One further aspect of historical change can be seen from the developments given in (3), namely that distinctions made at one period in the history of a language may be lost at a later stage.

8.3 Umlaut

The next change we want to discuss crosses the boundaries of phonology and morphology, namely Umlaut. Phonetically, as we saw in chapter 5, Umlaut is the fronting of back vowels. Even in OHG this is what Umlaut was; throughout the history of German, Umlaut has always been the fronting of back vowels. Two things have changed, however: firstly, the phonetic exponents in particular lexical sets have changed, as with MHG *hûs* : *hiuser* versus NHG *Haus* : *Häuser*, and secondly, and perhaps more significantly, Umlaut is no longer predictable because the original phonetic trigger of the fronting has disappeared. If we go back to the earliest period of German, to the time just before the West Germanic group split off from the other groups, we find that there are many words which have *i* or *j* in the syllable following the stressed one. By the time OHG was being written down there is one instance where a vowel change is indicated in the spelling, when an *i/j* follows, namely, the alternation of short *a* and *e*, as in (4).

(4) OHG gast (NHG *Gast*)   plural: gesti (NHG *Gäste*)
     OHG nezzi (NHG *Netz*)   from PGmc *natjo

In some cases, even at this time, the trigger had disappeared: compare OHG *brennen* with Gothic *brannjan*. Although it was not indicated by the spelling, it is usually assumed that all the other back vowels in OHG were fronted by a following *i/j*, because of the vowels found in MHG and modern German. Consider the examples in (5).

(5) PGmc *horjan   NHG hören
     OHG oli   NHG Öl
     OHG lohhir   NHG Löcher
     OHG furi   NHG für

The sound changes in the high vowels discussed above have altered the distribution of the Umlaut pairs in the lexicon. (6) gives the development from OHG to MHG then to NHG of *Haus/Häuser*.

(6) OHG hus > MHG hus > NHG [haʊs]
     OHG husir > MHG hiuser > NHG [hɔɪzʌ]

The [uː]–[yː] pair now occurs in *Stuhl/Stühle*, for example, which had [uə] and [yə], respectively, in MHG.

By the end of the OHG period the unstressed *i* had been reduced to [ə] (usually spelled *e*) or had been lost completely in many dialects. (*j* had disappeared earlier in the OHG period.) This meant that by the MHG period the trigger for Umlaut was no longer there in a large number of cases. By this time, too, the Umlaut vowels were all represented in the spelling, for example, *hœren*, *drücken*, *mære*, etc. With the loss of the trigger Umlaut was no longer predictable: there is no phonological reason why the masculine monosyllabic noun *Stuhl* has an Umlaut stem vowel in the plural, whilst *Schuh*, also a masculine monosyllable, does not, even though it has the same stem vowel [uː]. In PGmc and the earliest phase of OHG Umlaut was a system of vowel harmony: the frontness of *i/j* spread to the stem vowel so that both stressed and unstressed vowels shared the same feature. In modern German, however, Umlaut is lexically determined, that is, it depends on the individual word or morpheme, not phonologically determined, even though it is phonetically regular. (For a detailed treatment of Umlaut in modern German, see Lieber 1981; also chapter 3 above.)

The result of the changes to the vowel system means that there are two forms of Umlaut: alternating and non-alternating. Strictly speaking, whatever the historical origin, if Umlaut is to be equated with the fronting of back vowels in modern German, then it is only the first type that should be interpreted as Umlaut, because it involves alternating morphological forms. Thus we can say that the stem vowels in *Füße* and *käme* are the Umlaut partners of the stem vowels in *Fuß* and *kam*. On the other hand, *für*, *Käse*, *Zyklus*, *Ökonomie* all have stressed front rounded vowels, but they are not partners of any back vowels: there is no **fur*, no **Kase*, and *Zyklus* and *Ökonomie* are loan words with spelling pronunciations.

8.4 Morphology

If we compare a number of OHG forms with their modern German equivalents, it can be seen that their morphological structure has changed in certain respects. In (7) and (8) we give the OHG and modern German equivalents of some nouns and verbs. The macron over a vowel, *ā*, indicates length in OHG.

(7)

	OHG	NHG	OHG	NHG
Nom, Acc	geba	⎫	gast	Gast
Gen	gebā	⎬ Gabe	gastes	Gast(e)s
Dat	gebu	⎭	gaste	Gast(e)
Nom, Acc	gebā	⎫	gesti	Gäste
Gen	gebōno	⎬ Gaben	gesto	Gäste
Dat	gebōm	⎭	gestim	Gästen

Nom	boto	Bote	lamb	Lamm
Acc	boton	⎫	lamb	Lamm
Gen	boten	⎬ Boten	lambes	Lamm(e)s
Dat	boten	⎭	lambe	Lamm(e)

Nom, Acc	boton	⎫	lembir	Lämmer
Gen	botōno	⎬ Boten	lembiro	Lämmer
Dat	botōm	⎭	lembirum	Lämmern

(8)

OHG	NHG	OHG	NHG
nimu	nehme	hōru	höre
nimis(t)	nimmst	hōris(t)	hörst
nimit	nimmt	hōrit	hört
nememēs	nehmen	hōremēs	hören
nemet	nehmt	hōret	hört
nemant	nehmen	hōrent	hören
nam	nahm	hōrta	hörte
nāmi	nahmst	hōrtōs(t)	hörtest
nam	nahm	hōrta	hörte
nāmum	nahmen	hōrtum	hörten
nāmut	nahmt	hōrtut	hörtet
nāmun	nahmen	hōrtun	hörten

Some of these changes have their origin in phonological ones. For instance, the reduction of the quality of post-tonic unstressed vowels to [ə] meant that some distinctions were lost, for instance *-un, -ōn, -an* in different verb forms reduced to an undifferentiated [-ən]. Similarly, the distinction between the past tense and the subjunctive II forms in regular verbs has been lost in modern German because of vowel reduction, as exemplified in (9).

(9)

Past	lebēta	⎫		lebētut	⎫	
		⎬ lebte			⎬ lebtet	
Subjc II	lebēti	⎭		lebētit	⎭	

On the other hand, morphological changes can come about for other reasons. One of the commonest is levelling out of stem-form alternations to produce regularity. There is pressure on morphological systems to avoid too many alternant forms of one and the same morpheme (see Bauer 1988a and Kiparsky 1982a). Levelling out can be exemplified in both verbs and in nouns.

The strong verbs in OHG and MHG had, in most cases, a different stem vowel in the singular of the past tense from in the plural. Consider the MHG examples in (10).

(10)   sanc sungen   half hulfen   gap gâben   streit striten

Some of the other irregular verbs followed this pattern, too, for example
ward, wurden. Towards the end of the medieval period the stem vowel
was levelled out in favour of either the singular or the plural and the
other stem disappeared. Note that a few verbs hung on to the distinction: *ward* was used in standard German into the eighteenth century but
is now restricted to poetry. It eventually gave way to the plural stem, in
this case: *wurde*. The modal verbs still retain two stem forms in the
present tense: *kann, können; darf, dürfen*. (The historical name for these
verbs is **preterite-presents**, meaning that their present tense forms are
like those of the past [= preterite] tense in the strong verbs.) An interesting parallel can be found in the English strong verbs, with dialect variation as to which form was retained, resulting in inconsistency in the
standard language, for example, *sang* but *stung*. The apparently irregular subjunctive II stems in German, such as *hülf-*, can be seen as deriving
from the old plural stem of the past tense, whereas the present-day past
tense has the old singular stem.

   Another verbal example relates to the small set of so-called mixed verbs,
for example, *bringen, denken*, which have different vowels in the present
and past stems but regular past endings. In MHG this class was much
larger and the relationship was in most cases between an Umlaut vowel in
the present and its non-Umlaut partner in the past, as exemplified in (11).

(11)   MHG hœren horte   NHG hören hörte
       MHG decken dahte   NHG decken deckte
       MHG füllen fulte   NHG füllen füllte
       MHG setzen sazte   NHG setzen setzte

It is interesting to note that the Umlaut forms with *e* were not spelled *ä*,
as one might expect, and it is these verbs in particular that have stayed in
this class in modern German. By NHG most of these verbs had levelled
out their stem vowels in favour of the present tense, thereby becoming
normal regular verbs, as indicated. The reason for the different stem
vowels relates to the triggering of Umlaut. If one considers the OHG
forms of *hören* in (8), one can see that there is an *i* in some of the
endings which triggered Umlaut in the stem which was levelled out to all
forms in MHG. On the other hand, the endings of the OHG past tense
did not have an Umlaut trigger, hence the non-Umlaut stem in MHG.

   In OHG Umlaut occurred in the noun stem of the case forms that had
endings with *i/j*, whereas no Umlaut occurred in those with other endings. Thus, a word like *oli* 'oil' in the nominative had an [ø]-type vowel
in the stem, but the genitive *oles* had the equivalent back vowel. Once
again, levelling out took place by the MHG period, usually in favour of

the nominative stem vowel. In other instances it was the other way round: no Umlaut in the nominative, Umlaut in the other cases, as in *kraft* 'power', genitive and dative *krefti*. In these feminine nouns the levelling out took place during the MHG period, although both *krefte* and *kraft* survived side by side for some time.

The other example from the noun system of German involves a sound change affecting short vowels in open syllables. In MHG these were lengthened, producing alternating long and short stem vowels in the paradigm of individual nouns. For instance, *tac* 'day' had a short vowel because it is a closed syllable, whereas *tages*, the genitive, has an open syllable which lengthened. In such cases the long vowel was extended to all case forms in the standard language, hence modern [taːk], though there is regional variation in this regard, for example, North German [tak] or [tax], but genitive [taːgəs] or [taːɣəs] (see further chapter 9).

A typical Germanic feature is provided by Ablaut (vowel gradation), although it was a feature of all the Indo-European languages, especially Latin, Ancient Greek and Sanskrit. In the Germanic languages it has been retained in the strong verbs and related nouns. Basically, Ablaut is the alternation of the stem vowel, as in the examples in (12).

(12)   ziehen   zog   Zug
        binden   band   gebunden
        gießen   goß   Guss
        helfen   half   geholfen   Hilfe

In modern German this is a relic phenomenon, that is, one that is no longer productive (see chapter 3), and outside the strong verbs it is difficult to know whether native speakers are aware of the historical connections. If the relationship in the meaning is straightforward, then one may reasonably assume that the morphological connection is recognized, for example, *singen – Gesang, binden – Band – Bund*. But to what extent do Germans see the connection between *ziehen* and *Zug* ('something that is pulled'; compare also English *draught*) or *Zucht* ('the process of bringing up', compare modern German *erziehen*)? In some cases the semantic disparity between forms connected in a straightforward way in earlier periods of the language means that some forms can no longer be considered morphologically related. For instance, *mögen* is historically related to *Macht*. The MHG equivalent *mugen* meant 'to have the ability or power (to do something)' and the present tense singular stem vowel was *a: mac*, modern *mag*. The *-t* ending created nouns and the fricative before [t] was regular; hence *Macht* meant and still means 'power'. But the modal verb has changed its meaning and the two are no longer connected. Similarly, *biegen* 'to bend' had a related noun, *Bucht* 'bay' (= 'something which is curved'), but the connection is not obvious to today's native speaker. The noun-forming suffixes *-t* and *-i* as in OHG *hôhi* 'height' (NHG *Höhe*) are examples of morphemes that were once productive but no longer are (see chapter 3).

8.5   Syntactic Changes

The basic system of syntactic structures of German has been in place since the beginning of OHG. It is only in details that the syntax has changed. With the loss of some of the morphological endings, which was caused largely by phonological changes in unstressed syllables, as exemplified in (7) above, a greater reliance on phrase order is evident. Unless the context of the previous text indicates otherwise, a sentence like (13) will be interpreted as having the following order: subject–verb–object.

(13)   Die Frau sah das Mädchen

In OHG and MHG *diu*, nominative, was distinct from *die*, accusative, so phrase order in such cases was not crucial. Nevertheless, the order of phrases in a German sentence is still more flexible than in English, which has lost its case system entirely.

Other changes include the development in MHG and subsequent loss of double negatives. As in many non-standard varieties of English (*I ain't got no money*) and in French (*ne . . . pas*), at least two negative words were used in MHG to indicate simple negation. The examples in (14) are from the poem *Iwein* by Hartmann von Aue.

(14)   und enlac niht langer dâ
       and lay there no longer

       Ichn gewan liebern tac nie
       I never had a more wonderful day

       ichn wil iu keine lüge sagen
       I do not want to tell you a lie

       ichn gehôrt . . . nie selhes niht gesagen
       I never heard such a thing

The negative clitics *n, en, ne* were sometimes prefixed to the verb, as in *enlac*, sometimes suffixed to the subject pronoun, as in *ichn*. Double negatives of this kind no longer occur in German, though many speakers use negative concord, that is, a negative in the main clause causes a negative in a dependent clause, as in (15).

(15) Das mache ich lieber nicht, bevor ich nicht von ihr gehört habe
      I'd rather not do that before I've heard from her

The modal verbs originally had no non-finite forms other than the infinitive and so did not form the perfect and pluperfect phrasal tenses. In MHG perfect infinitives were used with a simple modal form, as in (16).

(16) Ich kan gesehen haben
      Er solte gesehen haben
      Er müeste gekomen sîn

In early NHG the modern construction with two infinitives began to appear, as in (17).

(17) Ich habe sehen können
      Er hat sehen sollen
      Er hätte sehen müssen

After the new constructions were introduced the older ones took on a different meaning, as exemplified in (18).

(18) Er kann gesprochen haben
      He may have spoken

      Er hat sprechen können
      He was/has been able to speak

      Sie könnte es getan haben
      She might have done it

      Sie hätte es tun können
      She would have been able to do it

To demonstrate how little the syntax has changed, Priebsch and Collinson (1962: 384–5) reproduce a prose passage from the second half of the thirteenth century from West-Central Germany which is very close to a modern German text, as far as word order is concerned. In (19) we give an extract.

(19) Ein junger phaffe, einez richen mannes sun, gelobete unser vrowen sinen
      magetum und reine zu blibene, also daz er nummer wibes lip wolde gewaldik
      werden. Diz hilth er an den werken und och mith willen, aber sien herze waz
      vrolich und mit lichtekeit biegriffen. . . . Eines tages ershein ime unser vrowe
      und brachte einerhande spise, die waiz gar verwenet und gelustik zessene.

(The inconsistencies in spelling are a peculiarity of this particular scribe.)

The main changes in prose writing have been a gradual development of more explicit connections between sentences and the fixing of verb-final order in subordinate clauses. In OHG, and to some extent in MHG as well, sentences were placed next to one another with no explicit conjunction. This is usually referred to as **parataxis**. It is common in spoken language generally: consider the English example: *I'm sorry I'm late. I missed the bus*, where the causal connection is implicit. Sometimes the relationship is carried by a specific form in one of the sentences; Priebsch and Collinson (1962: 353) give an example of a negative conditional clause indicated by *en-* prefixed to a subjunctive verb form:

(20)   mich enmac getrœsten niemen, si entuoz.
        No one can comfort me, unless she does.

8.6   Lexical and Semantic Changes

Words change their meaning over time; some may disappear altogether, others are borrowed from other languages or from elsewhere in the lexicon to take their place. An example of the first kind is provided by PGmc. **guma*, OHG *gomo* ('man', which is cognate with Latin *homo*). This word disappeared during the OHG period, though it remains as an unidentifiable relic in modern German *Bräutigam*, 'bridegroom', literally 'man of the bride', the first part originally being the genitive, OHG *brutigomo*. Note that in English the equivalent component has been misidentified as *groom* in an attempt to make sense of it. This is called folk etymology and we will exemplify it from German below.

It is less easy to give general principles for semantic changes, though some general tendencies emerge (extension, reduction, amelioration, pejoration, metaphor, translation), but it is not always easy to see why particular changes occur, for instance, the loss of OHG *gomo*. The other point to make is that words do not, for the most part, change in isolation, but in relation to other words in the same lexical field. To illustrate this and some of the general tendencies referred to above, let us consider the semantic relationships involved in the development of MHG *maget/wîp/dierne/frouwe* to modern German *Magd/Weib/Dirne/Frau*.

In MHG *frouwe* meant a woman of rank to whom respect was due, a lady to whom men paid court. By today the meaning has been generalized to all women, an instance of extension. Such generalization can take place as part of a process of polite euphemism. The same kind of extension can be found in English, too: since it is impolite to suggest women are not 'ladies', the latter term is often used by many English speakers to refer politely to any woman (usually within earshot). *Maget* referred to a female child up until the loss of virginity; the modern equivalent *Magd* has been subject to reduction in terms of reference in that it refers to a serving girl or a dairy maid. On the other hand, the diminutives *Mädchen* and *Mädel* have been generalized to any young female child or adolescent. *Dirne* has undergone pejoration. In MHG it could be used of the Virgin Mary or a handmaiden; now it refers to a prostitute, but is not used very much, the loan word *Prostituierte* having taken its place. *Wîp* in OHG and MHG was the general word for 'woman'. During the MHG period it took on the meaning of a sexually mature woman, in contrast to *maget*, but as the word *Frau* became more and more general, *Weib* lost its neutral meaning and is now used in pejorative contexts such as *dummes Weib* 'stupid cow', *altes Weib* 'old cow', *tolles Weib* 'a bit of alright', all of which show a lack of respect when used by men. In fact, *Weib* would not normally be used by women, only ironically, as in the title of Hera Lind's book, *Das Superweib* (published in 1996).

It is important to note that meaning is affected by context. This is not a matter of pragmatics (see chapter 1), but a general factor in semantics. The same meaning does not attach to a word or morpheme in all its contexts of occurrence. Modern *Dirndl* has nothing to do with prostitutes and the generic meaning of *wîp* is retained in the adjective *weiblich*. General statements about the meaning of lexical items, therefore, have to be qualified with careful, detailed comments about collocations with other words and morphemes.

A form we gave as an example of morphological divergence in section 8.4 above was *Zucht*. Although the modern word refers to discipline and propriety, the earlier MHG meaning of 'upbringing', related to *ziehen* in the sense of 'to bring up', is still retained in the context of breeding animals and cultivating plants. A new verb has been formed, *züchten*, with the specific meaning of 'to breed, cultivate'. *Züchtig* retains the meaning of propriety, 'modest', 'demure', 'proper', whereas *züchtigen* has the meaning 'to discipline'. These words show how morphologically related forms may undergo changes of meaning in some contexts and not in others.

The extension of meaning sometimes involves a metaphorical use of a word or phrase with physical referents for something abstract or an emotion. For example, *Angst* 'fear' is related to *eng* 'narrow'; fear is presented as a feeling of being confined in a small space (compare the English expression *a tight spot*). More obvious perhaps are cases like *Vogelzunge*, a technical term meaning 'oval file', where the object in question is related to some other, more common entity, literally 'bird's tongue'.

In the early period of OHG, when the language was beginning to be given an orthographic form, in particular in the translations from Latin of ecclesiastical texts, borrowings were very common, especially in the form of loan translations. The words simply did not exist in the spoken language of the time but were needed to express the new ideas coming from an educated elite, where educated meant in particular having a knowledge of Latin. The words were often translated morpheme by morpheme as in the following examples with the modern German equivalents: *trans + ferre → über + tragen, ex + primere → aus + drücken*. It was only later that Latin words were regularly borrowed in their Latin forms, sometimes the same ones that had been translated earlier, for example *exprimieren*.

There are cases where a word has changed its original meaning or disappeared altogether as a separate word, but has been retained as an affix or in a compound. Affixes like *-bar*, from OHG *bari*, 'bearing' (adj.), and *be-*, from OHG *bî*, an adverb and preposition (= NHG *bei*), were once separate words, but had lost this status by the MHG period. We have already seen an example of a lost element in the former compound *Bräutigam*, but sometimes folk etymology steps in to interpret what has become uninterpretable (as in the case of English *bridegroom*). The word for 'crossbow' in modern German is *Armbrust*; this is a re-interpretation of the original medieval French word *arbaleste*, whereby some attempt has been made to render the German loan a compound of German words, though the relevance of the meanings of the component parts is no more obvious than that of *-groom* in *bridegroom*!

A fairly small semantic system which has undergone internal changes is that of the modal verbs. Basically the semantic system deals with possibility and necessity. There are two sub-types of these meanings: (i) relating to statements, usually referred to as epistemic and (ii) relating to commands, usually referred to as deontic. In German, as in English, the same auxiliaries are in many cases used for both. The examples in (21) show both types of necessity with *müssen*.

(21)   Er muss jetzt da sein
       He must be there by now

       Du musst jetzt gehen
       You must go now

The first sentence is an assessment of the definiteness of his being there; the second is a command, an indication of an obligation of some kind. Possibility and necessity, like permission and obligation, are related to one another by way of negation. If we assume that the sentence meaning has two parts, the modal element and the main proposition, we can represent the basic system as in (22) using English *possible that* for the epistemic type and *possible for* for the deontic type. The modal element is introduced by the impersonal *it is*, the proposition by *that/for*. An English equivalent with a modal verb form is given for each meaning.

(22) It is possible that he is there   He may be there
     It is possible for him to go   He can/may go

     It is not possible that he is there   He can't be there
     It is not possible for him to go   He can't/mustn't go

     It is possible that he is not there   He may not/needn't be there.
     It is possible for him not to go   He needn't go

     It is not possible that he is not there   He must be there
     It is not possible for him not to go   He must go

Necessity and obligation are interpreted as possibility and permission in combination with two negatives, one modal (neg(m)), the other propositional (neg(p)):

(23)   possible + neg(m) + neg(p) = necessity

In MHG some of these meanings were represented as in (24).

(24)   possible   muoz

       neg(m) possible   enmac (epistemic), ensol (deontic)

       possible neg(p)   endarf

       neg(m) possible neg(p)   sol

First of all it must be pointed out that there is not a one-to-one relationship between words and meanings, that is to say that lexical items overlap one another and/or may have a number of meanings. This is demonstrated above in the case of roots like *zieh-/Zucht*. It is this lack of rigid limits to meaning that allows semantic shifts. These may be rapid or gradual. In the case of modality the verbs used to indicate the basic meanings shifted gradually in relation to one another from OHG times onwards. In modern German the basic picture is as in (25) with the epistemic type first, then the deontic.

(25)   possible   mag, darf, kann (both)

       neg(m) possible   kann nicht, darf nicht

       possible neg(p)   mag nicht, muss nicht

       neg(m) possible neg(p)   muss (both)

A second point to make is that another consequence of the lack of rigid limits is that not all forms of a lexical item necessarily change in the same way. For instance, the use of the subjunctive II of *dürfen* in (26) retains the meaning of epistemic possibility from MHG which the other tense forms no longer have.

(26)   Er dürfte da sein
       He'll certainly be there

What should be noted in this exemplification is that the semantic system remains more or less the same; it is the lexical representations of the system that have changed.

8.7   External Influences

External influences are those aspects of change that have been brought about by circumstances outside the language itself, for example, the social and political circumstances in which the language was used as a means of communication. Many of these influences have effected a standardization and levelling out of the local differences that we will discuss in chapter 9. Although what is now Germany was for many centuries fragmented into small states, some no bigger than towns (for example, Lübeck and Augsburg), it did have the unifying structure of the Holy Roman Empire going back to the time of Charlemagne (742–814). The church, therefore, was one element in the cohesiveness of what was otherwise a group of potentially competitive principalities, which, from time to time, they became.

During the classical MHG period, say 1190–1250, the courtly ethos was important in determining the prized linguistic forms of the time. Hartmann von Aue, Gottfried von Strassburg and Walther von der Vogelweide were all respected poets of the day, whose portrayal of the ideals of courtly life were both popular and influential. The aristocracy used the language they felt was appropriate to the attainment of these ideals and it was through the written language that standardization of a kind occurred. Local dialects were appropriate for local matters and everyday speech was still locally determined. But greater matters were above local concerns and the language had to reflect this and be supraregional to some extent. This is a common feature of standardization and linguistic appropriateness in general. In Ancient Rome the spoken language of everyday life (Vulgar Latin) was not the same as the standard written form, Classical Latin, which was also spoken in certain formal contexts such as the Senate and the law courts. Similar situations arise in many modern African states, usually involving different languages, rather than standard and non-standard dialects. For example, in Kenya English is the language of higher education, some forms of literature and of international affairs, Kiswahili is used as the language of Kenyan nationality in government and general education (it has ousted English in these functions), and the local languages are used for local purposes indicating ethnic cohesion and loyalty. Often these local languages have no standard variety and often no written form either.

In medieval Germany, as in many other parts of Europe, power and influence changed gradually from the aristocratic elite, the kind of people portrayed by the *Minnesinger* poets in their romances, to the growing merchant and secular clerical classes of the ever-increasing towns and cities. Castles and monasteries, though still important, were joined by bourgeois communities. The *Bürger* demonstrated their own importance in the change from feudalism and the absolute dominance of the church. From around 1350 onwards standardization became a matter of secular politics and commerce. Along with this came an ever-more powerful civil service.

The other important issue in the development of German as a unified language was the displacement of Latin as the language of official writings and education by German. The use of German as an academic language did not take place until 1687, when Christian Thomasius lectured in German at the University of Leipzig (see Priebsch and Collinson 1962: 393), but this can be seen as the culmination of a process going back over 300 years.

In the fourteenth century the Imperial chanceries developed their own written versions of the language in order to keep records, write edicts and charters, and communicate with one another. These are known as **Kanzleisprachen**. Increased commercial interaction, too, meant that communications between different parts of the Empire had to be improved and made more efficient. A number of written forms emerged but they tended to suppress some of the local dialectal variation. For nearly 100 years under the Luxemburg emperors (1347–1437) the Imperial Chancery was at Prague. The language of this area contained both Upper and Central German elements. For example, it had the Upper German diphthongs written *ei, au, eu* rather than earlier *î, û, iu*, and the Central German monophthongs *î, û, ü* for the earlier diphthongs *ie, uo, üe* (see section 8.2 above; see also Priebsch and Collinson 1962: 386–7). More and more there is evidence of compromise between different dialectal areas with the emergence of what may be termed Common German.

In one particular instance there was a combination of two separate innovations which were of crucial importance in the establishment of the standard form of the language: the translation of the Bible into German and the invention of printing. Both of these ensured that the written form of German would be much more widely accessible all over the German-speaking area than anything that had gone before. Since printed materials were much cheaper than handwritten manuscripts, it made sense to keep variation to a minimum. The matter of imposing one version of the language for printed books was a pragmatic one, something proposed also by Caxton with respect to English in the 1480s (see Milroy and Milroy 1985). In Germany the *Druckersprache* followed the chanceries to a large extent for their spelling and grammatical conventions, but even went beyond them in the direction of Common German. For example, Strassburg and Basel printers introduced the diphthongs *ei*, *au*, *eu* in contrast to the local dialects. This general trend towards a standard written form detached from the spoken language facilitated communication all over the Empire and meant that books would sell over as wide an area as possible.

In the wake of this increased availability of reading material came an increase in literacy. Books on language became more important during the sixteenth century in that they were mostly manuals to instruct the learner in the rules of the new standards for both reading and writing. Luther himself engaged in considerable linguistic discussions in the process of translating the Bible, presenting the difficulties he faced in his *Sendbrief von Dolmetschen* (1530).

Luther's language was readily accepted in the Protestant North, pushing aside the written standard version of Low German in the process. Low German had developed in the North for official purposes, especially in the towns of the Hanseatic League such as Hamburg and Lübeck, but the last Low German Bible appeared in 1621. (For a historical survey of Low German, see Sanders 1982.) High German was even used in sermons in the Low German area from 1600 onwards (see Keller 1978: 377).

The main barrier to linguistic unification was the division between the Protestant block and the Catholic areas of Austria, Bavaria and the Rhineland. However, resistance dwindled until by the middle of the eighteenth century grammatical descriptions concentrated solely on the language descended from that of Luther and the period of great literature spearheaded by Lessing, Goethe and Schiller firmly established it as the literary standard. It should be pointed out, however, that even at this time the local phonology played its part. Goethe, for instance, rhymed what in the standard pronunciation would be rounded and unrounded front vowels, because in his local dialect the two sets had been collapsed into one unrounded set. We give two examples in (26), with the rhymed syllables underlined.

(26)   Sieh, diese Senne war so stark,
       Dies Herz so fest und <u>wild</u>,
       Die Knochen voll von Rittermark,
       Der Becher ange<u>füllt</u>;

                         (from *Geistesgruß*, 1774, see Boyd 1962)

Willst, feiner Knabe, du mit mir <u>gehn</u>?
Meine Töchter sollen dich warten <u>schön</u>;
    (from *Erlkönig*, 1782, see Boyd 1962)

This simply underlines the separation of speech and writing as different media that we referred to in chapter 5.

Codification of the language became a way of controlling the norms of at least the written form. Once standardization was under way for the pragmatic reasons we have set out, the linguistic forms that evolved soon came to be considered 'correct', 'ideal', 'beautiful', 'better than the rest'. This is not due to either linguistic or pragmatic considerations; it is a matter of social pressure. Education, a cosmopolitan outlook, knowledge of current political matters become prized attributes of a developing social order. By the eighteenth century the desire for purity in all matters applied to language as much as anything else (take the case of Gottsched, as discussed by Priebsch and Collinson 1962: 394, and Keller 1978: 500–9). Such value judgements have become part of the lay attitudes to language that we find in the present day and have long been a part of the education system. Such an approach to language can be seen as an attempt at social control by imposing conformity on a population. Individuality is a danger to the state. (For an interesting discussion of linguistic standardization and authority, see Milroy and Milroy 1985.)

In this brief sketch of the major influences on the development of the standard language we have attempted to show general trends that one also finds in the case of other languages, for example, the development of the printed word as a means of communication, as well as those circumstances that are specific to German. Standard languages are important cohesive forces in the daily dealings of a nation; this is why people tend to equate a language with a nation.

8.8 Further Reading

For general treatments of language change, see Aitchison (1981), McMahon (1994), Trask (1996); for a detailed discussion of some of its social aspects, see Labov (1972).

For details of the history of German, see Wright (1907), Priebsch and Collinson (1962), Lockwood (1965), Chambers and Wilkie (1970), Keller (1978), Schmidt (1980), Wells (1985), von Polenz (1970), (1991), (1994).

For a discussion of various aspects of linguistic change, see several of the papers in Kiparsky (1982a) in addition to McMahon (1994) and Trask (1996).

EXERCISES

1 Collect sets of English and German words that are related by the High German sound shift; look for examples in different environments in the words, e.g. *ten/zehn* in onset position, *open/offen* in intervocalic position and *book/Buch* in coda position. Note that in many cases in English what was in Old and Middle English an intervocalic environment has in modern English become word-final because of the loss of unstressed syllables, e.g. *make* [meɪk] but German *machen* [maxən].

2 Attempt an English translation of the text in example (19).

3 Find a list of strong verbs in MHG and compare it with the list of modern German strong verbs. What processes can you suggest connect the two sets?

CHAPTER NINE

Contemporary Variation

9.1 Preliminaries

We discussed in chapter 7 how in German, as in any other language, the same meaning can be represented in a number of different ways. Active, passive and nominalized versions of the same underlying syntactic relationships are possible, as in (1), and this variety of possible structures is of stylistic significance.

(1) Der Bischof begründete die Abtei im zwölften Jahrhundert
     Die Abtei wurde vom Bischof im zwölften Jahrhundert begründet
     Die Begründung der Abtei durch den Bischof im zwölften Jahrhundert

But this is not the only kind of variation that is of interest to linguists. Each grammatical system has stylistic variation and different registers (see section 9.2 below), and most native speakers operate variant grammatical systems as well. These may be closely overlapping systems or they may diverge considerably. An example of the latter from the German-speaking context is Switzerland, where most speakers use both standard German and Schweizerdeutsch, depending on the context of situation. This is often referred to as **diglossia** (Ferguson 1959). (See Barbour and Stevenson 1990, and Russ 1994, for more details of Swiss German.) Similarly, in North Germany some speakers will use both standard German and Plattdeutsch. But although these varieties are presented as separate entities used in mutually exclusive contexts, a closer look at a person's linguistic habits will show us a rather more complicated picture, in particular in that they move from one system to another even within one and the same utterance, a phenomenon referred to as **code-switching**. For example, a North German speaker may use a Plattdeutsch form (*dat*) in an otherwise standard utterance:

(2)   Sie hat ihren Geburtstag vergessen; dat ist nich' schön

In fact, for some northern speakers this form will be their only version of this particular lexical item, along with *wat* rather than *was*.

Before we consider any more details of linguistic variation in German we need to look at the traditional terminology for different varieties of a language and then see if it is appropriate to be applied to what we actually find.

Slang is a term that is often used by non-specialists to refer to any non-standard linguistic form. As a technical term, though, it refers to short-lived, fashionable and often invented vocabulary; for instance, *geil* meaning 'brilliant', *cool*, a loan word from English, and *Trollo* 'idiot', invented. These forms may be used in any linguistic variety; their presence does not define one particular variant.

Dialect is used to refer to a local variety of language which is identifiable from particular characteristics which may be lexical, syntactic, morphological or phonological.

Accent is used to refer exclusively to phonological variation.

Colloquial speech is used to refer to a style of language used in informal contexts with characteristics on any of the linguistic levels, for instance, the use of *kriegen* for *bekommen* ('to get'), the use of *gucken* rather than *sehen* ('to see') in some areas, the use of *kaputt* ('broken'), the use of *würde* + the infinitive rather than the simple subjunctive II in all cases, or a high level of assimilation and deletion.

Standard language refers to the linguistic system used in formal contexts such as education, the media, the law and central government. It is also the variety taught to foreigners. For many linguists it is a non-regional dialect: 'a dialect with an army and a navy' (attributed to Max Weinreich by Chomsky 1986: 15). The term is also often used in contrast to poetic or literary language, to mean language that is not stylistically marked (see chapter 7).

Can we actually classify variants according to these categories? We may note first of all that they do not all have exclusively linguistic definitions and that they may, therefore, suffer from the shortcomings we noted in chapter 1 with regard to definitions of the German language. One particular difficulty for the observer is to get a complete picture of variation, especially if the observer is a non-native speaker, who has normally only been introduced to the standard language. (Even native speakers of a language cannot predict all its possible varieties; see Trudgill 1983.) Clearly, not all variants are available to all speakers and this leads us back to the problem of saying just what German is. It has long been a temptation for observers, especially non-specialists, to say that standard German is the 'real' language and other varieties are deviations from it. However, if we consider how standard languages come about (see section 8.7; see also sections in Keller 1978; Wells 1985; von Polenz 1991, 1994; Barbour and Stevenson 1990: 45–53), then we can see that the standard variety is consciously and artificially created. A standard language is codified by experts and to a large extent prescribed by this process of codification. But the criteria used in this standardization process are obscure and rarely made explicit. How standard is *bräuchte* as the subjunctive II of *brauchen* and how are we to decide? When and how did *das ist der meinige* and all the related forms cease to be widely used and get replaced by *das ist meiner*, etc.? The distinguishing feature of standard languages from a historical point of view is that they do not develop like other varieties, the non-standard dialects, because of this 'interference'. So, in terms of native-speaker acquisition, the standard is often a variety learnt after the acquisition of one's local variety. In linguistic terms it is rarely the naturally acquired variety, and is taught via the educational system.

Another aspect of standard languages is that they tend to be thought of as the written form rather than as one of the spoken variants. It is true that most languages have a standard pronunciation, too, but in fact the standard language is pronounced with a variety of accents. To take two simple examples, standard German spoken in the North and in central Germany mostly has [ʀ] initially in words like *Rat*, whereas in the South and in Austria we find [r], an apico-alveolar trill (or sometimes a tap). ([r], incidentally, is the form prescribed for stage use.) Similarly, northerners have only voiceless obstruents in syllable-final position (see chapter 5), for example, [bliːp], *blieb*; [baːt], *Bad*; [tsoːk], *zog*, whereas southerners have voiced ones in such words: [bliːb], [baːd], [tsoːg]. These are not dialect forms, they are standard ones pronounced with a southern accent.

So standardization relates in particular to the written form (*Schriftsprache*) and as such is central to the process of education. In that sense most German speakers have two varieties at their disposal, the local one acquired when they were children and the standard one taught to them at school. The latter will be used in writing and in supraregional communication, the former in local contexts, in particular with family and friends. But again the notion of partially overlapping systems means that slippage from one system to another is not always clear-cut. That is to say, in cases where code-switching takes place it may be difficult to determine the boundaries between the two systems precisely. The 'mixed' system for some speakers may even be the norm, so it would constitute a variety in its own right.

This is where the traditional distinction between dialects and standard in German does not reflect the linguistic facts. A traditional dialect (*Mundart*) is seen as a self-contained system, quite distinct from its neighbours, with clear historical origins and development. But this assumes that local communities are hermetically sealed from one another. Individuals within a community may, of course, be very limited in their mobility, but with the advent of general literacy and mass communications there are very few people who have no access to varieties other than their own. Furthermore, because the aim of traditional dialectology was the search for historically 'uncontaminated' varieties of local speech, it concentrated almost exclusively on rural communities, pretending that urban varieties were not true linguistic systems and not worthy of study. Urban language is characterized in this view as 'bastardized'. Once again, if one considers the way language actually works and changes (see Aitchison 1981, McMahon 1994, Trask 1996), such notions of contamination are misleading and usually disguise value judgements of a non-linguistic nature. Country life is good and healthy (!), so the language of rustics is equally good; urban life is hard and unpleasant, so urban language is equally unpleasant. Human beings intermingle and this, in part, has an effect on their linguistic systems, so we should not be surprised to find linguistic features shared by a number of different varieties: variety A may thus have twelve characteristics in common with variety B and eight different ones in common with variety C. This is how overlap works. So, rather than a set of basic, distinct varieties (local dialects), a standard language, and a mishmash of the two, dialect and standard, used by uneducated people, we can establish a slow gradation from standard to dialect with all kinds of possibilities in between.

A common distinction in sociolinguistic terms is that drawn between variation by use and variation by user (see Halliday et al. 1964: 75–110, and Halliday 1978: 35). This distinction relates roughly to those characteristics of texts that are seen as being determined by the use to which the language is put and the context in which it is used, and to those that are determined by the speaker's own linguistic system, referred to as dialectal variation, or idiolect, if referring to one speaker's personal and idiosyncratic characteristics. This is a somewhat oversimplified way of considering linguistic variation, especially as the two aspects are closely linked, but it is a suitable starting point. We should also note that stylistic variation straddles both the area of language use and that of language universals: the kind and function of a text will determine its style, but also there are universal, systematic aspects of style which operate irrespective of use, as we showed in chapter 7. We shall start, then, by looking at variation according to use.

9.2   Variation by Use

Variation according to use can be seen as a type of pragmatic variation. In chapter 1 we define pragmatics as the study of language use. The commonest term for the types of variable linguistic output in texts of all kinds is **register**. This term was developed by Halliday in particular in a number of publications (see references in the previous section). Each text is assumed to have particular linguistic characteristics determined by its context of use. This is a **functional** view of variation. The reason a particular text has the form it does has to do with its function in that context and the relationship between the text producer and its recipient(s). (The term **text** is used in relation to both writing and speech; in other words, a conversation is a text, just as much as a novel.) To take a simple example: an instruction manual or a cookery book will contain a lot of imperative verb forms because their function is to tell the reader (or hearer, if the medium is speech) how to carry out certain tasks. It is important to be aware that this type of functional view is not necessarily at odds with the non-functional view of the style of texts expounded in chapter 7. This is because the functional view developed by Halliday and others can be seen to apply to the choice among existing stylistic and non-stylistic possibilities, whereas the actual generation of possible stylistic features cannot, according to the system set out in chapter 7, be reduced to functional principles. The Hallidayan term register is complex and it was developed into a subtle analytical tool (see, for example, Halliday 1973: 103–43, and the references given above). It is subdivided into three aspects: **mode, tenor** and **field**.

Mode is the actual medium of language, such as speech or writing; tenor is the reflection of the relation between speaker and audience, such as familiar or formal; and field is the subject matter. Register has often been considered important to stylistic studies because it is a way of characterizing the style of a particular text and of characterizing particular elements of style of a whole set of texts related by one of the elements given above, usually the field. Thus, the register of, for example, scientific texts can be characterized by reference to particular stylistic features, such as use of agentless passives, use of specific scientific terminology, and so on. The concept of register has been further developed in particular by Fowler et al. (1979) and Fowler (1996: esp. 185–209) into a way of looking at the social meaning of texts. (In relation to German, see Good 1985.)

In the sense in which we used the term **style** in chapter 7, however, that is, to mean a body of linguistic knowledge which has both universal as well as language-specific aspects, stylistic features of a register are only one type of feature by which a register may be characterized. Lexical choice, frequency of particular syntactic structures, complexity of morphology will also form part of such a characterization. The sum of typical characteristics, stylistic or otherwise, of a particular set of texts is seen to constitute a norm or an idealized stereotype of that particular text-type. And indeed much of what is studied as register in English comes under the heading of **Textsorten** or **Texttypen** in German of the kind proposed, for example, by Gülich and Raible (1972) and Möhn and Pelka (1984). Although the English term register is often a more theoretically based notion than the German descriptive terms **Texttypen** or **funktionale Stile** (the latter often used in the former GDR, as in Fleischer and Michel 1975, and Riesel 1970), we shall assume for our purposes that there is no essential difference.

German studies of register or functional styles often divide the possible styles up into categories such as:

- Stil des öffentlichen Verkehrs
- Stil der Wissenschaft
- Stil der Presse
- Stil des Alltagsverkehrs
- Literaturstil.

The types of register which are assumed to exist vary from author to author as do the types of text assigned to a specific register (see, for instance, the debate in Gülich and Raible 1972). In the view of style we discussed in chapter 7, we could say that the principles of style apply to different degrees in the different registers. Thus, considering the classification above, which is based on Riesel (1970), it appears that the journalistic register (**Stil der Presse**) is characterized among other things by the application of the Principle of Ambiguity and the Principle of Compression. There have been studies specifically of the headlines of German newspapers (for example, Sandig 1971) which show that headlines are typically compressed in that they omit prepositions and articles. They are therefore potentially ambiguous. A headline such as (3) has several instances of compression in the omission of an article and a verb.

(3)   Schlechtes Garten-Geschäft
      poor   garden-business

It could be made less compressed by the addition (or the assignment at the semantic level) of such elements, as in (4), but some types of ambiguity still remain.

(4)   Das Garten-Geschäft ist im Moment schlecht
      The garden-business is poor at the moment

One type rests in the systematic ambiguity of non-relational compounds mentioned in chapter 7; we do not know what relation to assign between *Garten* and *Geschäft*. As with any compressed structure, various readings are possible:

(5) (a) Das Geschäft, das Gegenstände für den Garten verkauft
     (b) Das Geschäft, das einem Garten ähnlich ist
     (c) Das Geschäft, das von einem Garten aus betrieben wird

The number of readings is increased by the ambiguity of the word *Geschäft*. (5a) is based on the meaning 'shop', (5c) on the meaning 'business', and (5b) could be either a business which grows and flourishes like a well-tended garden or a shop full of plants and seats which looks like a garden.

Stil der Wissenschaft, or scientific style, would be characterized by the absence of many of the principles of style, as would everyday language, **Stil des Alltagsverkehrs**, and literary style, **Literaturstil**, would be characterized by their presence. **Stil des öffentlichen Verkehrs** roughly corresponds to what we described in the previous section as standard language.

Many of the characteristics of the different registers are universal in nature. Thus the depersonalization of scientific texts achieved by the absence of agents and the use of passive constructions is a universal characteristic. The use of metaphor or repetition in literary texts is also universal, as indicated in chapter 7. But the language-specific features of texts come about not only because universal stylistic principles interact with the resources of the language in order to produce a particular type of figure but also because a text will be characterized by other features such as lexis and syntactic structures which are not directly related to stylistic principles, and these will either be language-specific (lexis) or language-specific manifestations of universal principles (syntax).

Some of the categories presented above are rather broad, for example the language of newspapers. Certainly, there are linguistic characteristics specific to this type such as layout, headlines, columns and different typographical devices, all of which have a particular function within news reporting. On the other hand, the syntactic and lexical characteristics of news reporting depend to a large extent on the type of newspaper and its editorial stance (see further Fowler 1991, and Good 1985). Describing narrower categories according to function does not necessarily help: advertising, for example, may have one basic function, to sell products, but the means of achieving this are more varied than the styles of newspaper reporting. However, many of the categories correlate well with a complex of linguistic features and we shall consider a few examples from German and discuss their linguistic characteristics, concentrating in particular on lexical choice and syntactic structures.

To start with we shall look at academic writing, which we assume to be the same as scientific writing or *Stil der Wissenschaft*; indeed, German does not generally make a distinction between the academic and the scientific, as terms such as *Literaturwissenschaft* ('literary science' or 'literary studies') indicate. Lexical choice will be determined by which academic discipline the text relates to. In (6) we have italicized the technical terms that define the text as art-historical.

(6) Mächtige *Streben gliedern* die *Fassade*, die in *Türmen* aufgipfelt. Das erst 1432 in die *Front* eingebrochene große *Maßwerkfenster* zerstört die Geschlossenheit des *Blocks* und lockert die *Fassade* im Sinne der englischen *Spätgotik* auf

(Adam 1963: 147)

In (7) we give the English equivalents in the order they occur in the text.

(7) buttresses, articulate, façade, towers, front, tracery window, block, façade, late Gothic period

The syntactic forms, on the other hand, belong to the more general genre of academic writing, which aims to depersonalize and objectivize what is being discussed. This is usually achieved by a large number of agentless passives, a characteristic of scientific texts we referred to above. In (6) there is one instance, *eingebrochene*, 'let in', an adjectivally subordinated version of the structure in (8).

(8) Das große Maßwerkfenster wurde erst 1432 in die Front eingebrochen
     The great tracery window was not let into the front until 1432

The text from which (6) is taken contains many such instances and we give in (9) an example of a *werden* passive and one of a *sein* passive (simplified for convenience).

(9) a. Die Turmhelme wurden nie ausgeführt
         The spires were never built

     b. Die dreischiffige Basilika war ursprünglich flachgedeckt
         The three-aisled basilica was originally flat-ceilinged

A related structure in academic texts is the nominalized form of verbs. In this case a whole sentence can be reduced to an NP (see also the discussion of the Principle of Compression in newspaper headlines above). Our nominalized example in (1) could be reduced in any of the following ways:

(10) Die Begründung der Abtei im zwölften Jahrhundert
      Die Begründung der Abtei
      Die Begründung

This also gives rise to compound nouns and adjectives being used and even coined in many cases. In (11) we give a selection from art-historical texts.

(11) Gesimsunterteilung   *division by means of cornices*
      Längenausdehnung   *extension of the horizontal axis*
      flachgedeckt   *flat-ceilinged*
      vogelbelebt   *populated with birds*

Another way of avoiding reference to persons in texts is to put inanimate objects in subject position, as in (6), (12) and (13).

(12) Der dicke kräftige Vierungsturm steigert den Eindruck des Blockhaften noch
      The wide, heavy crossing tower enhances the blocklike impression even more

(13) Wie in der Normandie fallen auf ein Mittelschiffquadrat zwei Seitenschiffquadrate
      As in Normandy, two side-aisle squares adjoin one square of the nave

In (6) the subjects of the two sentences are *Streben* and *Maßwerkfenster*. They are actually the instruments whereby the effects described in the sentences were produced, not the agents, who were presumably human. Instrumental subjects are very common in art-historical texts and (12) is yet another example. A human agent as subject requires the instrument to be expressed by a PP, as demonstrated in (14).

(14) Der Erbauer steigert den Eindruck des Blockhaften durch den Vierungsturm
      The builder increases the blocklike impression by means of the crossing tower

In example (13) the choice of verb, *fallen*, with the meaning 'to adjoin', rules out the possibility of having a human agent in the sentence because it requires only inanimate subject NPs. In other words there are no German sentences such as (15).

(15) *Der Erbauer fällt auf ein Mittelschiffquadrat

So, as characteristics of academic texts we can give at least agentless passives, nominalizations and instrumental subjects. For a detailed discussion of German art-historical texts, see Lodge (1982).

The kinds of technical vocabulary given in examples (6) to (13) are instances of **jargon**, which, in its technical, linguistic sense, has no pejorative overtones. In many cases it is easy to tell the specialist field to which a text belongs on the basis of the lexicon:

(16) Antritt, Setzstufe, Trittstufe, Wange, Geländer, Podest, Handlauf, Austritt, Treppenpfosten

If the words in (16) all occur in a text, it is immediately recognizable as being about the construction of staircases. We give the English equivalents in (17), in the same order.

(17)   bottom step, riser, tread, stringer, banisters, landing, hand-rail, top step, newel post

However, this tells us nothing about the function any text may have. It is the syntax and the layout that give us that information. For instance, Möhn and Pelka (1984: 69) give an example of a manual for carpenters explaining the terminology, of which we give a brief extract in (18).

(18)   Die unterste Stufe heißt *Antritt*, die oberste *Austritt*. Alle Stufen zusammen ergeben den *Treppenlauf*

Notice that in its defining function the text is made up of simple sentences with a Subject–Verb–Object structure. The verb forms *heißt, wird bezeichnet, (man) nennt* are the commonest; a number of different verbs are used to avoid repetition of the same lexical item. The tense is present, the mood indicative without exception. On the other hand, the words could be presented quite differently. If they were presented in columns with French and English terms by the side of them, as in (19), with a numbered illustration of a staircase for reference, then we would be dealing with a trilingual dictionary (see, for instance, Huber and Rieth 1985: 151), in which definitions are given by lexical equivalences. (In some of the entries there is a German definition as well with a similar structure to those in (18).)

(19)   1   Antritt – marche de départ – bottom step
       2   Setzstufe – contre-marche – riser
       3   Trittstufe – giron – tread
       4   Wangenstärke – épaisseur du limon – thickness of string
       5   Eckpodest – repos d'angle – corner landing
           Viertelpodest – repos en équerre – quarter landing
       6   Wandwange – contre-limon – wall string

Two different presentations, two different functions, but the same specialized subject.

   In some cases, as we have already noted, it is not possible to be so precise about the lexical choice and syntactic structures. If we take poetry to be a register (or sub-register of *Literaturstil*), then by its very nature, its creativity, we cannot expect an easily definable set of characteristics similar to the ones we have just discussed for art-historical texts. On the other hand, poems are usually recognizable from different kinds of characteristic. In their written form their layout signals poetry: short lines one under the other, sometimes capital letters at the beginning of each line, sometimes no punctuation, usually a title. In their spoken form they possess particular features of presentation: rhythmic patterns not always found in ordinary speech, a 'performing' voice quality, often rhyme, assonance and alliteration. In (20) we give an extract of an unrhymed poem, *Fragen eines lesenden Arbeiters* by Bertolt Brecht. It does contain alliteration and assonance, for example the word-initial [z] in *seine, sonst, siegte* (twice), *Sieben-, Seite, Sieg*, and the alternation of [aɪ] and [iː] in *weinte, seine, Seite* on the one hand, and *niemand, Sieben-, Krieg, siegte, Sieg*, on the other. Line-initial capital letters interrupt sentences, as in *Wer Siegte außer ihm?* On the lexical level there is a lot of repetition, for instance, the morpheme *sieg* (see chapter 7).

(20)   Philipp von Spanien weinte, als seine Flotte
       Untergegangen war. Weinte sonst niemand?
       Friedrich der Zweite siegte im Siebenjährigen Krieg.
       Wer Siegte außer ihm?
       Jede Seite ein Sieg.

In the case of advertising, which uses all kinds of linguistic and non-linguistic devices together, we can see that there is a specific and functional relationship between the verbal and the visual aspects. Certain linguistic features recur: direct address, short, sometimes incomplete sentences, the visual and/or oral emphasis of certain words or phrases, repeated catch-phrases, (pseudo-)technical details.

9.3   Variation by User

In chapter 1 we showed how the notion of one particular language is not a useful linguistic concept. Rather the notion 'language X' has to do with matters of politics, society and nationhood. The alternative picture is that linguistic systems exist on a continuum of variation and that they overlap one another in terms of structure in varying degrees. In addition, as we pointed out in section 9.1, an individual speaker will normally have a number of variants at his or her disposal from which to draw on various occasions. A speaker's linguistic output is to some extent a badge of identity, and this may change depending on the circumstances a speaker is in. People will also indicate their reaction to others in their linguistic usage; basically, if they approve of their interlocutors and want to get on with them, they will shift their language use (slightly) in the direction of those they are talking to. This is not usually a conscious decision. It is referred to as **accommodation**. If people disapprove of their interlocutors and want to dissociate themselves from their perceived values, they will emphasize and even exaggerate their own linguistic variety in contrast to the alien one. This is **disaccommodation**. A form of institutional disaccommodation occurred in Germany after the partition; each half tried to establish its values in contrast to the other one. (For a discussion of the linguistic consequences of this, see Good 1975, and there are also discussions in Barbour and Stevenson 1990: 174–9, and Clyne 1995.)

If people accommodate to one another linguistically, or not, as the case may be, then we also need the notion of an **act of identity** to explain this behaviour. The notion of act of identity was developed by LePage (1980) and LePage and Tabouret-Keller (1985) (see also Downes 1998: 272–4). It has also been applied to British and American English by Trudgill (1983: 141–60) in an attempt to explain the variable linguistic output in the songs of British pop-singers in the 1960s and 1970s. Both accommodation and acts of identity have been postulated to explain the reasons for a speaker's choice of one linguistic variety over another in different contexts of situation.

Bearing in mind the background to variation and its great complexity, we now want to consider some particular aspects of German variation from a purely linguistic point of view. Two points in particular need to be made: firstly, variation has its origins in history, as we have already noted in chapter 8; secondly, whatever the origin, linguistic variation is constrained at all levels by universal characteristics of language of the kind presented briefly in chapter 1 and mentioned throughout this book, except, perhaps, for lexical variation, because of the arbitrary nature of naming. Lexical variation in particular can lead to misunderstandings; consider, for example, the regional variation in English of *crumpet*, *pikelet* and *muffin*, or *carpenter* and *joiner*, where the different lexical items can refer to the same object or person in different parts of the British Isles.

9.3.1 Regional Accents

In chapter 5, section 5.8 most of what we said related to standard German in a colloquial speech style. It is important to distinguish this from dialect pronunciations. Example (40) in chapter 5 (*Was soll ich ihm geben?*) must not be considered dialect just because it contains forms which are found in informal conversation (and, incidentally, which are rarely taught to foreigners). We have already distinguished between dialect and accent. A dialect differs from other variants on all linguistic levels: phonology, morphology, syntax and lexis. An accent is simply phonological variation. The standard language can be pronounced with a variety of regional accents and we have already made the point that in any particular instance there may be a mixture of regionalisms and dialect forms. Dressler et al. (1972) provide a particularly good example of this from

Viennese German, from which we give a selection of their examples in
(21).

(21) Wir haben alle ein Auto gehabt, aber trotzdem sind
      wir mit der Straßenbahn nach Hause gefahren

      a. [viːər haːben ale aen aoto gehaːpt aːber trɔtsdeːm sint viːər mit deːr
          ʃtraːsenbaːn naːx haoze gefaːren]

      b. [viə haːbm alə aen aoto gəhapt abɐ trɔtsdəm sin viə mitə ʃtrasnban
          nəx haoze gefaːrn]

      c. [miəm ɔlə ɐ aoto kɔpt əwə drɔtsdəm simə mitə ʃtrɔsnbãn tsaos kfɒn]

(We have omitted some of their transcriptional devices and ignored the
stress marks for the sake of simplicity. Final [r] they write as a superscript.) (21a) is standard German with an Austrian accent, as indicated
by the [r]-realization of /r/, initial /s/ and final unstressed [e] (presumably
centralized). (21b) is a faster tempo with reduced vowels and some dele-
tions. (21c), on the other hand, contains elements of Austrian dialect, for
instance, the use of *mi* for the first person plural pronoun rather than *wir*
(a fairly widespread feature of German dialects), instances of [ɔ] and [ɒ]
where standard German has [a(ː)], [d] rather than [t] in initial position
of *trotzdem*, and the use of *zu Hause* instead of *nach Hause*. In different
degrees a speaker of standard German will have indicators of his or her
regional background, usually features of accent, even if they are limited
to just one or two. These regional features are not necessarily dialect
forms; according to Keller (1961: 200) the gradual transition between
dialect and standard found characteristically in Austria and Bavaria is
not found in northern and central Germany. Colloquial speech in North
Germany will certainly be regional, but it is not directly influenced by
the local dialects spoken in rural areas. This is probably due to the
differences in the consonantal systems of Low German and High German, so that the two types of variety do not overlap to any great extent,
as far as the phonology is concerned. We should also point out here that
phonological variation is much greater than that in the areas of morphology and syntax. That is why this section is rather longer than the
others in this chapter.

In this section we shall look at variation in particular in the stops and
fricatives, /r/ and some of the vowels. As we saw in the previous chapter,
the development of the PGmc voiceless stops served as the basis for the
split between the High German variants and all the other varieties of
Germanic. If we take the two basic systems as in (22) with the corre-
spondences indicated by the lines, we will find mixes of the two as well.

(22)   p t k ⟍⟍⟍⟍⟍⟍⟍⟍⟍ pf ts kx

    f s x ⟍⟍⟍⟍⟍⟍⟍⟍➤ f s x
   Low German   High German

The traditional dialects are different mixes of these two systems; in historical terms the High German sound shift spread unevenly through the varieties covering the area of modern Germany, as we noted in chapter 8, and as discussed by Barbour and Stevenson (1990: 77–81). But colloquial standard German speech will offer up even more possible mixes; for instance, a central German speaker who uses [f] rather than [pf] in word-initial position only, so *Pferd* is [feːɐt], but *Apfel* is [apfl]. (Many of the examples referred to in this section are taken from various recordings of native speakers at UEA.)

The voiced stops /b/ and /g/ also interact and vary with fricative realizations, for example, *bleeven* = standard *bleiben*. In many northern dialects [v] relates to standard [b] and [ɣ] to [g] with voiceless variants in syllable-final position, for instance, *bleef*, past tense of *bleeven*. The velar fricative is very widespread in colloquial speech in the North and in parts of central Germany. For instance, *Tag* is often [tax]; note that this is not the Low German form, which is [dax]. In chapter 5 we discussed the fricativization rule that applied only to word-final, unstressed -*ig* in the standard language. What we see in colloquial varieties is that some North German speakers extend the fricative rule to cases after any stem vowel, for example *Krieg* [kʀiːç], *klug* [kluːx]. On the other hand, we find many southern speakers who do not have a fricativization rule, so *König* is entirely regular in accordance with the devoicing rule, pronounced [køːnɪk], or with a voiced stop finally, [køːnɪg]. So, if we include other fricative realizations found in the North, for the standard phoneme /g/ in stem-final position we find at least the alternatives set out in (23), all of which count as variant pronunciations of the standard.

(23)

	Tag	Tage	König	Könige
Standard	[k]	[g]	[ç]	[g]
Variety 1	[x]	[ɣ]	[ç]	[j]
Variety 2	[x]	[g]	[ç]	[g]
Variety 3	[k]	[g]	[k]	[g]
Variety 4	[g]	[g]	[g]	[g]

The realization of /ç/ is different in Bavaria and Austria. Many speakers use [x] in all circumstances, in contrast to the standard allophonic distribution discussed in chapter 5, section 5.3; yet others, when using the standard language, have a different distribution of [x] and [ç] in the context /Vr____(t)/, if they have a vocoid realization of the post-vocalic /r/ (see further below). For such speakers [x] follows a back nuclear vowel, [ç] a front one, with a variable realization of the /r/ as well, as in [fʊɐxt], *Furcht* (compare with standard [fʊʌçt]) and [fʏ̝çtətə], *fürchtete* (standard [fʏʌçtətə]); in unstressed words the /r/ may not be realized, as in [dʊx], *durch*.

Word-initial [s] and [ʃ] have a variable distribution. In the South words like *Sonne, Sohn, sagen* have initial [s] rather than standard [z], and the use of [ʃ] before voiceless stops occurs in all circumstances, that is, not only in *Spott* and *Stamm*, but also in *ist, Wurst, lispeln*. On the other hand, northern speakers use [sp-] and [st-] in initial position, as in *Speise* and *Student*.

In addition to all the various realizations of /r/ discussed in section 5.6 of chapter 5, we find alternatives to the [ʀ]-realization: namely, an alveolar trill [r], which is sometimes reduced to a single tap, [ɾ], and a voiced uvular fricative [ʁ]. The former is a regional variant, used, for example, in Bavaria, Austria and Schleswig-Holstein; the latter does not seem to be associated with any particular group of speakers. In the case of the [r]-realization we must note that the post-vocalic variant is [r] or [ɾ] (see, for instance, *gefahren* in example (21b)). The tap is also used in intervocalic position, as in [andəɾəs], *anderes*. When southerners use a vocoid articulation for post-vocalic /r/ it is often more open and centralized than the standard [ʌ]-realization, namely [ɐ], as in the transcription of *Furcht* above. For some speakers, for instance, those in the area of Bonn and Cologne, post-vocalic /r/ has been lost altogether with compensatory lengthening of the preceding vowel, as in standard British English, so that *Wort* is [vɔːt] and *Bart* is [baːt]. In such accents contrasts are still maintained where necessary by having short stem vowels, as in *Bad* [bat]. (For a more detailed discussion of the variability of German /r/, see Wiese 2001.)

The vowel systems are also very varied. We referred in passing to some of the variation in the previous chapter, specifically the long high vowels, the diphthongs, the unrounding of the front rounded vowels and long–short alternations. We give a few more details here.

Alemannic speakers have retained diphthongs in words like *bieten, müde* and *gut*. In those parts where unrounding of front vowels has also taken place, for example, in Austria, the first two have the same stem vowel: [iə]. Similarly, the MHG monophthongs *î, û* and *iu* have not diphthongized to [aɪ], [aʊ] and [ɔɪ], respectively, as they have in the standard. Roughly speaking, the North and Alemmanic have retained the monophthongs of MHG and the rest have diphthongs. (For a map, see Barbour and Stevenson 1990: 91.) These varied developments lead to the establishment of at least four varieties, as indicated in (24).

(24)   Zeit   Haus   heute   bieten   gut   müde

	Zeit	Haus	heute	bieten	gut	müde
Standard	[aɪ]	[aʊ]	[ɔɪ]	[iː]	[uː]	[yː]
Variety 1	[aɪ]	[aʊ]	[ɔɪ]	[iə]	[uə]	[yə]
Variety 2	[aɪ]	[aʊ]	[ɔɪ]	[iə]	[uə]	[iə]
Variety 3	[iː]	[uː]	[yː]	[iə]	[uə]	[yə]
Variety 4	[iː]	[uː]	[yː]	[iː]	[uː]	[yː]

Note that Variety 3 is like MHG and in Variety 4 the six distinctive phonemes of standard German have been collapsed into three.

We referred to the unrounding of front rounded vowels in relation to Goethe's rhymes chapter 8, section 8.7 and again just above. In many varieties /yː/, /ʏ/, /øː/, /œ/ have fallen together with /iː/, /ɪ/, /eː/, /ɛ/, respectively. This means that for some speakers *fühlen* and *vielen* will be **homophonous**, that is, they are pronounced in the same way, with the stem vowel [iː]. Similarly, the following pairs rhyme: *zehn* : *schön*, *Mütze* : *Hitze*, *können* : *kennen*. (For a map relating to this phenomenon in the traditional dialects, see Barbour and Stevenson 1990: 93.)

In the South the vowels equivalent to standard /a/ and /aː/ have a range of realizations: they are always low but can be completely back and even rounded, as can be seen in (21c) above, but [ɐ] and [ɑ] are also to be heard. This backing of the vowel is assumed to have its origins in the late medieval period.

In section 8.4 of chapter 8 we referred to the development of long vowels in open syllables so that certain stems alternated depending on the syllable structure produced by adding the inflectional endings. Thus, MHG *tac* had a short vowel, *tages*, with an open stressed syllable, a long one. In many areas, especially in the North, these alternations are still maintained. In some cases the base form is long, but in some inflected forms short, as in [zaːɣən] *sagen*, [zaxtə] *sagte*. We have also noted that loss of post-vocalic /r/ produces long vowels, but that homophony does not necessarily ensue, as in *Bart* long versus *Bad* short. Rather than just seeing these developments from the point of view of one variety, usually the standard language or MHG, it is more helpful to compare systems in order to discover the extent of overlap, that is, the similarities and dissimilarities between them. In the case of Bavarian-Austrian backing we are dealing with a difference of phonetic realization, that is, the low phonemes (long and short) are realized as [ɑ(ː)], not [a(ː)]. In the case of /r/-loss and long–short alternations the systems are such that the differences are located in the lexicon, that is, it is a matter of **lexical incidence**. With /a/ and /aː/ we can demonstrate the difference in lexical incidence as in (25). Variety 1 has no post-vocalic /r/.

(25)   /a/   /aː/   /a/   /aː/

	Standard		Variety 1	
	hat	sagen	hat	sagen
	was	sagte	was	Tage
	lachen	Tag	lachen	Bades
	sanft	Tage	sanft	Bart
	hart	Bad	sagte	hart
		Bades	Tag	
		Bart	Bad	
		Heimat	Heimat	

9.3.2 Morphological and Syntactic Variation

We treat these together, as there is clearly a close correlation between the two, as we have noted in earlier chapters. Furthermore, some changes in morphology are due to phonological changes. If we consider the case system, first of all we may note that many varieties of German have no genitive. Further, the unstressed nature of the words that typically carry the case markers has led to further losses of contrast, so that in many varieties it is only the accusative masculine singular that remains distinct. For instance, Low German varieties have the following set of forms for the definite article (26) and the indefinite article (27), in phonetic transcription.

(26)   *m*   *f*   *n*   *pl*
Nom	[də]			
		[də]	[dat, dət]	[də]
Acc	[dən, n]			

(27)   *m,n*   *f*
       [ən, n]   [ənə, nə]

In fact, some speakers have no distinct case forms, so they could be said to have a two-gender system as in Dutch, Danish and Swedish (see also Barbour and Stevenson 1990: 163). Since singular and plural are not differentiated by the article, those nouns with non-distinct plurals, for instance those ending in the suffix -*er*, use the dialect plural marker -*s*, as in [də faːʀʌ], [də faːʀʌs], as equivalents of standard *der Fahrer, die Fahrer*, respectively.

Those Low German varieties that are closest to the traditional dialects also use two or three different personal pronouns: *he*, rather than *er*, *ji* or *ju* for 'you' in the plural and as the polite form, and *et*, which is the same word as standard *es*, without the consonantal sound shift.

In many central areas and most of the South final [n] in unstressed syllables often does not occur. This has an effect on many of the morphological endings. In the extreme case masculine singular nominative and accusative are both realized as [də] for the definite article, and adjectives are not distinctive either: [də gʊətə mɑn] may be either *der gute Mann* or *den guten Mann*. This occurs in the West and South of the German-speaking area, for instance, in Luxemburg, Alsace and parts of Switzerland (see Shirer 1965 for details). Dative final [m] is maintained, however. The final [n] does occur, if the following word begins with a vowel. Thus, in sentence-final position *gestanden* is [kʃtɒndə], but in *gestanden ist* the [n] separates the two vowels: [kʃtɒndən ɪʃ]. This intervocalic link may be extended to any two vowels, even where it is not historically justified, as in *wo er*: [vonɐʁ]. (This is exactly like linking [ɹ] in English, see Wells 1982, and Lodge 1984; on linking [n] as a dialectal feature in German, see Keller 1961: 54, and Russ 1990: 371.)

Detailed information on syntactic variation is difficult to come by, though there are treatments of the traditional dialects (see, for instance, Keller 1961, and Russ 1990). Given what we have said about the loss of case distinctions, it is clear that several varieties rely on word-order to signal subject and object, as does English. The standard language can have object-first sentences, especially where the accusative case is signalled by the determiner, as in (28).

(28)   Meinen Freund hat ihr Mann gestern gesehen

If no such distinguishing markers are used then the order of the phrases in the clause is crucial, as demonstrated by the English pair in (29).

(29)   Her husband saw my friend yesterday
       My friend saw her husband yesterday

The flexibility of phrase order that we find in the standard is not available to those varieties that have lost a lot of their inflectional morphology.

The dative follows prepositions which take the genitive in the standard: *trotz, wegen, während,* and *von* + the dative replaces the simple genitive: *die Hand von der Frau, der Kopf vom Kind.* The other, non-standard alternative to the genitive is the dative + noun with a preceding possessive determiner: *der Frau ihre Hand, dem Kind sein Kopf.*

Separation of morphemes which would be kept together in the standard is found in several non-standard varieties. This affects prepositions and an accompanying *da* or *wo* in particular. Examples (30) and (31) show that German shares tendencies found extensively in English varieties, including the standard.

(30)   Da sind die Suppelöffel für
       That's what the soup spoons are for

(31)   Der Zug, wo ich gefahren bin mit, ...
       The train that I travelled by . . .

It is very difficult to know the extent of such forms in everyday speech.
(30) is certainly a continuation of a standard construction in MHG, but
the normative pressure of the modern standard written language means
that forms such as (31) are simply considered 'wrong'.

A distinction between the North and the South can be seen in the use
of the simple past tense (North) versus the perfect tense (South). Not
only does this reflect the dialectal basis of much colloquial speech in that
the Upper German local dialects have long ceased to have a simple past
tense form for any verb, but Barbour and Stevenson (1990: 166–8) see
the increasing use of the perfect in formal written German too as a
preference for flexible word-order in the sentence in order to avoid the
fixed V2 position of the main, lexical verb (see chapter 2). So where the
North has *fragte, lief*, the South has *hat gefragt, ist gelaufen*. The point
about flexibility can be exemplified by cases where an emphatic contrast
is made between two verbs, as in (32).

(32)   A: Hat sie sich das Auto selbst gekauft?
            Has she bought the car herself?

       B: Nein, gewonnen hat sie es, beim Lotto
            No, she won it in the lottery

As Barbour and Stevenson (1990) point out, this flexibility is also found
in the non-standard use of *tun* as an auxiliary in similar circumstances,
as in (33).

(33)   Arrangieren tu' ich sehr gern
       Flower-arranging is something I love doing

We referred above to the variable use of the subjunctive tenses. In
this case it is a matter of formal versus colloquial usage. Use of the
subjunctive I in reported speech is a mark of the formal written language; it is not used in colloquial speech. In the latter the subjunctive
II of the tense and modal auxiliaries is used. This means that the
periphrastic construction *würde* + the infinitive (often referred to as
the conditional) replaces not only the non-distinctive subjunctive II
forms of the regular verbs, as in the written standard, for instance,
würde leben for *lebte*, but also any other subjunctive II form, such
as *würde gehen* for *ginge*. Basically, the difference between the two
types of language is that formal written German uses more subjunctive
forms.

9.3.3   Lexical Variation

One of the foci of traditional dialectology has always been lexical variation. A lot of material has been collected and published in this area – for
instance, the bibliographies compiled by Keller (1978), much of which is
no longer current. Nevertheless, the variation of lexical items today has
a historical basis. Forms spread and recede from areas they were used in
in OHG or MHG times. For instance, in the Middle Ages the word *kno-
kenhouwer* (High German *Knochenhauer*) for 'butcher' was widespread
in the North, but *Schlachter* (sometimes with an Umlaut) is the normal
term today. *Fleischer* has been used in the East since the fifteenth century,
and the rest of the German-speaking area mostly uses *Metzger*. The latter
word is from MHG *metzjære*, < late Latin *matiarius* 'sausage-maker'.

Another way in which variation comes about is when technical terms
which are differentiated by those who use the objects in the course of
their work are used by lay people without such differentiation. For
instance, *Axt* and *Beil* are used for 'axe' all over the German-speaking
area, for the most part without any differentiation, though technically
they refer to different types of axe with differently sized handles and
blades. It is also in this area of the lexicon that we find the same word
used with different meanings in different geographical areas. For
instance, in parts of Bavaria and Austria *Hacke* is used for 'axe', which
elsewhere means 'hoe' or 'pickaxe'.

There are thus at least two ways in which variation takes place: the
use of a word particular to its own area, or the use of the same word
with different meanings in different areas. Sometimes the local word is
from the local dialect, though it is used even when speakers are using the
standard. An Austrian will say *Polster* rather than *Kissen* for 'cushion'; a
speaker from Schleswig-Holstein will use *feudeln* rather than *aufwischen*
'to mop up', and *fegen* rather than *kehren* 'to sweep'. In the North Low
German words may be used rather than their High German equivalent,
for instance *Deern* 'girl' (*not* 'prostitute'), which is the equivalent of
Dirne, is used rather than *Mädchen*.

We also want to look briefly at slang. Again there are different types
and different statuses. We can differentiate between words which are
made up with only a slang status and those words that are standard but
used with a different meaning in a slang context. In (34) we give a
selection of each type with English slang equivalents where possible.

(34)	Trollo	nutter	Fraß, Futter	nosh, fodder
	Fummel	togs	toll	great, brill
	Glotze	goggle-box	Plattenaufleger	DJ

There are also loan words that come into the slang lexicon often via English,
for example, *cool, down, happy, oldie, kids*, with the same meanings as in

English slang. Sometimes the slang meaning becomes widely accepted and it is possible to see a semantic shift taking place. For instance, *wahnsinnig* 'insane', 'frantic' has come to mean 'fantastic', 'amazing', 'unbelievable' in a very positive sense, as well as retaining its original meaning, as in (35).

(35) Du bist wahnsinnig!
      You're mad!

We defined slang above as short-lived, fashionable vocabulary, but sometimes words last for more than a century with a slang connotation. They can also change status under certain circumstances. *Schwul* was an abusive term for a male homosexual and goes back to the nineteenth century. During the 1970s, however, homosexual men themselves adopted the adjective and made it a positive term as a description of themselves (compare this with *gay* in English, which, however, did not have derogatory origins), though people may still use it derogatorily, too. (The same kind of change occurred in English with the adjective *black* in reference to people's ethnic origins.) On the other hand, external circumstances can terminate the currency of a slang word. In the 1950s and early 1960s homosexuals were also referred to as *hundertfünfundsiebziger*. This was a reference to the law (clause 175) which made homosexuality illegal in Germany. Once this law was repealed, the term had no relevance and ceased to be used by speakers under the age of about fifty. Similarly, in the mid-1960s the word *Beatle* was used in the German popular press to mean 'yob'; this, too, has ceased to be current. The somewhat old-fashioned-looking *Plattenaufleger* has been used in particular by the recent German rap singers; since vinyl records have been made obsolete by CDs, it remains to be seen how long this term will survive. (For details of various German slang words and expressions, including historical information, see Küpper 1955–64.)

There are examples of lexical variation, which are not related to dictionary meaning but to the way language is used in context. These would, therefore, normally be considered instances of pragmatic variation. One such example is the use of the definite article with first names, as in (36).

(36) Ist der Franz da?
      Is Franz there?

In North Germany this would not be used at all but be considered a southern feature. In parts of central Germany such a form would indicate a patronizing tone. In the South, however, this is a normal textual device for indicating intimacy. Certainly, even here, use of the article with the name of someone who was only an acquaintance would also indicate that the speaker was being patronizing or dismissive. Furthermore, the relationship between speaker and named person can be signalled by the diminutive in Bavaria, Austria and Switzerland: *'s Betli* 'Beth' with the diminutive ending -*li* indicates that the speaker likes/approves of/is pleased with the person referred to. On the other hand, *d'Bet* with feminine gender and no diminutive indicates that the speaker dislikes/disapproves of/is displeased with her. In Bavaria use of the diminutive is a textual marker of intimacy without any necessary connotations of smallness; indeed, forms such as *Schweindl* 'piggy', *Katzl* 'pussy', etc. are used by adults to children because the addressees are small, not the animals referred to. (This is just like the use of the -*y* ending in English when adults speak to children.) In the North, however, use of -*chen* or -*lein* always refers to size and is not a marker of intimacy. All this is part of a native speaker's local communicative competence; it is learned from the social environment.

9.4   Further Reading

With reference to the difference between dialect and standard and problems relating to this in the school system, see, for example, Ammon (1972), (1973), (1978).

For a description of various German dialects, see Keller (1961) and Russ (1990).

For a discussion of the differences between traditional dialectology and sociolinguistics, see Trudgill (1983: 31–51). For an extended discussion of the Berlin dialect, see Dittmar and Schlobinski (1988); for an introductory discussion of variation in German, see Stevenson (1997).

The term 'accommodation' is used by Giles and Powesland (1975), and Giles and Smith (1979); Labov (1972) contains an interesting investigation of disaccommodation on the island of Martha's Vineyard, off the eastern coast of the United States; see also Downes (1998: 271–2).

For further details of variation in the case system, see Koss (1982–3).

For a discussion of written German in school, see Good (1980) and (1986).

EXERCISES

1   Collect a number of different text-types and comment on the linguistic features that are characteristic of those types.

2   Find a text and change it into another style or register, e.g. a radio commentary turned into a newspaper report. Note: Barbour and Stevenson (1990: 3–5) have a number of examples of textual variation.

3   Choose a text and pick out all the examples of nominalization; work out possible alternative formulations using the same lexical root.

REFERENCES

Abney, S. (1987) 'The English noun phrase in its sentential aspect'. PhD dissertation, MIT, Boston, Mass.

Abraham, W. (1975) *A Linguistic Approach to Metaphor*. Lisse: Peter de Ridder.

Abraham, W. (1983) (ed.) *On the Formal Syntax of Westgermania*. Amsterdam: Benjamins.

Abraham, W. (1985) *Erklärende Syntax des Deutschen*. Tübingen: Narr.

Adam, E. (1963) *Baukunst des Mittelalters*, vol. 1. Frankfurt: Ullstein.

Aitchison, J. (1981) *Language Change: Progress or Decay?* London: Fontana.

Aitchison, J. (1992) *The Articulate Mammal*. London: Routledge.

Allen, M. (1978) 'Morphological investigations'. PhD dissertation, University of Connecticut.

Ammon, U. (1972) *Dialekt, soziale Ungleichheit und Schule*. Weinheim: Beltz.

Ammon, U. (1973) *Probleme der Soziolinguistik*. Tübingen: Niemeyer.

Ammon, U. (1978) *Schulschwierigkeiten von Dialektsprechern*. Weinheim: Beltz.

Anderson, J. M. and Ewen, C. J. (1987) *Principles of Dependency Phonology*. Cambridge: Cambridge University Press.

Anderson, S. (1982) 'Where's morphology?' *Linguistic Inquiry* 13: 571–612.

Archangeli, D. (1988) 'Aspects of underspecification theory'. *Phonology* 5: 183–207.

Aronoff, M. (1976) *Word Formation in Generative Grammar*. Cambridge, Mass.: MIT Press.

Ausländer, R. (1977) *Gesammelte Gedichte*, ed. H. E. Käufer and B. Masblech. Cologne: Literarischer Verlag Helmut Braun.

Bach, E. (1962) 'The order of elements in a transformational grammar of German'. *Language* 38: 263–9.

Baker, C. L. and McCarthy, J. J. (1981) (eds) *The Logical Problem of Language Acquisition*. Cambridge, Mass.: MIT Press.

Ball, M. J. and Rahilly, J. (1999) *Phonetics: The Science of Speech*. London: Edward Arnold.

Barbour, S. (2000) 'Germany, Austria, Switzerland, Luxembourg: the total coincidence of nations and speech communities?' In *Language and Nationalism in Europe*, ed. S. Barbour and C. Carmichael. Oxford: Oxford University Press.

Barbour, S. and Stevenson, P. (1990) *Variation in German*. Cambridge: Cambridge University Press.

Bauer, L. (1983) *English Word-formation*. Cambridge: Cambridge University Press.

Bauer, L. (1988a) *Introducing Linguistic Morphology*. Edinburgh: Edinburgh University Press.

Bauer, L. (1988b) 'What is lenition?' *Journal of Linguistics* 24: 381–92.

Beckman, B. J. (1980) *Underlying Word Order: German as a VSO Language*. Frankfurt: Peter Lang.

Beedham, C. (1995) *German Linguistics: An Introduction*. Munich: Iudicium.

Behagel, O. (1929) 'Zur Stellung des Verbs im Germanischen und Indogermanischen'. *Zeitschrift für vergleichende Sprachforschung* 56: 276–81.

Behagel, O. (1930) 'Von deutscher Wortstellung'. *Zeitschrift für Deutschkunde* 44: 81–9.

Bendor-Samuel, J. T. (1960) 'Segmentation in the phonological analysis of Terena'. *Word* 16: 348–55.

den Besten, H. (1983) 'On the interaction of root transformations and lexical deletive rules'. In Abraham (1983).

den Besten, H. (1984) 'The ergative hypothesis and free word order in Dutch and German'. In Toman (1984).

Bierwisch, M. (1963) *Grammatik des deutschen Verbs*. Berlin: Akademie Verlag.

Bird, S. (1995) *Computational Phonology: A Constraint-based Approach*. Cambridge: Cambridge University Press.

Blakemore, D. (1992) *Understanding Utterances*. Oxford: Blackwell.

Boase-Beier, J. (1987a) *Poetic Compounds: The Principles of Poetic Language in Modern English Poetry*. Tübingen: Niemeyer.

Boase-Beier, J. (1987b) 'Word-formation and poetic language: non-lexicalised nominal compounds in the poetry of Kevin Crossley-Holland'. In *Functionalism in Linguistics*, ed. R. Dirven and V. Fried. Amsterdam: Benjamins.

Boase-Beier, J. and Toman, J. (1986) 'On θ-Role assignment in German compounds'. *Folia Linguistica* 20: 319–40.

Boase-Beier, J. and Vivis, A. (1995) (trs. and eds) *Rose Ausländer: Mother Tongue*. Todmorden: Arc Publications.

Boyd, J. (1962) (ed.) *Goethe's Poems*. Oxford: Basil Blackwell.

Brekle, H. E., Boase-Beier, J., Toman, J., Beier, D. and Stöhr, I. (1983–5) *Kommunikative und pragmatisch-semantische Bedingungen der Aktualgenese, der Verwendung und des Verstehens von Nominalkomposita im Deutschen*. Nuremberg: Microfilm Computer Service.

Bright, M. (1990) *The Dolittle Obsession*. London: Robson.

Brooks, C. and Penn Warren, R. (1950) *Fundamentals of Good Writing: A Handbook of Modern Rhetoric*. London: Dobson.

Bruner, J. (1975) 'From communication to language – a psychological perspective'. *Cognition* 3: 255–87.

Caplan, D. (1987) *Neurolinguistics and Linguistic Aphasiology: An Introduction*. Cambridge: Cambridge University Press.

Carr, P. (1993) *Phonology*. Basingstoke: Macmillan.

Carston, R. (1985) 'Lexical concepts'. In Hoppenbrouwers et al. (1985).

Chambers, W. W. and Wilkie, J. R. (1970) *A Short History of the German Language*. London: Methuen.

Chomsky, N. (1957) *Syntactic Structures*. The Hague: Mouton.

Chomsky, N. (1964) *Current Issues in Linguistic Theory*. The Hague: Mouton.

Chomsky, N. (1965) *Aspects of the Theory of Syntax*. Cambridge, Mass.: MIT Press.

Chomsky, N. (1970) 'Remarks on nominalization'. In *Readings in English Transformational Grammar*, ed. R. A. Jacobs and P. S. Rosenbaum. Waltham, Mass.: Ginn.

Chomsky, N. (1980) *Rules and Representations*. Oxford: Blackwell.

Chomsky, N. (1981) *Lectures on Government and Binding*. Dordrecht: Foris.

Chomsky, N. (1986) *Knowledge of Language: Its Nature, Origin and Use*. New York: Praeger.

Chomsky, N. (1993) 'A minimalist program for linguistic theory'. In *The View from Building 20*, ed. K. Hale and S. J. Keyser. Cambridge, Mass.: MIT Press.

Clahsen, H. (1982) *Spracherwerb in der Kindheit. Eine Untersuchung zur Entwicklung der Syntax bei Kleinkindern*. Tübingen: Niemeyer.

Clahsen, H. and Smolka, K. D. (1986) 'Psycholinguistic evidence and the description of V-second phenomena in German'. In H. Haider and M. Prinzhorn (1986).

Clahsen, H. (1988) *Normale und gestörte Kindersprache*. Amsterdam: Benjamins.

Clark, J. and Yallop, C. (1995) *An Introduction to Phonetics and Phonology*. Oxford: Blackwell.

Clyne, M. (1995) *The German Language in a Changing Europe*. Cambridge: Cambridge University Press.

Coleman, J. (1995) 'Declarative lexical phonology'. In Durand and Katamba (1995).

Conrady, K. O. (1977) (ed.) *Das große deutsche Gedichtbuch*. Kronberg: Athenäum.

Cook, V. J. and Newson, M. (1996) *Chomsky's Universal Grammar: An Introduction*. Oxford: Blackwell.

Crystal, D. (1987) *The Cambridge Encyclopedia of Language*. Cambridge: Cambridge University Press.

Davenport, M. and Hannahs, S. J. (1998) *Introducing Phonetics and Phonology*. London: Arnold.

Delbrück, B. (1878) *Syntaktische Forschungen, III: Die altindische Wortfolge aus dem Çatapathabrāmaṇa*. Halle: Buchhandlung des Waisenhauses.

Delbrück, B. (1920) *Grundlagen der neuhochdeutschen Satzlehre. Ein Schulbuch für Lehrer*. Berlin and Leipzig: Vereinigung wissenschaftlicher Verleger.

Di Sciullo, A. M. and Williams, E. (1987) *On the Definition of Word*. Cambridge, Mass.: MIT Press.

Dittmar, N. and Schlobinski, P. (1988) (eds) *The Sociolinguistics of Urban Vernaculars: Case Studies and their Evaluation*. Berlin: de Gruyter.

Dorian, N. C. (1982) 'Defining the speech community to include its working margins'. In *Sociolinguistic Variation in Speech Communities*, ed. S. Romaine. London: Edward Arnold.

Downes, W. J. (1998) *Language and Society*, 2nd edn. Cambridge: Cambridge University Press.

Dressler, W. U. (1981) 'External evidence for an abstract analysis of the German velar nasal'. In *Phonology in the 1980s*, ed. D. Goyvaerts. Ghent: E. Story-Scientia.

Dressler, W. U., Leodolter, R. and Chromec, E. (1972) 'Phonologische Schnellsprechregeln in der Wiener Umgangssprache'. *Wiener Linguistische Gazette* 1: 1–29.

Durand, J. (1990) *Generative and Non-linear Phonology*. London: Longman.

Durand, J. and Katamba, F. (1995) (eds) *Frontiers of Phonology: Primitives, Architectures and Derivation*. London: Longman.

Durrell, M. (1996) *Hammer's German Grammar and Usage*. London: Arnold.

Eagleton, T. (1983) *Literary Theory: An Introduction*. Oxford: Blackwell.

Edmondson, J. (1982) *Einführung in die Transformationssyntax des Deutschen*. Tübingen: Narr.

Empson, W. (1930) *Seven Types of Ambiguity*. London: Chatto and Windus.

Epstein, E. L. (1975) 'Language and style'. In Fowler (1975).

Erben, J. (1975) *Einführung in die deutsche Wortbildungslehre*. Berlin: Schimdt.

Erben, J. (1984) *Deutsche Syntax: Eine Einführung*. Berne: Peter Lang.

Erdmann, O. (1886–98) *Grundzüge der deutschen Syntax nach ihrer geschichtlichen Entwicklung*. Stuttgart: Cotta.

Fabb, N. (1997) *Linguistics and Literature*. Oxford: Blackwell.

Fabb, N. and Durant, A. (1990) *Literary Studies in Action*. London: Routledge.

Fanselow, G. (1981) *Zur Syntax und Semantik der Nominalkomposition. Ein Versuch praktischer Anwendung der Montague-Grammatik auf die Wortbildung im Deutschen*. Tübingen: Niemeyer.

Fanselow, G. (1984) 'What is a possible complex word?' In Toman (1984).

Fanselow, G. (1988a) 'Word formation and the human conceptual system'. In Motsch (1988).

Fanselow, G. (1988b) ' "Word syntax" and semantic principles'. In Motsch (1988).

Fasold, R. (1984) *The Sociolinguistics of Society*. Oxford: Blackwell.

Felix, S. and Fanselow, G. (1987) *Sprachtheorie*. Tübingen: Francke.

Ferguson, C. A. (1959) 'Diglossia'. *Word* 15: 325–40.

Ferguson, C. A. (1978) 'Phonological processes'. In *Universals of Human Language*, ed. J. H. Greenberg et al. Stanford, Cal.: Stanford University Press.

Fischer, A. (1999) 'Graphological iconicity in print advertising'. In Nänny and Fischer (1999).

Fischer, O. and Nänny, M. (1999) 'Introduction: iconicity as a creative force in language use'. In Nänny and Fischer (1999).

Fischer, O. and Nänny, M. (2000) *The Motivated Sign*. Amsterdam: Benjamins.

Fleischer, W. (1975) *Wortbildung der deutschen Gegenwartssprache*. Leipzig: VEB Verlag Enzyklopädie.

Fleischer, W. and Michel, G. (1975) *Stilistik der deutschen Gegenwartssprache*. Leipzig: VEB Bibliographisches Institut.

Fodor, J. A. (1983) *The Modularity of Mind*. Cambridge, Mass.: MIT Press.

Fourquet, J. (1974) 'Genetische Betrachtungen über den deutschen Satzbau'. In *Studien zur deutschen Literatur und Sprache des Mittelalters*, ed. W. Besch et al. Berlin: Schmidt.

Fowler, R. G. (1975) (ed.) *Style and Structure in Literature: Essays in the New Stylistics*. Oxford: Blackwell.

Fowler, R. G. (1991) *Language in the News*. London: Routledge.

Fowler, R. G. (1996) *Linguistic Criticism*. Oxford: Oxford University Press.

Fowler, R. G., Hodge, R., Kress, G. and Trew, T. (1979) *Language and Control*. London: Routledge and Kegan Paul.

Fox, A. (1984) *German Intonation: An Outline*. Oxford: Oxford University Press.

Fox, A. (1990) *The Structure of German*. Oxford: Clarendon.

Freeborn, D. (1996) *Style*. London: Macmillan.

Freeman, D. C. (1976) 'Iconic syntax in poetry: a note on Blake's "Ah! Sunflower" '. *University of Massachusetts Occasional Papers in Linguistics* 2: 51–7.

Garvin, P. L. (1964) (ed.) *A Prague School Reader on Esthetics, Literary Structure, and Style*. Washington, DC: Georgetown University Press.

Gazdar, G., Klein, E., Pullum, G. and Sag, I. (1985) *Generalized Phrase Structure Grammar*. Oxford: Blackwell.

Geckeler, H. (1971) *Strukturelle Semantik und Wortfeldtheorie*. Munich: Fink.

Giegerich, H. J. (1985) *Metrical Structure and Metrical Phonology: German and English*. Cambridge: Cambridge University Press.

Giegerich, H. J. (1986) *A Relational Model of German Syllable Structure*. Duisburg: LAUDT.

Giegerich, H. J. (1987) 'Zur Schwa-Epenthese im Standarddeutschen'. *Linguistische Berichte* 112: 449–70.

Giles, H. and Powesland, P. (1975) *Speech Style and Social Evaluation*. London and New York: Academic Press.

Giles, H. and Smith, P. (1979) 'Accommodation theory: optimal levels of convergence'. In *Language and Social Psychology*, ed. H. Giles and R. St Clair. Oxford: Blackwell.

Gleason, H. A. (1955) *An Introduction to Descriptive Linguistics*. New York: Henry Holt.

Good, C. H. (1975) *Die deutsche Sprache und die kommunistische Ideologie*. Frankfurt: Peter Lang.

Good, C. H. (1980) 'Hochdeutsch – a sociolinguistic perspective'. *New German Studies* 8: 221–51.

Good, C. H. (1985) *Presse und soziale Wirklichkeit*. Düsseldorf: Schwann.

Good, C. H. (1986) ' "Du mußt deine Sprache verbessern", or the transmission of linguistic norms'. *New German Studies* 14: 1–20.

Greenberg, J. (1961a) 'Some universals of language with particular reference to the order of meaningful elements'. In Greenberg (1961b).

Greenberg, J. (1961b) (ed.) *Universals of Language*. Cambridge, Mass.: MIT Press.

Gülich, E. and Raible, W. (1972) (eds) *Textsorten*. Frankfurt: Athenäum.

Gussmann, E. (1987) (ed.) *Rules and the Lexicon*. Lublin: Wydawnictw.

Haider, H. (1984) 'The case of German'. In Toman (1984).

Haider, H. (1986) 'V-second in German'. In Haider and Prinzhorn (1986).

Haider, H. and Prinzhorn, M. (1986) (eds) *Verb Second Phenomena in Germanic Languages*. Dordrecht: Foris.

Haiman, J. (1974) *Targets and Syntactic Change*. Paris: Mouton.

Halliday, M. A. K. (1971) 'Linguistic function and literary style'. In *Literary Style: A Symposium*, ed. S. Chatman. London: Oxford University Press.

Halliday, M. A. K. (1973) *Explorations in the Functions of Language*. London: Edward Arnold.

Halliday, M. A. K. (1975) 'Learning how to mean'. In *Foundations of Language Development: A Multidisciplinary Approach*, ed. E. H. Lenneberg and E. Lenneberg. New York: Academic Press.

Halliday, M. A. K. (1978) *Language as Social Semiotic*. London: Edward Arnold.

Halliday, M. A. K. (1994) *An Introduction to Functional Grammar*. London: Edward Arnold.

Halliday, M. A. K. and Hasan, R. (1976) *Cohesion in English*. London: Longman.

Halliday, M. A. K., McIntosh, A. and Strevens, P. (1964) *The Linguistic Sciences and Language Teaching*. London: Longmans.

Handke, P. (1969) *Die Innenwelt der Außenwelt der Innenwelt*. Frankfurt: Suhrkamp.

Harris, M. (1992) *Language Experience and Early Language Development: From Input to Uptake*. Hove: Lawrence Erlbaum.

Helbig, G. and Buscha, J. (1987) *Deutsche Grammatik*. Leipzig: VEB Verlag Enzyklopädie.

Henzen, W. (1965) *Deutsche Wortbildung*. Tübingen: Niemeyer.

Hockett, C. F. (1958) *A Course in Modern Linguistics*. New York: Macmillan.

Hopper, P. (1975) *The Syntax of the Simple Sentence in Proto-Germanic*. Paris: Mouton.

Hoppenbrouwers, G., Seuren, P. and Weijters, A. (1985) (eds) *Meaning and the Lexicon*. Dordrecht: Foris.

Hornstein, N. and Lightfoot, D. (1981) *Explanation in Linguistics*. London: Longman.

Huber, R. and Rieth, R. (1985) (eds) *Glossarium Artis 5: Treppen Escaliers Staircases*. Munich: K. G. Saur.

Hyman, L. M. (1975) *Phonology: Theory and Analysis*. New York: Holt, Rinehart and Winston.

Hymes, D. (1972) 'On communicative competence'. In *Sociolinguistics*, ed. J. B. Pride and J. Holmes. Harmondsworth: Penguin.

Jackendoff, R. (1975) 'Morphological and semantic regularities in the lexicon'. *Language* 51: 639–71.

Jackendoff, R. (1977) *X Syntax: A Study of Phrase Structure*. Cambridge, Mass.: MIT Press.

Jackendoff, R. (1983) *Semantics and Cognition*. Cambridge, Mass.: MIT Press.

Jackendoff, R. (1993) *Patterns in the Mind*. Hemel Hempstead: Harvester Wheatsheaf.

Jacobs, J., von Stechow, A., Sternefeld, W. and Vennemann, T. (1993) (eds) *Syntax: Ein internationales Handbuch zeitgenössischer Forschung*, vol. I. Berlin: de Gruyter.

Jakobson, R. (1956) 'Two types of language and two types of aphasic disturbance'. In R. Jakobson and M. Halle (1956).

Jakobson, R. and Halle, M. (1956) (eds) *Fundamentals of Language*. The Hague: Mouton.

Jones, D. (1950) *The Phoneme: Its Nature and Use*. Cambridge: Heffer.

Kager, R. (1999) *Optimality Theory*. Cambridge: Cambridge University Press.

Katamba, F. (1994) *English Words*. London: Longman.

Katz, J. J. (1980) 'Chomsky on meaning'. *Language* 56.1: 1–41.

Kaye, J. (1995) 'Derivations and interfaces'. In Durand and Katamba (1995).

Keller, R. E. (1961) *German Dialects*. Manchester: Manchester University Press.

Keller, R. E. (1978) *The German Language*. London: Faber and Faber.

Kempson, R. (1977) *Semantic Theory*. Cambridge: Cambridge University Press.

Kiparsky, P. (1973) 'The role of linguistics in a theory of poetry'. *Daedalus* 102: 231–44.

Kiparsky, P. (1979) 'Metrical structure assignment is cyclic'. *Linguistic Inquiry* 10: 421–41.

Kiparsky, P. (1982a) *Explanation in Phonology*. Dordrecht: Foris.

Kiparsky, P. (1982b) 'Lexical morphology and phonology'. In *Linguistics in the Morning Calm*, ed. I. S. Yang. Seoul: Hanshin.

Kiparsky, P. (1985) 'Some consequences of lexical phonology'. *Phonology* 2: 85–138.

Kohler, K. J. (1977) *Einführung in die Phonetik des Deutschen*. Berlin: Schmidt.

Koss, G. (1982–3) 'Realisierung von Kasusrelationen in den deutschen Dialekten'. In *Dialektologie: ein Handbuch zur deutschen und allgemeinen Dialektforschung*, 2 vols, ed. W. Besch, U. Knoop, W. Putschke and H. E. Wiegand. Berlin: de Gruyter.

Koster, J. (1975) 'Dutch as an SOV language'. *Linguistic Analysis* 1: 111–36.

Küpper, H. (1955–64) *Wörterbuch der deutschen Umgangssprache*, 3 vols. Hamburg: Claassen.

Labov, W. (1972) *Sociolinguistic Patterns*. Philadelphia: University of Pennsylvania Press.

Ladefoged, P. (1982) *A Course in Phonetics*, 2nd edn. New York: Harcourt, Brace and Jovanovich.

Ladefoged, P. (1993) *A Course in Phonetics*, 3rd edn. New York: Harcourt, Brace and Jovanovich.

Lakoff, G. and Johnson, M. (1980) *Metaphor We Live By*. Chicago: University of Chicago Press.

Lakoff, G. and Turner, M. (1989) *More than Cool Reason: A Field Guide to Poetic Metaphor*. Chicago: Chicago University Press.

Lapointe, S. (1981) 'General and restricted agreement phenomena'. In M. Moortgat et al. (1981).

Lass, R. (1984) *Phonology*. Cambridge: Cambridge University Press.

Lees, R. B. (1960) *The Grammar of English Nominalizations*. Bloomington, Ind.: Indiana University Research Center in Anthropology, Folklore, and Linguistics, no. 12.

Lehmann, W. (1971) 'On the rise of SOV patterns in New High German'. In *Grammatik, Kybernetik, Kommunikation*, ed. K. G. Schweisthal. Bonn: Dümmler.

Lenerz, J. (1981) 'Zur Generierung der satzeinleitenden Positionen im Deutschen'. In *Sprache: Formen und Strukturen*, ed. M. Kohrt and J. Lenerz. Tübingen: Niemeyer.

Lenerz, J. (1984) 'Diachronic syntax: verb position and COMP in German'. In J. Toman (1984).

LePage, R. B. (1980) 'Projection, focussing, diffusion'. In *York Papers in Linguistics* 9: *Festschrift R. B. LePage*, ed. M. W. S. DeSilva.

LePage, R. B. and Tabouret-Keller, A. (1985) *Acts of Identity*. Cambridge: Cambridge University Press.

Levin, S. R. (1971) 'The analysis of compression in poetry'. *Foundations of Language* 7: 38–55.

Lieber, R. (1981) *On the Organization of the Lexicon*. Bloomington: Indiana University Linguistics Club.

Lieber, R. (1983) 'Argument linking and compounds in English'. *Linguistic Inquiry* 14: 251–85.

Local, J. K. (1992) 'Modelling assimilation in non-segmental rule-free synthesis'. In *Papers in Laboratory Phonology II*, ed. G. Docherty and R. D. Ladd. Cambridge: Cambridge University Press.

Lockwood, W. B. (1965) *An Informal History of the German Language*. Cambridge: Heffer.

Lodge, K. R. (1971) 'The German strong verbs: a prosodic statement'. *ArchL* [new series] 2: 71–94.

Lodge, K. R. (1981) 'Dependency phonology and English consonants'. *Lingua* 54: 19–39.

Lodge, K. R. (1982) 'Transitivity, transformation and text in art-historical German'. *Journal of Pragmatics* 6: 159–84.

Lodge, K. R. (1984) *Studies in the Phonology of Colloquial English*. London: Croom Helm.

Lodge, K. R. (1989) 'A non-segmental account of German Umlaut: diachronic and synchronic perspectives'. *Linguistische Berichte* 124: 470–91.

Lodge, K. R. (1992) 'Assimilation, deletion paths and underspecification'. *Journal of Linguistics* 28: 13–52.

Lodge, K. R. (1997) 'Some handy notes on phonology'. *Journal of Linguistics* 33: 153–69.

Lodge, K. R. (forthcoming) 'Underspecification without derivation: German /r/ revisited'. *Lingua*.

Lyons, J. (1977) *Semantics*, vol. I. Cambridge: Cambridge University Press.

Lytton, B. (n.d.) (trs. and ed.) *The Poems and Ballads of Schiller*. London: Finch.

MacCarthy, P. A. D. (1975) *The Pronunciation of German*. Oxford: Oxford University Press.

McMahon, A. (1994) *Understanding Language Change*. Cambridge: Cambridge University Press.

Malicka-Kleparska, A. (1987) 'Potential forms and lexicons'. In E. Gussmann (1987).

Marchand, H. (1964) 'Die Ableitung desubstantivischer Verben mit Nullmorphem im Englischen, Französischen und Deutschen'. *Die neueren Sprachen* 10: 105–18.

Marchand, H. (1969) *The Categories and Types of Present-Day English Word-Formation: A Synchronic-Diachronic Approach*. Munich: Beck.

Meister, E. (1979) *Ausgewählte Gedichte 1932–1979*. Darmstadt: Luchterhand.

Milroy, J. and Milroy, L. (1985) *Authority in Language*. London: Routledge and Kegan Paul.

Mohanan, K. P. (1986) *The Theory of Lexical Phonology*. Dordrecht: Reidel.

Möhn, D. and Pelka, R. (1984) *Fachsprachen*. Tübingen: Niemeyer.

Moortgat, M., van der Hulst, H. and Hoekstra, T. (1981) (eds) *The Scope of Lexical Rules*. Dordrecht: Foris.

Motsch, W. (1988) (ed.) *The Contribution of Word-Structure Theories to the Study of Word Formation*. Berlin: Akademie der Wissenschaften der DDR.

Mulder, J. and Hervey, S. (1972) *Theory of the Linguistic Sign*. The Hague: Mouton.

Nänny, M. (1985) 'Iconic dimensions in poetry'. In *On Poetry and Poetics*, ed. R. Waswo. Tübingen: Narr.

Nänny, M. and Fischer, O. (1999) *Form Miming Meaning: Iconicity in Language and Literature*. Amsterdam: Benjamins.

Nerbonne, J., Netter, K. and Pollard, C. (1994) (eds) *German in Head-driven Phrase Structure Grammar*. Stanford, Cal.: Center for the Study of Language and Information.

Newton, B. (1970) *Cypriot Greek, its Phonology and Inflections*. The Hague: Mouton.

Newton, B. (2001) *Savage Girls and Wild Boys*. London: Faber.

Nischik, R. (1991) *Mentalstilistik: Ein Beitrag zu Stiltheorie und Narrativik*. Tübingen: Narr.

Odmark, J. (1979) (ed.) *Language, Literature and Meaning I: Problems of Literary Theory*. Amsterdam: Benjamins.

Olsen, S. (1984) 'On deriving V-1 and V-2 structures in German'. In J. Toman (1984).

Olsen, S. (1986a) ' "Argument-Linking" und produktive Reihen bei deutschen Adjektivkomposita'. *Zeitschrift für Sprachwissenschaft* 5: 5–24.

Olsen, S. (1986b) *Wortbildung im Deutschen*. Stuttgart: Kröner.

Ortony, A. (1979) (ed.) *Metaphor and Thought*. Cambridge: Cambridge University Press.

Ouhalla, J. (1994) *Introducing Transformational Grammar*. London: Arnold.

Peirce, C. S. (1931–58) *Collected Papers*, vols 1–18, ed. C. Hartshorne and P. Weiss. Cambridge, Mass.: Harvard University Press.

Pinker, S. (1994) *The Language Instinct*. Harmondsworth: Penguin.

Pinker, S. (1997) *How the Mind Works*. New York: Norton.

von Polenz, P. (1970) *Geschichte der deutschen Sprache*. Berlin: de Gruyter.

von Polenz, P. (1991) *Deutsche Sprachgeschichte vom Spätmittelalter bis zur Gegenwart*, vol. I. Berlin: de Gruyter.

von Polenz, P. (1994) *Deutsche Sprachgeschichte vom Spätmittelalter bis zur Gegenwart*, vol. II. Berlin: de Gruyter.

Porzig, W. (1934) 'Wesenhafte Bedeutungsbeziehungen'. *Beiträge zur deutschen Sprache und Literatur* 58: 70–97.

Posner, R. (1980) 'Ikonismus in der Syntax. Zur natürlichen Stellung der Attribute'. *Zeitschrift für Semiotik* 2: 57–82.

Priebsch, R. and Collinson, W. E. (1962) *The German Language*. London: Faber and Faber.

Püschel, U. (1980) 'Linguistische Stilistik'. In *Lexikon der Germanistischen Linguistik*, ed. H. P. Althaus, H. Henne and H. E. Wiegand. Tübingen: Niemeyer.

Pustejovsky, J. (1993a) 'Introduction'. In Pustejovsky (1993b).

Pustejovsky, J. (1993b) (ed.) *Semantics and the Lexicon*. Dordrecht: Kluwer.

Putnam, H. (1975) 'The meaning of "meaning"'. In *Language, Mind and Knowledge*, ed. K. Gunderson. Minneapolis: University of Minnesota Press.

Radford, A. (1988) *Transformational Grammar: A First Course*. Cambridge: Cambridge University Press.

Radford, A., Atkinson, M., Britain, D., Clahsen, H. and Spencer, A. (1999) *Linguistics: An Introduction*. Cambridge: Cambridge University Press.

Rappaport, M., Langhren, M. and Levin, B. (1993) 'Levels of lexical representation'. In J. Pustejovsky (1993b).

Reiners, L. (1990) *Stilfibel*. Munich: Beck.

Ricoeur, P. (1975) *Métaphore vive*. Paris: Éditions du Seuil.

van Riemsdijk, H. and Williams, E. (1986) *Introduction to the Theory of Grammar*. Cambridge, Mass.: MIT Press.

Riesel, E. (1970) *Der Stil der deutschen Alltagsrede*. Leipzig: Reclam.

Roberts, I. (1997) *Comparative Syntax*. London: Arnold.

Roca, I. and Johnson, W. (1999) *A Course in Phonology*. Oxford: Blackwell.

Romaine, S. (1982) 'What is a speech community?' In *Sociolinguistic Variation in Speech Communities*, ed. S. Romaine. London: Edward Arnold.

Ross, J. R. (1980) 'Ikonismus in der Phraseologie. Der Ton macht die Bedeutung'. *Zeitschrift für Semiotik* 2: 39–56.

Russ, C. V. J. (1990) (ed.) *The Dialects of Modern German*. London: Routledge.

Russ, C. V. J. (1994) *The German Language Today: A Linguistic Introduction*. London: Routledge.

Sanders, W. (1973) *Linguistische Stiltheorie*. Göttingen: Vandenhoeck and Ruprecht.

Sanders, W. (1982) *Sachsensprache, Hansersprache, Plattdeutsch. Sprachgeschichtliche Grundzüge des Niederdeutschen*. Göttingen: Vandenhoeck and Ruprecht.

Sanders, W. (1986) *Gutes Deutsch – besseres Deutsch*. Darmstadt: Wissenschaftliche Buchgesellschaft.

Sandig, B. (1971) *Syntaktische Typologie der Schlagzeile*. Munich: Max Hueber.

Sandig, B. (1986) *Stilistik der deutschen Sprache*. Berlin: de Gruyter.

de Saussure, F. (1916) *Cours de linguistique générale*, ed. C. Bally, A. Sechehaye and A. Riedlinger. Lausanne: Payot.

Scaglione, A. (1981) *The Theory of German Word Order from the Renaissance to the Present*. Minneapolis: University of Minnesota Press.

Scalise, S. (1984) *Generative Morphology*. Dordrecht: Foris.

Schmidt, W. (1980) *Geschichte der deutschen Sprache*. Berlin: Volkseigener Verlag.

Selkirk, E. O. (1982) *The Syntax of Words*. Cambridge, Mass.: MIT Press.

Selkirk, E. O. (1984) 'On the major class features and syllable theory'. In *Language Sound Structure*, ed. M. Aronoff and R. T. Oehrle. Cambridge, Mass.: MIT Press.

Shirer, M. (1965) 'Case systems in German dialects'. *Language* 41: 420–38.

Short, M. (1996) *Exploring the Language of Poems, Plays and Prose*. London: Longman.

Siegel, D. (1979) *Topics in English Morphology*. New York: Garland.

Simpson, A. (1998) 'Accounting for the phonetics of German *r* without processes'. *ZAS Papers in Linguistics* 11: 91–104.

Smith, F. (1995) 'The day after tomorrow'. *Language* 35: 156–206.

Smith, N. V. and Tsimpli, I. M. (1995) *The Mind of a Savant*. Oxford: Blackwell.

Smith, N. V. and Wilson, D. (1979) *Modern Linguistics: The Results of Chomsky's Revolution*. Harmondsworth: Penguin.

Sowinski, B. (1972) *Deutsche Stilistik*. Frankfurt: Fischer.

Spencer, A. (1991) *Morphological Theory*. Oxford: Basil Blackwell.

Sperber, D. and Wilson, D. (1995) *Relevance: Communication and Cognition*. Oxford: Blackwell.

Sproat, R. (1985) 'On Deriving the Lexicon'. PhD dissertation, MIT, Boston, Mass.

Stanford, W. B. (1939) *Ambiguity in Greek Literature: Studies in Theory and Practice*. Oxford: Blackwell.

von Stechow, A. and Sternefeld, W. (1988) *Bausteine syntaktischen Wissens*. Opladen: Westdeutscher Verlag.

Steen, G. (1994) *Understanding Metaphor in Literature*. London: Longman.

Steinbach, C. E. (1724) *Kurtze und gründliche Anweisung zur deutschen Sprache*. Rostochii et Parchimi: Georg Ludwig Fritsch.

Steriade, D. (1995) 'Underspecification and markedness'. In *The Handbook of Phonological Theory*, ed. J. A. Goldsmith. Oxford: Blackwell.

Stevenson, P. (1995) (ed.) *The German Language and the Real World: Sociolinguistic, Cultural and Pragmatic Perspectives on Contemporary Germany*. Oxford: Clarendon.

Stevenson, P. (1997) *The German-Speaking World*. London: Routledge.

Stillings, J. T. (1975) 'The formulation of gapping in English as evidence for variable types in syntactic transformations'. *Linguistic Analysis* 1: 247–73.

Stowell, T. (1981) 'The Origins of Phrase Structure'. PhD dissertation, MIT, Boston, Mass.

Su, Soon Peng (1994) *Lexical Ambiguity in Poetry*. London: Longman.

Thiersch, C. L. (1978) 'Topics in German Syntax'. PhD dissertation, MIT, Boston, Mass.

Thornborrow, J. and Wareing, S. (1998) *Patterns in Language*. London: Routledge.

von Törne, V. (1981) *Im Lande Vogelfrei*. Berlin: Wagenbach.

Toman, J. (1983) *Wortsyntax: Eine Diskussion ausgewählter Probleme deutscher Wortbildung*. Tübingen: Niemeyer.

Toman, J. (1984) (ed.) *Studies in German Grammar*. Dordrecht: Foris.

Toman, J. (1988) 'Issues in the theory of inheritance'. In W. Motsch (1988).

Toolan, M. (1998) *Language in Literature*. London: Arnold.

Trask, L. (1996) *Historical Linguistics*. London: Arnold.

Traugott, E. (1969) 'Toward a grammar of syntactic change'. *Lingua* 23: 1–27.

Trier, J. (1934) 'Das sprachliche Feld. Eine Auseinandersetzung'. *Neue Jahrbücher für Wissenschaft und Jugendbildung* 10: 428–49.

Trudgill, P. J. (1983) *On Dialect*. Oxford: Blackwell.

Vickers, B. (1970) *Classical Rhetoric in English Poetry*. London: Macmillan.

Vikner, S. (1990) 'Verb movement and licensing of NP-positions in the Germanic languages'. PhD dissertation, University of Geneva.

Wackernagel, J. (1892) 'Über ein Gesetz der indogermanischen Wortstellung'. *Indogermanische Forschungen* 1: 333–436.

Wales, K. (1989) *A Dictionary of Stylistics*. London: Longman.

Weinrich, H. (1964) *Tempus: Besprochene und erzählte Welt*. Stuttgart: Kohlhammer.

Weisgerber, L. (1954) 'Die Sprachfelder in der geistigen Erschließung der Welt'. In *Festschrift für J. Trier*, ed. B. Wiese. Meisenheim: Hain.

Wells, C. J. (1985) *German: A Linguistic History to 1945*. Oxford: Oxford University Press.

Wells, J. C. (1982) *Accents of English*, vols 1 and 2. Cambridge: Cambridge University Press.

Wiese, R. (1996) *The Phonology of German*. Oxford: Oxford University Press.

Wiese, R. (2001) 'The unity and variation of (German) /r/'. In H. Van de Velde and R. van Hout (eds) *'r-atics: Sociolinguistics, Phonetic and Phonological Characteristics of /r/*. Brussels: Etudes et Travaux.

Willberg, H.-J. (1989) *Deutsche Gegenwartslyrik: Eine poetologische Einführung*. Stuttgart: Reclam.

Williams, E. (1981) 'Argument structure and morphology'. *Linguistic Review* 1: 81–114.

Wright, J. (1907) *Historical German Grammar*. London: Oxford University Press.

Zwicky, A. (1972) 'Casual speech'. *Chicago Linguistic Society* 8: 607–15.

Zwicky, A. (1985) 'Heads'. *Journal of Linguistics* 21: 1–29.

INDEX